Women in the Americas: Bridging the Gender Gap

Published by the Inter-American Development Bank
Distributed by The Johns Hopkins University Press

Washington, D.C.
1995

The views and opinions expressed in this publication are those of the authors and do not necessarily reflect the official position of the Inter-American Development Bank.

Women in the Americas: Bridging the Gender Gap

1300 New York Avenue, N.W.
Washington, D.C. 20577

Distributed by
The Johns Hopkins University Press
2715 North Charles Street
Baltimore, Maryland 21218-4319

Library of Congress Catalog Card Number: 95-79063
ISBN: 0-940602-98-9

Acknowledgments

Many people and institutions have made this book possible. *Women in the Americas* evolved from background papers prepared for the Regional Forum on Women in Development held in Guadalajara, Mexico, in 1994, and special thanks go to the authors of the original studies. These papers include "The Gender Issue in Social Policy: The Latin American and Caribbean Case" by Vanessa Cartaya; "Reforma Social con Perspectiva de Género: Aportes para la Discusión" by Cecilia López and Margarita Ronderos Torres; "Women and Democracy: Consolidating the Role of Women in the Democratic Process in Latin America and the Caribbean" by Alda Facio, Beverly Anderson-Manley, Ligia Delgadillo and Gladys Acosta; "Women and Democracy: Strengthening Women's Role in the Democratic Process in the Anglophone Caribbean Region" by Beverly Anderson-Manley; "Sustainable Development and Women: Management and Protection of the Environment" by Lourdes Arizpe, Michael Paolisso, Margaret A. Lycette, Margarita Velázquez, and Fernanda Paz; "Women's Contributions to Economic Growth in Latin America and the Caribbean: Facts, Experience, and Options" by Mayra Buvinić and Margaret A. Lycette; and an overview by Molly Pollack.

Women in the Americas also benefitted greatly from the insightful discussions that took place at the Guadalajara forum. The forum's "Agenda for Action," which appears here as an annex, represents the contributions of all forum participants.

Jane Jaquette, Mary Hill Rojas, Richard Webb, Elizabeth Jelín and Lourdes Benería reviewed the original background papers, and the points they raised were important contributions to this book.

Special recognition should go to Beth Woroniuk as principal author of the chapter, "Women in the Americas," and to Marguerite Berger, Chief of the IDB Women in Development Unit, as the main author of the case study, "Gender Equity and Changing Institutions."

For the book's final form, we are indebted to the contributions of Beth Woroniuk, Catherine Gander and Lucie Bazinet as writers and editors and to Lora Pietrantonio, Jane Fuller, Adèle Lamoureux and Sheila Faure for their research support. Many members of the Women in Development Unit and other IDB departments were also involved in conceiving, writing, and editing *Women in the Americas,* particularly Barbara Rietveld, Sarah Howden, Gabriela Vega, Clotilde Charlot, Chris Delboni, Michele Lemay, Jane Sevier Sãnchez and Susanne Ihre. Sarah Howden also coordinated the book's preparation, and Luz Stella Gomez of the Women in Development Unit provided excellent support throughout the process.

Foreword

The Inter-American Development Bank (IDB) believes that the goals of economic and social development cannot be achieved unless both women and men are able to participate freely in all spheres of life, unhindered by discrimination. The principal goal of Latin American and the Caribbean countries today is to combat poverty. Women play a decisive role in that fight, as demonstrated during the economic crisis of the 1980s. The effects of that crisis are still being felt among the poorest sectors of society, where women are most often the backbone of the household. In addition to their pivotal role in alleviating poverty and administering scarce resources, both within the household and through their role as community leaders, women make significant contributions to economic growth in the region. To strengthen these efforts, we must focus attention on expanding their employment opportunities and on providing complementary services that support women's multiple roles.

The IDB, in conjunction with the Economic Commission for Latin America and the Caribbean (ECLAC) and the United Nations Development Fund for Women (UNIFEM), sponsored a regional forum on women's participation in the development process in the Americas in Guadalajara, Mexico, in April 1994. Heads of state, cabinet ministers, first ladies, parliamentarians, representatives of nongovernmental organizations and academics were among the 400 people who attended this meeting.

Women in the Americas grew out of discussions at the forum, which focused on strategies to expand economic opportunities for women, improve social services that respond to women's needs, promote women's political participation, and support the contributions that women make to sustainable development. The forum's "Agenda for Action" calls for increased collaboration with governments and non-government groups of member countries. The challenge is to build gender considerations into all programs. Needs and incentives of both women and men must be considered in the design and execution of projects. The different impact of projects on women and men must be assessed and priority given to those projects that tend to reduce the gap between them and improve the quality of life of both women and men in the region.

To be successful in our endeavors, we must continue the fruitful dialogue initiated at the forum to heighten public awareness and knowledge about the status of women in the region, as well as their contributions to the region's development. By sharing the results of the forum and by contributing to the body of research emerging on this topic, we hope this book will help advance that effort.

Enrique V. Iglesias	Nancy Birdsall
President	Executive Vice-President

Contents

Chapter 1

Women in the Americas

"Women in Latin America and the Caribbean" is used extensively but cautiously in the chapters that follow. The region's women are not a homogeneous group. "La mujer" or the composite woman does not exist.

Generalizations across the entire Latin American and the Caribbean region can be misleading, given economic, geographic, racial, historic, political, linguistic and cultural differences (Radcliffe and Westwood, 1993). Life for a young woman in a poor Kingston, Jamaica neighborhood is different from that of an elderly Quechua woman in the Bolivian highlands. Change is the one constant in the region. With evolving economies and the rapid movement of ideas and images (propelled by international media), a snapshot of a particular community today may not be relevant five or even two years from now.

As Peruvian feminist Virginia Vargas says:

> The development of the Latin American women's movement shows that it is no longer possible to speak of women's identity, anchored and built on their experiences as a subordinate gender. Instead, we need to recognize the plurality of experiences, the possibility of multiple representations and identities (1992: 196).

The growing field of gender analysis, although far from being fully developed and refined, offers several important starting points from which to explore women's lives. But "gender analysis" now has many different meanings. It behooves policy makers, politicians, activists and academics to define this term and to specify what it means.

One definition of gender analysis constitutes a good starting point for the chapters that follow:

> ... the concept of gender [is] a system of socially ascribed roles and relationships between men and women, which are deter-

> mined not by biology but by the social, political and economic context. Gender roles are learned, and they can change over time. It is the analysis of these roles and relationships which shows the imbalances in power, wealth and workload between women and men, and it is this analysis which may then lead to the ***possibilities and necessity*** of change (GENESYS, 1994:60).

The central thesis of this book is that understanding gender differences is vital to development planning. A gender analysis is important for three basic reasons—equity, efficiency and empowerment.

First, gender analysis can promote the just distribution between men and women of costs and benefits of development in general, or of specific initiatives. Evidence has shown that women do not "automatically" benefit from development initiatives to the same degree as men.[1] Different starting points (for example, different access to and control over resources, varying responsibilities, social and cultural expectations) translate into different abilities to take advantage of new opportunities or to participate in programs. Generally, those most able to take advantage of new resources are better off, male, educated and well-informed (Chambers, 1983; Cernea, 1985; Coady International Institute, 1991). An understanding of women's and men's roles and relations can help offset this problem.

Second, a clear understanding of differing needs, interests, access to resources, and work of women and men can greatly facilitate successful development planning and promote economic growth. General categories such as "the poor," "urban dwellers" or "agricultural workers" fail to capture significant differences important for planning. For example, when faced with the possibility of participation in a credit scheme or housing project, poor women have different constraints and often start with a different level of resources compared to poor men. They may have less free time to spend on volunteer labor, responsibility for child care often restricts their mobility, and they may face discrimination from project administrators. Understanding and programming around these differences can greatly increase efficiency and effectiveness.

Third, gender analysis is an important tool in the promotion of women's (and men's) participation in development. It can highlight imbalances in resources and power and help to identify ways to strengthen women's role in decision making and promote women's empowerment. Thus, gender

[1] Just as given the differences among women, women will not all benefit equally.

analysis not only helps policy makers design policies informed by existing relationships, but it also helps in the construction of alternatives that, in addition to being more efficient, are also more equitable and supportive of women's empowerment.

Building on these basic insights, this book sketches the broad panorama of issues in economic policy, political participation, the environment and sustainable development, and social policy. Experiences from recent projects and programs are documented, and the range of considerations that should be taken into account are reviewed.

Although the focus of this book is on women—women's work, women's roles, women's contributions, and women's empowerment—this does not imply that women should be looked at in isolation. Nor does it mean differences among women should be ignored. Throughout this collection, both the multiplicity of women's relationships and what has been termed the "diversity of gendered identities" are a constant (Radcliffe and Westwood, 1993).

With this diversity in mind, this overview examines the factors that both divide and unite women. Understanding the nature and complexity of the lives of women who are directly and indirectly—and intentionally and unintentionally—affected by policies and programs is an important starting point.

The issues this book addresses are also reflected in the *Agenda for Action,* the final document of the Regional Forum on Women in the Americas: Participation and Development organized by the Inter-American Development Bank, ECLAC and UNIFEM in April 1994. The *Agenda for Action* recommends objectives and definitive measures for both the IDB and the governments of Latin America and the Caribbean in three main areas:

- promotion of equitable and sustainable economic and social reform;
- promotion of the participation of women in the public decision-making process; and,
- strengthening of the institutional capacity of the IDB and of its counterparts to enable them to implement the *Agenda for Action.*

What Divides Women?

Women are not a unified group. They do not always share the same set of interests, nor are they united political actors (Radcliffe and Westwood, 1993; Jaquette, 1994; Cañadell, 1993; Safa, 1990). One of the major themes running through the chapters that follow is the importance of understanding the specifics of each situation. It is necessary to have a clear picture of the target group or the people—women and men, boys and girls—affected by a policy decision or specific program—the work they do inside and outside the home, the resources they have access to and the resources they control, their priorities and needs, their history and past involvements, their education and skills, the barriers they face, and their dreams.

Economic Position

Perhaps the most significant variation among women is class difference. For the majority of women in Latin America and the Caribbean, "the theme of gender is articulated...with that of subordinate classes" (Jelin, 1990: 1). Just like men in the region, women find themselves in very different economic situations. Women do not share economic interests. An *obrera* (worker) in the Mexican *maquilas,* a Cuban doctor, an executive with a multinational corporation in Santiago, and a domestic worker in São Paulo have very different economic needs and interests. Guzmán (1991) points out how the needs, problems and demands of *obreras* (urban women workers) are different from those of *mujeres pobladoras* (poor, urban women), even though they may share the same basic cultural and peasant background. Women workers may identify primarily with a union movement and promote increases in wages, whereas *pobladoras* may argue in favor of keeping prices (and thus even wages) down. Changes in the structure of the economy, government policies and trade flows will affect them in a variety of ways.

Class differences have played an important role in the women's movement in Latin America and the Caribbean. For example, the debate around the relative importance of class versus gender issues has been fundamental to the Chilean women's movement (Chuchryk, 1989). Some women have chosen class-based demands over gender ones, arguing that they have more in common with men who share their economic situation than with women who do not. Others have sought to combine the two. Still others have focused primarily on "women's issues" (Vargas, 1992).

The chapter on women as economic actors reviews women's participation in several sectors and highlights discrepancies that are often hidden by aggregate numbers. One must go beyond national statistics and understand the role of women within each sector within each country. With the economic crises of the 1980s came increased rates of female participation in the labor force, particularly in urban areas. The impact of economic crises and structural adjustment programs prompted women to enter the workforce. Given class differences, women enter the workforce in a number of ways.[2] A woman's economic position also influences her possibilities for education and skills development. An analysis that goes beyond gender aggregates is necessary to document these differences.

Race and Ethnicity

Women are also divided by race and ethnicity. The racial and ethnic diversity of the region is well-known. Indigenous people account for more than half the population of both Bolivia and Guatemala. Blacks in Brazil number over 8 million, and Colombia, Venezuela and Guyana also have sizable black populations. There are significant minority populations along the Atlantic Coast of several Central American countries including Nicaragua, Costa Rica and Panama (Gõmez, Shallat, Torres, et al., 1992).

Race and ethnicity issues are also important in the Caribbean. According to a recent ECLAC report, "a major problem which has confronted Caribbean societies since the emancipation of enslaved Africans and the ending of indentureships has been the task of fashioning a functional harmony out of the disparate social, racial and cultural elements that comprise them." Racial divisions are further complicated in countries such as Trinidad and Tobago and Guyana where racial lines coincide with divisions according to social class, religious and political party affiliation (ELCAC, 1994).

Many indigenous women have chosen to organize around general community demands, leaving aside their gender-specific concerns. Others have formed autonomous women's organizations that seek to articulate gender issues alongside those of indigenous people in general (Gõmez, et al., 1992).

Family Structures

The diversity of family structures in the region has received increasing attention in recent years. As the social policy chapter makes clear, policy makers are slowly recognizing that there are many types of family structure, for example, female-headed households; one, two or more income earners; multi-generational and extended families. Discussions of family survival strategies in the face of economic adjustment have spotlighted how women within different

[2] Given gender differences, women's starting point to enter the workforce also differs from that of men. This point is elaborated below.

family structures draw on a range of resources in the struggle to support their families (Benería and Roldán, 1987).

Family structure is also an important issue in household decision making. Analysts and critics of traditional economic approaches have argued that there is a need to examine the internal dynamics of the household and not treat it as an indivisible unit (Kabeer and Joekes, 1991). It cannot be assumed, they argue, that resources are shared in an equitable fashion or that decisions are made in the best interests of all members (Moser, 1993a). Also, the manner in which a family member responds to a change in policy or an incentive to participate in a project will depend on his or her position within the household. The chapter on women as economic actors explores this chapter further.

The theme of families and family structures is raised in various chapters. The chapter on social policy considers discussions around female-headed households, while the chapter on women's political participation examines women's politicization through their role as mothers.

Stage in Life Cycle

Women of different ages with different family responsibilities also have diverse interests and control different resources (Benería and Roldán, 1987). For example, young women with no family responsibilities may have better employment possibilities. They are often preferred employees in Export Processing Zones (EPZs). A woman with young children may prefer to seek employment in the informal sector, where working conditions are more amenable to juggling child care with income-generating opportunities.

Older women may have more flexibility in life choices than younger women. In some situations, however, women with grown children may still be expected to provide child care for their grandchildren. A Tantie or Grannie who looks after young children is a familiar figure throughout the Caribbean (Saint Victor, 1986). Young girls may face risks specific to their age groups. Economic pressure on the family may lead parents to pull daughters out of school to help with domestic tasks (Moser, 1993a) or may force to girls into alternatives such as street prostitution (Dimenstein, 1994).

So it is clear that not all women—even in a given community—will have the same options or control the same set of resources.

National Situations

The nation of a woman's birth and where she makes her home will strongly influence her life, both politically and economically. A woman born in Haiti has options different from those of a woman born in Chile.

As was clearly evident throughout the 1980s, a country's political system—for example, the degree of militarization and the level of political openness has profound effects on the way both women and men live their lives. Women both influence and are influenced by that system.

Military governments throughout the Southern Cone stressed conservative social values and emphasized women's roles as mothers. At first glance, this type of government seems to limit women's political participation, and at one level this was true. There was limited freedom or opportunity to organize and conduct political activity for traditional political parties and trade unions. Yet, as has now been extensively documented, women were often able to organize and speak out against military regimes where men were not (Jaquette, 1989 and 1994). The case of the *Madres de la Plaza de Mayo* is often cited. As the chapter on women and political participation explains, these women did not seek to "enter politics" in the traditional way. Rather their political participation was something that they felt compelled to do, given what had happened to their children and relatives.

Political regimes in Central America posed a different set of circumstances for women. In both Nicaragua and El Salvador, women were active in military organizations throughout the region, often challenging traditional views of femininity and women's capabilities. In the 1980s in Nicaragua, women organized around a variety of issues and entered into a debate on how best to advance their interests (Chinchilla, 1994).

How each country fits into the international economy will, in turn, affect opportunities open to women. Government policies, natural resource endowments and past economic relations all influence women's options. Governments that create export promotion zones (EPZs) and offer incentives for international companies may provide employment for some women. The economic policy chapter reviews the debate over this type of employment creation.

Religion

Different religious affiliations also divide women—the church people say they belong to, the meaning of church membership in their daily lives and the role for, and of, women within each church.

Although much of Latin America is traditionally Catholic, significant religious diversity is developing across the region. The vast majority of Latin Americans still consider themselves members of the Roman Catholic Church. Estimates of the growing trend of Evangelical Protestant churches vary. One author argues that the number of practicing Protestants is greater than the total number of all other kinds of voluntary organizations in culture, sports and politics combined, or over 15 percent in many countries. Given that relatively few of the people who identify themselves as Catholic regularly attend mass, the numbers of Evangelicals may approach the number of practicing Catholics (Berryman, 1994). Within the Catholic Church itself, the "popular church" has articulated a different vision of "liberation theology" that has enjoyed varying degrees of popularity in different places at different times in the last two decades.

Although images of women are closely linked with religion, and almost all religions have a clearly proscribed role for women, there is very little written on the participation of women within various religious movements in the 1990s.

Participation in Organizations

Women organize themselves in many ways. The chapter on women's political participation delves extensively into questions of women in politics and organizations. It reviews how women have become politically active in traditional ways and how they have "done politics" in new ways.

Women in the region have set different priorities and organized around issues as diverse as family law, domestic violence, reproductive rights, basic social services, human rights, land rights, prostitutes' rights, and the environment. While not generally contradictory, these different priorities have produced disagreements over strategy and forms of organization.

One of the major differences among women is between those who established women's organizations and those who joined with men in organizations with broad social goals. Whether women's interests are best advanced through autonomous women's organizations that can maintain control over their own agenda but run the risk of being marginalized has long been a subject of debate. Some feel that women will be more successful working through more mainstream organizations that hold more sway in society but where it is harder to have women's voices heard (Chinchilla, 1994). The chapter on women's political participation explores the tensions between these two ways of organizing.

There have been many debates on "feminism." What is it? Is it relevant for women in Latin America and the Caribbean? Is there only one strand or many? Is it a concern of middle-class women? Although use of the term is growing, the word feminism still provokes unease in many quarters. Within the women's movement itself various "feminisms" are now accepted. There is a growing recognition of the importance of not only respecting the diversity among women, but also of building on that diversity (Vargas, 1992).

What Do Women Have in Common?

Despite all the differences among women, they share vital similarities as well—not all of them and not all the time, but there are general things that bring women together. In recent years, there has been much discussion around the concepts of women's practical gender needs and strategic gender interests.

First conceived by Maxine Molyneux (1985), this distinction has generated heated debate. Molyneux argued that it is important to distinguish between two sets of interests. Practical gender interests arise from specific circumstances (the need for clean water, housing, etc.) and do not challenge the gender division of labor. Strategic gender interests, on the other hand, could be derived from an analysis of women's subordination and require a feminist consciousness to struggle for them. Molyneux used this distinction to assess women's status in Sandinista Nicaragua, concluding that more ground had been gained in practical gender needs than in specific gender interests. The use of these terms (and the debate around their usefulness) has taken off.

Several elements of this debate are worth highlighting. First, there has been a disagreement around whether this general issue is best phrased in terms of needs or interests. Perhaps the most well-known use of these concepts is that explored by Caroline Moser in her "gender planning framework" (Moser, 1993b). In attempting to develop a clear framework that is easily accessible for policy analysts and development planners, Moser reworked Molyneux's distinction and proposed practical and strategic gender needs as central planning tools within her framework. Moser argued that meeting women's practical gender needs (ie., clean water or health care) could alleviate women's day-to-day burden but did little to challenge women's subordination.

Kabeer (1994) and others have been critical of the focus on needs and sought to shift emphasis to a discussion of interests. Kabeer writes that "the language of need is thus associated with a top-down planning approach which constructs, in this case, women as clients of bureaucratic provisioning, while that of interests positions them as social actors, disempowered but not powerless" (p. 297).

Second, there has been considerable discussion around whether or not these two types of needs or interests constitute an either-or programming option or a way of categorizing women's actions. In her discussion of two women's organizations in Central America, Schirmer (1993) argues against the dichotomy of practical vs. strategic, stressing that women have "*multiple* 'strategic' and 'pragmatic' interests that change over time and that they themselves do not deem separate" (p. 61).[3]

Finally, other analysts have questioned the entire notion of the distinction between practical and strategic gender needs (Rodríguez, 1994). Wieringa (1994) argues that labelling of problems as either "practical" or "strategic" by development planners is overly simplistic and misses the "diversity of women's experiences and the conflicting, at times contradictory, nature of the interests of the women they are concerned with" (p. 835). She goes on to say that women's gender interests can be discussed only in specific socio-historic contexts.

Perhaps one way out of this debate is to pull back slightly and see the basic distinction between the two types of needs or interests as useful but to avoid a sharp dichotomy that categorizes practical as "bad" and strategic as "good." As the chapter on political participation stresses, categorizing one form of women's mobilization as "better" than another is difficult at best and is often misleading. It is also important to view these terms as analytical tools that should be applied to the extent they are useful and then put aside.

Turning away from the theoretical debate, one thing women clearly have in common is the "invisibility" of several important aspects of their lives. Domestic work (or reproductive work, as explored in the chapter on social policy)—although it can involve heavy tasks and is time consuming—is not counted as work in national accounts, nor is it figured into policy calculations. Furthermore, women's contributions to agricultural production and sectors of the informal economy (primarily home-based production) are also generally underestimated.

A second major factor women shared is that they are not a "vulnerable group" or simply one more "special interest group." The chapter on social policy argues that to consider women only as a vulnerable group does considerable disservice to women and constitutes a faulty premise on which to build policies or programs. Women are actors both collectively and individually at

[3] Emphasis is in the original.

political, social, economic and cultural levels. They are not passive individuals buffeted about by winds of change. Women are also not a special interest group to be added to a list of possible target groups such as the poor, urban dwellers, workers in the informal sector or indigenous people. Although it seems obvious that women generally constitute at least half of all these groups, there does appear to be an ongoing need to remind policy makers of this fact.

A number of other factors affect women's lives in the Latin American and Caribbean region. These include women's lack of time; their distance from macro policy making; their difficulties in accessing credit, services and land; their low levels of educational attainment and employment possibilities; and their lack of access to and knowledge of their legal rights. The chapters in this book stress interests that women have in common, including the need for greater access to public life; assistance in, and recognition of, their multiple roles; changes in cultural stereotypes about the place of women in society in relation to men; and the creation of development projects that do not rely on them as volunteers, but place the proper value on their time.

Misconceptions

Planners and policy makers across the region hold numerous misconceptions about what women do and about their positions inside social institutions, including the family. The chapters that follow scrutinize numerous important and often widespread assumptions.

The chapter on women and the environment reviews and criticizes three commonly held suppositions: that women's fertility (and thus population growth) is directly linked to environmental degradation, that poor women's survival strategies are substantially responsible for environmental decline and that women have a special and natural relationship with the environment. The usefulness of each of these is limited and point policy makers and organizers down futile paths.

The chapter on women as economic actors highlights the invisibility of much of women's work. Despite the importance of women's domestic work to families and to society, this work is undervalued and overlooked. It is not measured in national accounts and is not captured by national censuses. It is rarely factored into development plans or compensated for in employment schemes aimed at women (although there are increasing examples of day care services incorporated into specific projects). The all-too-common assumption that women are "only housewives" and have plenty of time to volunteer in community-based programs has also been proved false.

Under-reporting women's contributions to agricultural work is explored in the same chapter. Data from a recent IDB-IICA study demonstrate how women's participation rates in this sector are significantly higher than those generally recorded and estimated.

The chapter on women and social policy explores faulty assumptions about family structure. It is difficult to generalize about composition, resource allocation, and decision-making processes within households. This chapter also looks at how the narrow equation of women's health with childbearing fails to consider other women's health issues.

Yet perhaps the most widespread assumption in need of debunking is that most policy—particularly policy at the macro level—is gender neutral. Analysts, researchers and activists have worked hard over recent years to point out how various macroeconomic choices, social policy options and environmental decisions affect women differently from men, a theme throughout this book.

The Need for Employment

Women's participation in paid employment has increased dramatically in recent years. The chapter on economic policy examines this trend in detail. Women's need to support themselves and their families has fueled this increase. Yet the type of employment open to women has generally been limited to low-paying, low-skilled jobs with few opportunities for advancement.

Women face discrimination in their work lives, although the form of that discrimination may vary across sectors. The chapter on women as economic actors summarizes efforts to document and understand this discrimination. Occupational stereotyping and segregation are major problems. The sectors in which women work are still predominantly "female" occupations, often related to the service industry. This fact, combined with limited exposure to vocational training in non-traditional occupations, leads to poor employment opportunities and limited opportunities for women to enhance their careers, incomes and status.

The role women play in agriculture, the extent to which the nature of their input remains largely unrecognized, and the implications this has for access to resources such as technology, land and agricultural extension services are also considered. The 'invisibility' of women farmers has contributed greatly to the impoverishment of female-headed households in rural areas.

Buvinić has argued that poverty causes increased female work that, in turn, exacerbates women's and children's deprivation and poverty unless women find work that pays adequately (Buvinić, 1994). Women's need for secure, stable and productive employment parallels their need for support in their reproductive role. The inability to obtain or finance day care for children is a significant obstacle that inhibits women's ability to take advantage of work or educational opportunities. The chapter on social policy further explores this issue.

There is a clear correlation between women's increased access to education at both the primary and secondary levels and improvements in their health and well-being, as well as that of their children. Although statistics for female literacy and completion of primary school years are comparable to those of males, issues should be raised about the quality of female education. The educational and vocational training women require is in non-traditional occupations that can give them access to better paying and more secure employment.

Domestic Responsibilities

Almost universally in the region, women are responsible for domestic work. It is women who wash clothes, shop for and prepare food, clean houses, care for small children and the elderly, and ensure that there is cooking and heating fuel. Even when a woman has the financial resources to hire someone to do this work, she is responsible for supervising that employee.

The chapter on social policy discusses women's "reproductive" work and highlights the challenge of developing programs that assist women with current responsibilities while opening the possibility for a more equitable division of responsibilities between women and men.

Juggling Multiple Roles and the Pressure on Time

Almost all women face the challenge of juggling a diverse set of responsibilities and roles. They are mothers, workers and often active members of their communities with responsibilities for cultural, religious or political organizations. They are responsible for holding their families together and stretching scarce resources. Current literature often makes note of the *doble* or *triple jornada* (double or triple workday) the majority of women maintain.

It is important to recognize the pressure on women's time and acknowledge the multifaceted nature of women's lives. For the vast majority of women in Latin America and the Caribbean, time is an extremely precious resource. The social policy chapter cites studies that document women's days and shows how women who work outside the home often have a workweek of over 90 hours. Rising early, going to bed late and forgoing leisure activities are often the only options available to these women with multiple responsibilities.

Policies and programs must recognize women's multiple roles. These roles are not identities that women change like pieces of clothing as they move from one task to another. Rather they are roles that women inhabit simultaneously. Every day as they sell goods in the market place, women may be planning meals. Or, as they wait in line with a sick child at a medical clinic, they may be talking with other women about constructing a new school. These spheres spill over and influence each other. For example, a woman's domestic responsibilities will influence her choice of paid work (Stephens, 1992).

Vulnerabilitv to Gender-based Violence

The issue of violence against women is receiving growing attention. In the national reports on the status of women prepared for the Fourth World Conference on Women, every report from the Caribbean raised this issue. "There is a tone of anger, disgust, sometimes mixed with frustration at the unending stream of violent crimes being committed in the region against women, from rape to brutal murder" (ECLAC, 1994). In addition to sexual abuse, battery, rape and murder, the same report cites other manifestations of violence against women such as using rape as a political tactic against Haitian women and the traffic in women from the Dominican Republic in the sex industry.

Domestic violence is one issue that has united women. Explored in both the social policy and political participation chapters, violence and the threat of violence cross classes, religions, ages and ethnic differences. It is not confined to urban slums or to one racial group. Violence against women in the home or on the streets hinders the ability of women to participate in economic and social activities. In addition to the medical costs, it destroys self-esteem and prevents women from being active participants in the development process (Carillo, 1992).

Concerns about Reproductive Health

The health risks associated with pregnancy and childbirth touch almost all women's lives, yet the quality and availability of medical care vary across the region. Women have a general interest in controlling their fertility in a safe, dignified and affordable fashion. The chapter on social policy explores the issue of women's health, arguing that although there is a clearly felt need for women-centered reproductive health policies and facilities, it is also important not to limit the definition of women's health to reproductive health issues. Other issues—including nutrition, women-specific diseases such as cervical and breast cancer, violence against women, occupational health issues, HIV-AIDs, tobacco, drugs, and alcohol—also warrant attention.

Limited Access to National Decision-making Bodies

The level of women's public and political participation across the Latin American and Caribbean region varies from country to country. However, the general trend is one of limited participation in leadership positions both within political organizations and in government.

Although evidence points toward the increased participation of women in municipal politics, NGOs, and community-based organizations, increased involvement at this level has been slow to translate into meaningful positions at the national level.

The chapter on political participation outlines the obstacles women face, including the nature and organization of the bodies themselves, the cultural stereotypes surrounding women's participation and the influence of the military and the church in inhibiting women's participation. Each of these issues poses significant problems for women who attempt to move into the political process. Other problems such as women's lack of time for such participation and their inability to finance political careers are also considered.

The chapter on political participation also raises questions about what changes are necessary to promote not just an increase in the number of women in national decision-making positions, but also what is required to construct a political system that takes women's needs and interests into account.

Reassembling the Pieces

This book argues that women do have enough in common to warrant consideration apart from men and that gender is a relevant variable in development planning. However, the differences among women clearly must be taken into consideration as well. Drawing on a wide range of recent research, each chapter explores how women's circumstances differ from those of men and demonstrates how major policies, although they may intend to be "gender neutral," do indeed have a different impact on women and men.

Grouping women is also relevant because significant numbers of women have voiced gender concerns and have mobilized around these issues.

Latin America and the Caribbean are seeing the "constitution of a new collective subject" (Jelin, 1990). Women at the local, national and international levels are voicing gender-specific demands and are organizing to change the way the political system operates.

Given this diversity, a final caution using a sectoral approach is in order. A sectoral approach is helpful in understanding various aspects of national development. After all, different disciplines offer insights into what we call "development." Yet it is also important to put the entire picture back together again after dissecting the various elements of women's lives and pulling apart the sectoral elements. The pieces should once again fall into place. After this analysis, they should reveal more than they conceal. Women are not just workers or mothers or environmental activists, they are all of these at the same time. Women are complex actors working in complex circumstances. Understanding that complexity is only the first step. Developing appropriate policies and programs is the second.

Chapter 2

Challenging Inequality: Women and Social Policy

Social policy has become a central concern of public policy making in the 1990s. The well-known social costs of the economic adjustments of the 1980s, together with evidence that progress is impossible without major reforms to address the huge inequalities found in Latin American and Caribbean societies, has made clear the absolute necessity for social reform.

In attempting to tackle inequality among citizens of the hemisphere, one of the most difficult areas is the persistent inequity between men and women—inequity in the burden borne in times of crisis, in the degree of participation in the struggle for development and in the enjoyment of the benefits of that struggle.

Most countries in Latin America and the Caribbean have managed to improve the quality of life for their people. In general, women have benefitted from that progress. However, when the money runs out and priorities have to be set, the unequal distribution of power means it is women who suffer most. In many areas the status of women continues to be precarious, or may have even worsened. Additional burdens may have been imposed on women, or the resources essential for them to perform their tasks efficiently and equitably may have been denied.

Recent research has revealed the inadequacy of prevailing social policies, which have been based largely on the out-dated perception of men as income earners and women as a "vulnerable group" (with a focus on their roles as wives and mothers). Women's roles as income earners, community organizers and political leaders have been neglected. Since the United Nations Decade for Women was declared in 1975, substantial research has documented the widely varying conditions in which women work and live, the enormous diversity of family groups, and the make-up of gender roles and relations. Recent research reveals a picture very different from that assumed by many policy makers. These findings have had only a minimal impact on the way social programs are devised and executed, but they underscore the inadequacy of social policies. It is no longer possible to base these policies on a model that is outdated.

Looking at how women have maintained and redefined their functions and tasks to meet changing circumstances, the question immediately arises whether it is efficient, effective or just—for women, men, and society—to go on considering women as "a vulnerable group." The latest findings in research, planning, and administration of public services point rather to an extraordinary wealth and complexity in women's contributions, to the burdens they bear, and to the difficulty they have in achieving a balance between them.

A broader understanding of women's lives enhances social development and helps redefine the way social programs are devised and executed. The first part of this chapter provides an overview of recent findings on the situation of Latin American and Caribbean women, including a discussion of the varying incarnations of the family, the multiple roles of women, an expanded vision of women's health and the persistence of gender biases in women's education. The second section looks at the differing economic and social burdens of women and men. It also examines social policy formulation from a gender perspective. The authors propose general criteria or guidelines for program design and indicate areas in which concrete action is needed.

Women Today in Latin America and the Caribbean

To a large extent, the circumstances faced by Latin American and Caribbean women reflect the full range of conditions found in the region. In this respect, women—like men—are affected by influences as diverse as their country's level of development and availability of resources. Women may be urban or rural, of different races, very poor, newly poor or extremely wealthy. They live in countries in which the "average" level of development disguises huge disparities among the population. Cultures differ as well. Women may find themselves in Hispanic, indigenous, African or—in the case of the non-Latin countries of the Caribbean—Anglo-Saxon or Hindu environments. There are therefore major dangers attached to planning for specific populations on the basis of "averages."

In societies with a highly skewed income distribution, the living conditions of women are clearly not homogeneous. This means that the restrictions and opportunities individual women (or groups of women) face have to be studied case by case. If women are to be in a position to take advantage of opportunities that come with development, in addition to general policies, specific actions must be taken to overcome the particular hurdles that different groups of women face.

There is no doubt that there has been an enormous improvement in the status of women and in their contribution to development in Latin America and the Caribbean. Compared to several decades ago, women today are better educated, can expect to live longer and healthier lives, and have fewer children. The gap between their income and that earned by men has narrowed. Their participation in the generation of national income—through their invisible as well as visible work—is considerable. Nevertheless, the many advances in women's situations have obscured problems that must be addressed if further progress is to be made.

Gender roles are still distributed in such a way that women are at a disadvantage when it comes to reaping the benefits of their efforts. Persisting stereotypes of what men and women do and should do impede objective insight into the changes taking place in the real world. Since such behavior is considered "natural," it is not subjected to scrutiny, questioning, or reformulation when social policies are developed. Those stereotypes turn into seemingly insurmountable obstacles, thwarting efforts to incorporate what women have to offer and to broaden their access to development. Policy makers face several important challenges.

Family and Household Structures

Recent research has highlighted families and households. Several assumptions often held by policy makers and development planners about the family have been thrown into question. The issues of whether who heads the family is a useful concept and significance of the growing number of female-headed households have also been raised.

Moser (1993a) clearly documents three assumptions about the family that rarely hold, yet are commonly used as the basis of policy making and program design:

- The household consists of a nuclear family of husband, wife and two or three children.
- The household functions as a socio-economic unit within which there is equal control over resources and power of decision making among all adult members in matters influencing the household's livelihood.
- Within the household there is a clear division of labor based on

gender. The man of the family, as the "breadwinner," is primarily involved in productive work outside the home. The woman, as the housewife and "homemaker," takes overall responsibility for the reproductive and domestic work involved in the organization of the household.

Numerous analyses clearly show that families in Latin America rarely conform to this neat model (Folbre, 1991a; Lloyd, 1993). There is now growing recognition that family configuration must be treated as a variable and that variations from one type of family to another are the key to making sure that services match the needs of family members. It can no longer be assumed that the family is a unit composed of father, mother and children living under the same roof, sharing resources in an equitable fashion and functioning as a unified economy. Other family patterns are increasingly common: families headed by women, families in which both partners work regularly, or extended families in which other members look after domestic chores so that a mother can go to work.

These false notions surrounding the role and composition of households no longer match today's changing circumstances. This discrepancy between assumption and reality is distorting the impact of projects.

Research has revealed the need to analyze the status of individual family members. They may not all have the same access to resources and power, nor are they necessarily equally endowed with human capital, nor is the head of the family always the main user of services. The real behavior of each household member, as a consumer and producer, varies considerably depending on his or her position in the home. Yet, the most common method of diagnosis for planning purposes uses the data for the head of the household as the criterion for determining the type and quantity of services required.

It is also important to look at the links between family structures and poverty. Buvinić (1994) has argued that households headed by women are over-represented among the poor. Three sets of factors are cited to explain this trend. First, woman-headed households often carry a high dependency burden. In other words, they have a higher ratio of children and older people to working-age adults. Second, in general women earn 60 to 70 percent of what men earn. Finally, women may encounter additional constraints as females in charge of households (such as time and mobility constraints or discrimination in access to jobs and credit).

Discussions of households must address the notion of "headship" itself. Using data from Peru, Rosenhouse (1989) argues that the reported head of household generally fails to reflect who is the regular presence in the household, has overriding authority, and is the primary economic support). There-

Box 1: Women's Domestic Responsibilities

In Argentina, it was found that the more than 20 chores carried out by members of a family took on average 84.5 hours a week. Four-fifths of those hours were put in by housewives, even those who had another job outside the home. Whereas those who had another job put in 55.9 hours a week, the women who stayed at home worked 73.1 hours a week. In contrast, domestic labor by other members of the family amounted to about 45 minutes a day, or 5.3 hours a week.

If you add a working week of approximately 35.4 hours to the hours spent doing domestic chores, women with paid jobs work a 13-hour day and a 91.3-hour week (Feijóo and Jelin, 1987).

fore, this concept offers limited insight into the economic structure and support of the household. Handa (1994) also questions the use of this concept, citing reports that even in households with a designated male head of household, women may be the primary income earners. Both support a revision to incorporate the concept of "working head" and argue that this could provide a more accurate base from which to develop policy and programs.

Women's Work

Recent models describing women's work identify three dimensions: reproductive, productive and community management work (Moser, 1993a). Recognizing this triple role, women's lives have been described as "a balancing act with which women try to reconcile the demand for survival of the home and cultural and religious traditions which define work as a male realm" (Ward, 1990). That balance varies according to income strata, to different historical contexts, and as a function of the particular stages of the family cycle. Not all women are equally responsible for family chores. Income levels and positions in households determine how much and what kind of work they do in the home. It is also important to stress that these roles are not mutually exclusive. Elements overlap and influence each other. For example, decisions around productive work are often heavily influenced by domestic responsibilities. A woman may decide to work in the informal sector even though it offers limited income potential because it does offer flexibility in terms of child care.

Further examination of women's roles and responsibilities bring to light the complexity of women's lives and the corresponding need for strategies that address this reality.

Reproductive Work

Reproductive work refers not only to childbearing and -rearing responsibilities undertaken by women but also to the domestic tasks required to guarantee the maintenance and reproduction of the labor force. Such tasks include housework, shopping, food preparation and preservation, caring for the sick, and laundry. A rural woman's day may begin as early as 5 a.m. and finish at 9 or 10 p.m. (Stephen, 1992). Although women constitute an increasing proportion of the paid workforce, this work continues to be assigned primarily to women with no recognition of the social costs involved. Leisure time is a luxury unknown to many women throughout the region.

As economic analysis has been applied to the ways families function, the economic value of household chores has been clarified and has become increasingly evident (Benería, 1991). Yet, because national accounting systems and many household surveys fail to register and measure this work, it remains largely invisible. Waring (1989) has criticized current national accounts and argues that this invisibility has important negative effects for women:

> Non-producers (housewives, mothers) who are "inactive" and "unoccupied" cannot, apparently, be in need. They are not even in the economic cycle in the first place. They can certainly have no expectation that they will be visible in the distribution of benefits that flow from production.

Productive Work

The level of participation of women in the economy of Latin America and the Caribbean has leapt forward over the past three decades. Although this is explored in more detail in the chapter on women as economic actors, several important points are also presented here. The number of women with jobs has grown over 120 percent, a figure far higher than the growth of women with jobs worldwide. Whereas the number of men in the regional labor force is expected to double between 1995 and the year 2000, the number of employed women will have tripled (López and Pollack, 1992; see also Tables 4, 5 and 6).

The implications of women's participation in the labor market acquire particular importance when the absolute numbers are considered: 55 million women are involved (López and Pollack, 1992). It is impossible to refer to any other area of women's participation without taking this fact into account. It is one thing to define a woman's role in society when she is basically "wife and mother" or a "secondary worker." It is quite a different matter, however, when her economic activity becomes an everyday fact and necessity.

This underscores the opportunity cost of domestic chores, which used to be considered "natural." It also raises the question of whether families should continue to handle a number of welfare-related tasks—such as caring for the elderly, the sick, and children—and whether or not it should be up to the state or the market to create new social services.

As is documented in the chapter dealing with economic policy, the nature of women's paid work differs substantially from men's in terms of remuneration, sector concentration, opportunities, working conditions and training required.

It has also been shown that poor households frequently turn themselves into productive-reproductive units—a phenomenon that, far from disappearing, has become more and more common (Bonilla, 1993). In such units the family uses the entire infrastructure of the home for work and engages members of the family whom the statistics assume to be inactive, such as grandparents and children, in work activities.

There are advantages to paid work for both women and the family group. Apart from the benefits of control over funds, which gradually translates into a more egalitarian position in the household, it has been proven that women tend to allot a higher proportion of income to the needs of the household (Blumberg, 1985; Benería and Roldán, 1987). In Mexico, women contributed all their income to the home, as opposed to men, who only contributed three-quarters of their earnings (Roldán, 1988). Thus, although women earn less, their weighting in the family budget is greater.

Yet, women working outside the home need support. Without this support, there are at least three possible costs associated with women's entry into the labor market:

- The lack of reasonably priced support services means that other members of the family, often girls, will contribute unpaid labor.
- Some kinds of jobs are incompatible with raising children if there is no suitable child care. Modern paid positions offer better social benefits and higher wages. In informal activities, women often depend on men for transportation in cities and frequently must use up savings in order to cover family needs. As a result, their "enterprises" are too often at the lowest end of the scale in terms of productivity and income. In such cases, female labor means an even heavier burden for women (Lloyd, 1993).
- Under extreme circumstances, unless other members of the family help out with domestic tasks, women may reach their limits and children may be abandoned or begin to have behavior problems (Moser, 1987).

Appropriate social policies offer an opportunity to minimize these costs. A recognition of the specific situation and needs of women provides an important starting point for policy design.[1]

Community Management Work

Women's community management work is the last area of women's activity to win recognition. This dimension is especially interesting when links are established between social development and women's participation. Families—and particularly women—have played an important part in obtaining improvements for the local community and in administering social services beyond the bounds of their own homes. The state has usually relied on families to compensate for the deficient resources it allots to its own social welfare institutions.

Women step in in times of crisis as an extension of their domestic responsibilities. Since they often feel the pressure to provide for their families, they are active in struggles for housing, potable water, health care, food for their families and education for their children. Local organizations that have mobilized to obtain these services are often dominated by women.

Adjustment programs have often forced women to take on more such responsibilities. As public services are cut back, women have had to spend more time organizing and planning to support the survival of their families.

A gender-based division of community labor also causes problems. Such work tends to be paid when done by men and "voluntary" when performed by women. This split is reinforced by international organizations, NGOs, and governments who rely on that voluntary labor.

Women's Health

The new emphasis on women's health is on the whole human being, going beyond illnesses related simply to women's role as mothers (Koblinsky, Campbell and Harlow, 1993). More than a third of all illnesses suffered by women between the ages of 15 and 45, and more than one-fifth of those affecting women

[1]Two areas of work that pose very different social policy challenges are not covered in this chapter: prostitution and sex trade and illegal drugs. Anecdotal evidence on prostitution signals that this is a growing phenomenon in the region (Dimenstein, 1994). For example, the review of the status of women in the Caribbean developed in preparation for the Fourth World Conference on women cites a study estimating that as many as 25,000 women from the Dominican Republic are involved in the sex industry as far away as Asia and Europe (ECLAC, 1994). Little has been written on the impact on women of the drug trade, although it was also highlighted as an issue in the ECLAC study cited above (ECLAC, 1994).

Box 2: The Solanda Women's Center
Women Organizing the Community

Solanda is a new settlement south of Quito, established in 1982 as a pilot housing project for low-income families. A group of women founded the Solanda Women's Center with the following objectives: (1) the amelioration of barrio living conditions, especially the provision of services such as water, creches, a primary school, and a market; and (2) the improvement of women's status, including the learning of practical skills and a discussion of women's rights and other themes relating to women's daily lives. The first issues that women confronted were the problems with the water supply and education. They worked with their neighborhood committee and then represented their interests to the local municipality (Rodríguez, 1994).

Rodríguez (1994, p. 37) argues that there was a tacit division of labor between women and men in Solanda. "While men are particularly involved in housing needs, women are involved in a struggle for both housing and household needs associated with their reproductive role."

between the ages of 45 and 59, are exclusively or predominantly women's illnesses. Many such ailments could be dealt with or reduced if health services altered their narrow approach of treating women exclusively as mothers.

What kills men also kills women. The different biology and social roles of women and men, however, imply different health problems and health care needs. For example, the fact that women generally have a lower body weight than men and that their hormonal makeup is different means that they have different physical reactions to drugs and alcohol. Women have less leisure time or rest, given their multiple roles, which also has health implications (Smyke, 1991).

Reproductive Health

Although mother-child health initiatives often constitute a major emphasis for governments and international agencies, there is a growing recognition of the need to understand women's reproductive health needs within a broader framework.

All pregnancies and childbirth carry risks for the mother and baby. These risks increase when the woman's general state of health is poor, when there are only minimal health services or support available, when the pregnancies and deliveries are badly timed—very early or very late in the reproductive cycle, very close to one another, or unwanted—and when a woman already has many children.

Box 3: Reproductive Health in the Context of Reproductive Rights

Reproductive rights include the following:

- the right to safe motherhood;
- the right to plan one's family;
- the right to assistance in preventing and overcoming infertility;
- the right to full and timely knowledge about all aspects of reproductive health and sexuality (Smyke, 1991).

The most dramatic indicator of the consequences of the poor state of health of some Latin American women is maternal mortality (see Table 2). To a large extent, this can be prevented by improved access to health services. As an average, this indicator disguises huge discrepancies among different social strata. The risk of a woman dying from causes related to pregnancy is between 0.2 and 2 percent in Latin America and less than 0.01 percent in industrialized countries (De Vanzo and Haaga, 1991).

The provision of medical care before, after, and during childbirth fluctuates considerably within and among countries. For example, Table 2 documents the range of the percentage of births with a trained attendant present: 12 percent in Bolivia and 9 percent in Haiti to 96 percent in Chile, 100 percent in the Bahamas, and 100 percent in Uruguay.

Statistics from the countries in the region show a direct link between the levels of maternal mortality and the provision of medical care before and during childbirth. Countries such as Cuba, Chile and Costa Rica, which have the highest percentage of women receiving this medical care, have the lowest maternal mortality. Countries with the least medical coverage, such as Bolivia, have the highest maternal mortality.

Abortion, practiced under unsanitary conditions also influences maternal mortality. The greatest risk comes from infections, which may have long-term consequences such as chronic pain, ectopic pregnancies, infertility, hemorrhages, and damage to the cervix. In Latin America, about half the deaths of pregnant women are estimated to be due to illegal abortions (World Bank, 1993a).

On average for the region as a whole, 43 percent of the women who say they do not want more children do not practice any form of contraception.

Some researchers estimate that if the unsatisfied demand for birth control among married women were met, maternal mortality would drop 33 percent (Society for International Development, 1993). One indicator of the lack of access to reliable forms of contraception is the high sterilization rate. In 1986 in Brazil, 19 percent of women between 25 and 29 years old living with a partner had been sterilized. The figure was 29 percent for the Dominican Republic, and 33 percent in El Salvador (PAHO, 1990). These rates are far higher than those found in industrialized countries and suggest, according to De Vanzo and Haaga (1991), that contraception is used more to limit the total size of the family rather than to space births over time.

Adolescent pregnancies are a major social problem. The transition from childhood to adulthood is a critical period with long-term effects on the lives of individuals and those of their dependents. A woman who gets pregnant at an early age without a stable partnership and who stops going to school will have very few options open to her for the rest of her life, thereby affecting her child's future (Feijõo and Jelin, 1987).

After taking into account the drop in fertility, the proportion of births among women under 20 has increased in the region and it is higher than in other parts of the world (De Vanzo and Haaga, 1991). In 1992, adolescent mothers accounted for 16 percent of all births (World Bank, 1993a). Such births are most frequent among poor women. In Brazil in 1986, 65 percent of mothers under the age of 20 came from poor homes. In Venezuela, 23 percent of female adolescents without schooling had been pregnant at some point, compared to 10 percent among those who had received between one and five years' education (World Bank, 1993d).

Female Malnutrition

Women tend to suffer more than men from anaemia caused by iron deficiency, from stunted growth due to a lack of proteins and calories, and from iodine deficiency. On average, one-third of pregnant women in Latin America are estimated to suffer from anaemia (Huffman *et al.,* 1990). In Central America, the proportion is thought to be between one-half and two-thirds of all pregnant women (García and Gomariz, 1989).

As in many other parts of the world, women and girls in Latin America and the Caribbean often eat last and least. The high status of boys often gives them priority access to food. For example, a survey from the state of Tlaxcala in Mexico showed that girls received less of all nutrients than boys (O'Connell, 1994).

Box 4: Violence against Women

In one forensic clinic in Bolivia, 1,432 cases of aggression were reported, with women being the victims in two-thirds of the cases. In 61 percent of those cases, women were the victims of abuse by their husbands, 23 percent of them had been raped, and 17 percent were attacked by other relatives or neighbors.

In Lima, in the first nine months of 1989, 88 percent of all accusations against husbands or companions involved physical violence.

In Caracas, 89 percent of cases reported to the Municipal Shelter opened in 1985 had to do with severe physical abuse by a companion (PAHO, 1990).

Malnutrition in women carries over to the next generation. It causes the birth of underweight children and increases the rate of infant mortality. Inequality in nutrition is also reflected later in life. For instance, a smaller than average or ill-shaped pelvis may be the result of an insufficient intake of proteins, calcium, and vitamin D during childhood. This in turn may translate into problems during childbirth.

Women's Diseases

There is a very high incidence of cervical cancer in Latin America, and health services to detect it in time are extremely deficient. In Brazil, for instance, only 2 percent of women have been tested in the public health system. The mortality rate for cases of cervical cancer among women aged between 35 and 64 in the United States and Canada (1.4 percent and 1.3 percent, respectively) are considerably lower than those observed even in countries with good health conditions such as Costa Rica (5.4 percent), Chile (6.6 percent), or Trinidad and Tobago (3.2 percent) (De Vanzo and Haaga, 1991).

Violence against Women: A Public Health Issue

Violence against women, including rape, is very common but under-recognized. World Bank data (1993a) show that in both developed and developing countries, at least a fifth of all women say—when asked—that they have been hit by their partners. Such women are twice as liable to have miscarriages and four times more likely to give birth to underweight children. Only recently has such violence been seen as a health problem, despite the fact that it is a significant cause of female morbidity and mortality and a factor leading to psychological trauma, depression, injuries, sexually transmitted diseases, suicides, and murders. Only a very few health professionals have been trained to spot cases of violence and abuse.

Nobody knows the real extent of the phenomenon because of the reporting difficulties involved. Nevertheless all the evidence of experts points to the existence of violence on an alarming scale in all social classes.

In the opinion of those who handle such cases—whether lawyers (Valdez, 1994) or police officers—failure to recognize violence against women as a crime is the main barrier to preventing it. The laws do not lay down requirements, for instance, that sexual violence against a woman by her partner be considered a crime. In almost all countries, there are no legal provisions with which to tackle family violence. Access to justice is highly precarious. In Brazil, for instance, there are some provisions and customs that justify killing a woman if the deed occurs in what is known as the "legitimate defense of her husband's honor."

In the Caribbean, the deterioration of the social fabric grown out of frustration and despair over higher unemployment rates and lower earnings has been identified as the source of an escalation of intra-family violence (Gaskin-Reyes, 1992). For Moser (1993b), men in Latin America feel they have lost authority and a sense of identity because they associate the economic dependency of women with fidelity. To reestablish their authority they often resort to violence.

The growing numbers of centers for battered women, self-help groups, shelters, legal advice offices, police stations with women police officers and emergency telephone number services are indirect indicators of how widespread violence is. In Latin America, there are roughly 400 NGOs attempting to deal with various aspects of this problem (Moser, 1993b). Few preventive programs addressing the causes of aggression against women and the beliefs underlying it exist at this time.

Occupational Health

While it is true that there are major gaps in maternal health, in other areas such as occupational health, there is simply no basic information available for an assessment of the size of the problem. The state's failure to supervise safety conditions and hygiene at the workplace is exacerbated in this case by women's and men's ignorance of dangers and of safety standards. There are major health hazards for women both in their work with the new export crops and in the jobs they do at home—exposure to pesticides and other chemicals in cropwork, for example and eyestrain in housework (Østergaard, 1992).

Tobacco, Alcohol and Drugs

Although not thought to be as serious as other health issues, the impact of the use and abuse of tobacco, alcohol and drug products is serious and cause for concern. Most of the resulting problems are preventable. Once again men and women differ in how these substances affect them (Smyke, 1991).

The World Health Organization (WHO) has recently drawn attention to the increasing numbers of women using tobacco products in developing countries. It is estimated that in Bolivia and Brazil, for example, 50-60 percent of women use tobacco in one form or another. Women and young people are increasingly targeted in tobacco advertising.

Research has drawn attention to the different biological and social effects of alcohol abuse on women and men. Physically, women's smaller body size often means that they are more sensitive to alcohol effects. Women who drink heavily are more likely than men to develop cirrhosis of the liver. Socially, women alcoholics are often treated differently from their male counterparts. For example, a study in Paraguay found that nine out of 10 husbands leave wives who have drinking addictions, while only one out of 10 women leaves her husband when he is an alcoholic (Smyke, 1991).

HIV-AIDS

Latin America and the Caribbean are not exempt from the HIV-AIDS pandemic increasing around the world. The WHO estimates that there are already about 1.5 million HIV-infected adults in the region. Brazil has the highest number of reported AIDS cases in the Americas after the United States, yet higher rates of infection were noted in some Caribbean islands (WHO, 1994).

Since the mid-to-late 1980s, the pattern of transmission has changed. There has been a steady increase in heterosexual transmission, principally between bisexual men and their female sex partners, between male and female drug users (and their sex partners) and between female sex workers and their male clients (and between the clients and their regular partners). Given this changing pattern, women are increasingly affected, as is shown in Box 5.

Education

Educational levels in Latin America, like health services, correlate closely with the level of development of a country and are a function of the education budget within total expenditure for the social sector.

In 14 countries of the region, female illiteracy is 15 percent or more, and in two of them—El Salvador and Haiti—more than half the women are

Box 5: The Increasing Incidence of HIV Infection among Women

In Brazil, heterosexual transmission—linked to only 7.5 percent of reported AIDS cases up to 1987—accounted for 23 percent by 1992. Primarily for this reason, women are increasingly affected: the male/female ratio was 28 to 1 in 1985 and only 5 to 1 in 1992. Studies among pregnant women attending prenatal clinics in São Paulo state between 1987 and 1990 found that seroprevalence increased steadily during that period, from 0.2 percent to 1.3 percent (WHO, 1994).

illiterate. Although generally speaking, the figures for women roughly correspond with those for men, there are still differences of four points or more in a third of the countries. In Peru and Bolivia, the difference is as large as 20 percentage points (see Table 3).

At the primary school level, the gap has closed in almost all countries. Only in Guatemala, Haiti, and Bolivia is primary education for women far from universal. In eight countries of the region, half the female population has surpassed the basic education level, whereas in the five poorest countries, the mean is less than four years of education.

Both the quality and orientation of women's education remain areas of concern. In almost all countries, there are very pronounced differences in the types and fields of education chosen by men and women. According to a recent study by the World Bank, Latin American women are less likely to receive vocational training oriented toward better-paid jobs in growth sectors (De Vanzo and Haaga, 1991).

To tackle such cases of segregation and discrimination, it is necessary to study what gives rise to them. It is worth investigating, for instance, whether there is discrimination in entry requirements, or whether there are differences in the prior conditions for men and women—cultural and family values—that make women automatically discriminate against themselves. Another hypothesis to be tested is that women probably lack knowledge of the educational options open to them (Flórez, 1992).

Despite different methodologies, populations, and length of studies, the mother's education is found to be the consistent determining influence on the health of the family (World Bank, 1993a). Education considerably strengthens a woman's ability to maintain a healthy home. Improvements in family health and living conditions correlate with women's education. The repercus-

Box 6: Women in Education Case Studies

- In Colombia in the 1980s there was a drop in the proportion of high performance schools, but boys' schools maintained their 54 percent to 68 percent share of the high performance schools, almost doubling that of girls' schools (FEDESARROLLO 1992).
- Also in Colombia, there has been an increase in the number of women graduating from secondary schools, but only in areas that are traditionally considered "feminine" and that lead to paid jobs that are extensions of domestic work (Flórez, 1992).
- In Costa Rica, it was discovered that all those receiving training in agriculture were men. All those being schooled in household economics were women (World Bank 1992).
- Both in Venezuela and in Colombia the statistics for graduates from professional training institutes show a marked tendency towards gender segregation (Castillo *et al.* 1992; Flórez, 1992).
- In Honduras, a World Bank study (1993c) found that the number of women going to university has increased, but that their presence at institutes providing technical training courses continues to be minor.
- The National Agricultural College (Escuela Nacional de Agricultura) does not allow women students.
- In the informal education and training courses for women provided by government and non-governmental institutions, most students enrol in courses related to activities in the home, such as household management, sewing, and cooking.

sions of a father's improved education are largely felt in terms of increased earnings. In the mother's case, the impact is via better information. Educated women are, according to the World Bank, a key to the success of the health sector in low-income countries such as Costa Rica.

Given the crucial importance of women's education, it is surprising to note that relatively little attention has been paid to the barriers that prevent women's access to education. Two explanations surface again and again. When the figures favor women, the argument runs that the opportunity cost of men's education is higher due to men's greater chances of getting a paid job. The alternative explanation would be that the opportunity cost for girls is very high because they are able to substitute for the mother in doing the domestic chores. It has been discovered, for instance, that the demand for girls' education is more sensitive to income and prices than that for boys. This has been confirmed for several countries such as Mexico, Guatemala, Chile and Peru (King, 1990).

The formidable influence of these hidden barriers can be seen in a project supporting professional training financed by the Inter-American Development Bank in Chile. Although from the time the project was first de-

Box 7: Impact of Women's Education

Demographic and health surveys carried out in 25 countries have shown that an increase of as little as one to three years in mothers' schooling reduces infant mortality by about 15 percent. A similar increase for fathers has an impact of only 6 percent (World Bank 1993a). Further years of education increase the impact. In Peru, for example, the effect of six or more years of education for the mother is to cut the risk of infant mortality by 75 percent (World Bank 1993a). In Central America (Garcia and Gomáriz, 1989) women with no schooling produce an infant-mortality rate three to four times higher than that for women who have had secondary or a university education. A World Bank study for the region showed that for children of women with no education, the mortality rate for those under five years of age was 140 per 1,000. When the mother has four to six years of education, the mortality rate drops to 90, and with seven or more years, to about 50 per 1,000 (Summers, 1992).

Educated women also make greater use of prenatal health services and give birth with medical help. In Lima, a study examining the availability of services found that 82 percent of the women with over six years of schooling made use of prenatal services, compared with 62 percent of the women with no schooling (World Bank, 1993a).

signed precautions were taken to ensure young women would take part in non-traditional areas—including agreements with institutions devoted to child care, contracting of special consultancy services, and interviews with employers to make them more sensitive to the issue—a recent assessment of the project reveals that it has hit snags. Employers involved in the program have resisted, and some young women have given up for reasons associated with their traditional roles—to get married, because they got pregnant, or because their boyfriends protested. This experience draws attention to a whole set of factors, including cultural influences, that are common throughout the region but that, nonetheless, have hardly begun to be faced (IDB/Government of Chile, 1993).

Women's Access to Support Services

Child care constitutes one of the principal needs of working women throughout the region. In a study commissioned by the Inter-American Development Bank, six benefits to both individuals and societies were documented (Myers, 1994):

- increased employment and productivity—Children who are well-cared for will grow up to perform better at school and will most likely be in a

Box 8: Girls, Women and Education: Two Projects

Education Reform in Bolivia

Within an IDB-funded program designed to support both administrative and educational and pedagogical reforms to the education system, attention is being paid to gender-specific issues. For example, stereotypical presentation of men's and women's roles will be removed from educational material.

Special attention is also paid to girls' enrolment in schools to reduce their dropout rate, particularly in the rural areas where the situation is the most severe. Seventy percent of the country's illiterate are women. On average, girls complete only 60 percent of the number of school years that boys do. The problem is partly explained by safety concerns of parents and the opportunity costs of sending girls to school. Some of the incentives to keep girls in school will be scholarships, daycare for younger siblings whom girls are responsible for, and meals for girls in rural areas.

Support for Labor Force Adaptation in Argentina

Women's specific needs in a changing labor market are granted attention in a project funded by the IDB in Argentina. An analysis revealed that even though the participation rate of women in the economy had increased in recent years, there are still barriers that prevent many women from seeking and obtaining employment. Women's unemployment rate was higher than that of men.

The project developed a series of specific measures to expand women's opportunities to obtain the training they need to move into more productive and better-paying jobs. These included the promotion of the program to young women, training institutions and prospective employers; support for women with small children; and efforts to train women in non-traditional occupations (including placements with employers that offer on-the-job experience). The impact of these program measures is analyzed periodically to assess whether or not they are actually achieving the overall goal of increased women's participation.

better position to contribute to their families, communities and societies. In addition, child care programs facilitate increased labor force participation by women and can enable daughters to continue with their education.

- cost savings—Reduced absenteeism on the part of parents with inadequate child care arrangements can cut costs; health costs can be reduced because quality child care includes preventative measures; and inefficiency in the school system decreases by reducing repetition, dropout and remedial programs.
- reductions in social and economic inequities—Quality child care programs for children from poor families can promote healthy development and increase the probability of increased schooling.
- reductions in gender inequalities—By supporting the participation of girls in early development programs, girls gain basic skills that they often do

not receive otherwise. A child care program also offers an opportunity to provide children with positive examples of women and men in more equitable positions through the teaching materials used.

- strengthened values—Child care programs can provide an environment with culturally desirable values.
- social mobilization and community benefits—Parent participation in a child care center can often be an entry point for mobilization around other issues.

Little is known about existing child care arrangements, but current evidence suggests that in poor households child care is left up to other female members of the household or to informal networks set up among women friends and neighbors. The studies suggest that very little coverage is provided by "formal" services, including pre-school education for the poorest groups (World Bank, 1993c; Joekes, 1987b; Massiah, 1983).

Even less widespread are low-priced services designed to substitute for other domestic chores, such as food preparation, washing clothes, or looking after the sick, the handicapped, and the elderly. Programs for the poorest women workers are few in number and far from comprehensive. To the extent that the growing importance of such women workers has not yet been recognized, social services have also lagged behind.

Women and Social Security

It is surprising to find that although social security has been amply debated in recent years, the specific issue of women and social security has not been tackled. A review of a large number of studies reveals only marginal references to the different manner in which women are affected by social security programs as compared to men. In Latin America, social security often aims to provide coverage for a family group through the affiliation of a worker who is, generally speaking, an employee of a relatively large firm. The system design implies—as can be seen from a glance at the rules entitling people to various benefits—that the "wife and children" have access as qualified members of the family. In fact, legislation frequently establishes different norms for a male or female spouse, making it very clear that the latter is a "dependent."

The structure of the labor market is a fundamental determinant in a family's potential and actual access to social security. If job options open to men and women differ markedly, especially in the poorer strata, it follows that coverage will differ according to gender. If a woman is not herself affiliated, either because she does not undertake paid work or works in an activity not covered by social security, access to benefits as a member of the family depends on her maintaining a stable relationship with a man (husband or son) who has a salaried job covered by social security. This is particularly important when it comes to maternity benefits. The data on both the composition and stability of the "traditional" household and the structure of the labor market indicate that there is only a very remote likelihood that poor women meet these conditions.

An analysis of women's access to social security should include two crucial aspects: the costs of pre- and postnatal care and child support contributions from absent fathers. First, many labor codes include measures to protect maternity (paid maternity leave, job guarantees, and support for breastfeeding for example). These codes are based on the view that the costs of that function should be socialized and not be a private cost borne by women alone. In practice, such measures merely lead to fewer job opportunities for women, dismissals and lower wages, justified by managers who consider maternity leave a bad investment as a waste of working hours. A World Bank study in Honduras (1993c) shows how such laws have had the effect of reducing employment opportunities for women or of making their work more expensive than that of men. As well, measures to make work contracts more flexible affect women proportionately more than men. Labor instability is particularly serious for women because they are then left without maternity coverage.

Second, the vast majority of laws that oblige fathers to contribute to the upkeep of their children are woefully ineffective. Several studies (Folbre, 1991b; Massiah, 1983; and Rakowski, 1989) show that contributions from absent fathers are minimal. Procedures to enforce payment are highly limited and time-consuming for mothers. Moreover, mothers and fathers are generally ignorant of their rights and duties in this area and are often unaware of the legal and administrative remedies available to them.

The Impact of Crisis, Adjustment and Social Policy on Women

For over a decade, Latin American societies have developed in a context marked by economic adjustment programs and economic change juxtaposed with new social policy approaches.

There has been endless discussion regarding the impact of economic changes on social welfare. It is evident that the recession and structural adjustment programs have exacerbated various kinds of inequality. Traditional institutional mechanisms to counter inequality are increasingly ineffective. Within this overall deterioration, some segments of the population have been hit harder than others. Research indicates, in particular, different effects on men and on women according to their position within the social structure (UNICEF, 1987; Moser, Herbert, and Makonnen, 1993; Benería and Feldman, 1992).

The years of crisis and adjustment have added to the burden borne by women, who have had to do more paid work to offset the drop in family income. At the same time, deterioration in social services has meant that women must devote more time to either obtaining services or making up for the lack of them. Similarly, the higher cost of basic items has forced women to spend more time preparing meals and shopping. Time spent on communal work and managing collective services has also increased. All this has put women under a severe strain because of their multiple roles.

Women made some gains in equity during the 1980s in the sense that they started to broaden their participation in the outside world, "the world of men," but at a disproportionate cost. Women have taken on low-skilled, less-productive and therefore poorly paid jobs. Both poverty and the informal sector have become feminized (Pollack, 1991).

In the social sector, great changes are taking place in the roles played by states, markets and families in achieving welfare. At the same time, each institution is undergoing profound change. The repercussions of such phenomena on the economy or on the use or demand for social services traditionally provided by the state have not yet been adequately explored.

The Impact of Crisis and Adjustment

The 1980s, the so-called lost decade of Latin America, which affected different countries in many ways, was characterized by an increase in poverty levels, greater inequity in the distribution of income, a greater shift to the informal sector and a massive but unequal entry of women into the economic and social processes. In addition, social investments have been smaller, less equitable and less efficient (Grosh, 1993).

In the midst of this sombre panorama, women have played a crucial role in ensuring that economic adjustments do not result in even greater negative impact. Women have played a greater role in contributing to household income (Bonilla, 1990), not only in terms of salary but also in terms of the rationalization of expenditures (at the cost of their own time) and through their efforts to resolve community problems via local support networks.

It is worth noting that the crisis helped spark a process of collective action and opened the way for new relationships between the state and civil society. Within this process, women were at the forefront of community cooperation and developed an organizational capacity that resulted, in some cases, in a process of empowerment (Lago, 1986).

In urban environments, macroeconomic reforms affected the population mainly via changes in the prices of mass-consumption goods, the level of services, falling wages, downsizing of public sector employment, and changes in the amount and composition of public expenditure. The literature analyzing the situation of women vis à vis economic adjustment has focused on a number of topics—first, family survival strategies; second, the changes in each dimension of women's roles; and third, the impact of changes on women-headed households.

Family Survival Strategies

Faced with an uncertain present and future, families have sought to defend themselves in various ways. They have developed strategies to gain access to various mechanisms of participation in markets and of reciprocity. Such tactics aim to reduce vulnerability through a diversification of roles of family members. Women are invariably the protagonists of such mechanisms (Raczynski and Serrano, 1992a and 1992b). In addition, (and as is explored in the chapter on women's political participation), these strategies have had implications for women's broader political mobilization and participation.

Studies have pointed to a recomposition of family groups, either through incorporation of relatives or other family groups or as a result of sending younger children to live with relatives so the parents can work. There have also been changes in previous patterns, such as the withdrawal of girls or young women from school so that they can take over domestic chores and allow their mothers to work.

Within the family, two changes are worth noting because of their relevance for social services. First, the need to upset the existing pattern of activities has often led to pressures for a family breakup. Moser (1987) discovered that in Guayaquil, Ecuador, since women were already working between 12 and 18 hours a day, having to devote more time to the market and collective survival activities meant that they had less time to devote to domestic chores. With no additional time put in by fathers, there was a negative impact on the children and increased likelihood of the family disintegrating. Second, case studies (Benería and Roldán, 1987; Tovar, 1992; Feijóo, 1992) have found that when women begin to contribute to the family earnings and, at the same time, are exposed to elements outside the home as a result of participating in the community's social programs, the balance of power within the home is altered. Sometimes it has been possible to achieve what Roldán (1988) calls "renegotiation of the marital contract." In other cases, however, the weaker position of the men has led to an increase in family violence.

Patterns of family participation in the labor market changed as the minimum wage lost all significance as a basic wage for the family. There is evidence that it is impossible for poor families to survive on a single income. Even with several family members working, survival with an acceptable standard of living is not necessarily guaranteed (González de la Rocha, 1986). The strategies for incorporating poor women in the labor market vary according to the composition of the family group; those living with a partner and with small children participate least.

In addition to participation in strategies that entail socializing consumption—such as soup kitchens and cooperatives in Chile, communal meals in Peru, or informal child care systems in Jamaica—there has also been increasing recourse to non-residential family networks for swapping goods and services.

Households Headed by Women

Abundant research has pointed out that one of the most marked tendencies of the past decade has been the increase in the number of households headed by women and the fact that they are more likely to be among the poorer households (Folbre, 1990a and 1990b; Schaffner and Kremen, 1990; Buvinić, 1990). There are, indeed, disadvantages attached to such household from the point of view of welfare. They tend to be more vulnerable because they are usually more dependent upon the informal sector and have less chance of access to social benefits (social security, for instance). In addition, the children tend to go to work at an early age, abandoning school and thereby perpetuating poverty.

But the evidence is contradictory concerning two questions:

- whether the proportion of households headed by women is always greater among the poor compared to segments of the population that are not poor and whether such households are a majority in poor areas; and
- whether they are always at a disadvantage compared to households headed by men.

The discrepancies are a result of the heterogeneous nature of those households. To the extent that initial research—which was based on the average situation of households headed by women—has since been taken to a more detailed level, certain nuances have appeared. Researchers are investigating different stages in the family life cycle, taking into account the presence of other family members in the household and their contribution to earnings, and are incorporating the presence of younger children and of specific socio-cultural contexts into their analyses.

Studies in Colombia (Flórez, 1992) and Chile (Schkolnick, 1992) show that households headed by women have poverty levels very similar to those of households headed by men. The percentage of households headed by women is not significantly higher in poor homes than it is in non-poor homes. However, the average age of women heads of households is considerably higher than for male heads of households, and a large number of households are headed by widows. In Jamaica (Louát, Gosh and van der Gaag, 1993), 42 percent of all homes were found to be headed by women, but they are only 1.4 percent more likely to be poor than households headed by men, regardless of age, education, marital status or area.

Thus, the economic handicap of households headed by women varies in the course of the family life cycle. Although young female heads of households with children under five are at an enormous disadvantage—they are the poorest of the poor households—in homes where one or more of the children work, family income is not necessarily less than in households headed by a man (Flórez, 1992; Schkolnick, 1992). All studies show that the income earned by women heads of households is much less than that of men. This does not necessarily mean that the household income is less because total income is a function of which and how many members contribute (Schkolnick, 1992).

Finally, in Jamaica because women devote more of their earnings to the nutrition and welfare of the children—a phenomenon verified in other areas as well—no differences in welfare of children can be traced back to the gender of the heads of household (Louát *et al.,* 1993).

Recognition of these different nuances leads one to question the advisability of targeting women heads of household without distinguishing according to phase of family cycle and composition of the household. Targeting is a process with certain costs attached. If that effort is to be made to tackle the appropriate problems, it is necessary to go further and focus on individual family members.

Households headed by young women living on their own with small children—the poorest households, suffering a complex set of deprivations—require specific types of child-care programs. Apart from removing children from the vicious circle of poverty by feeding and teaching them, programs should also free mothers for training so that at some point they will be able to enter the labor market successfully. This is a relatively small segment of the households headed by women. They are the ones least in contact with social assistance networks. The cost of targeting such households tends to be very high, but the benefits from doing so are also considerable.

In households where the female head is an older person, attention must be paid to younger members, who usually sacrifice their schooling in order to maintain the home. These are the most common cases. They most often need social assistance. In such instances, one option would be to grant women heads of household non-contributory pensions to substitute for the income their children earn so that the children can continue to attend school. An alternative would be to target the young members of the household with training programs that could provide them with substitute income.

Unless a distinction is made between the household as the place of residence of people who share expenses and as family units, the plight and prevalence of single mothers will remain unrecognized. Action to assist them in becoming economically independent will be almost impossible. Households headed by women in the early stages of the family life cycle are a relatively small proportion of all such households and would appear not to be economically and socially viable. As a result they are forced to live with other relatives (Louât *et al.,* 1993).

The Participation of Women in Social Programs

Within new social policy approaches, women are given a more important part to play as agents in social development. These approaches use new combinations of market, state and family-community mechanisms as alternative channels through which welfare can be improved. The ideal beneficiary is no longer the worker but rather the family group. The criterion that governs benefits is not integration in the labor market but the fact that family members belong to some particularly vulnerable segment of the population. While there has been significant positive experience to date, gaps exist between the theory and practice of these approaches. These gaps have an impact on the effectiveness of programs.

Targeting the Most Disadvantaged Groups

Targeting seeks to increase the efficiency and equity of social policy by giving special status to the poorest, and within this group, to the categories considered to be most physically vulnerable (such as children under six years of age and pregnant or breastfeeding women). This entails paying special attention to the specific needs of women.

Box 8: Problems with Service Delivery

Women have limited access to certain health services due to the narrow focus on their reproductive function that ignores the occupational health problems.

The provision of services is often inconvenient from the point of view of women's multiple roles. For example, individual health services (pediatrics, gynecology, prenatal care) are available on different days. Thus, women have to come and go several times depending on their needs and those of other members of the family. No attempt is made to match medical office hours with the needs of mothers who work fixed hours outside the home.

In urban services, researchers have pointed to numerous problems that result from the failure to take into account the real pattern of activities of all household members:

- In Belo Horizonte, Brazil, women have to travel further and make more connections because public transport is planned to take into account only the working hours of the formal sector (Moser *et al.*, 1993).
- In many countries the eligibility criteria for access to housing projects exclude women (Brydon and Chant, 1989).
- Despite the fact that it is usually women who suffer most from the effects of inadequate housing and who devote their time to help make up for such shortages, little attention has been paid to development of technology for the home or alternative arrangements of services that could save time.

Social policy geared to the satisfaction of basic needs upgrades the importance of one of women's roles, that of being mothers and looking after other members of the household. It can increase the coverage and, in some cases, the efficiency of essential services. As previously demonstrated, attention to the needs associated with women's reproductive role is necessary to offset the unfair conditions that confront the female population. Such attention provides a levelling effect by enabling women to take up other opportunities that will lead to greater equity.

With an exclusive emphasis on women's reproductive role, the basic-needs approach frequently disregards the conflict between the reproductive and productive roles of women. Critics of this approach argue that it facilitates the irresponsibility of other household members through a reinforcement of the idea that domestic chores are women's work instead of favoring a fairer distribution of the burden. Also, programs designed to expand services frequently do not take into account the current complexity of women's roles.

New Targeting Mechanisms: Social Investment Funds

To reach a larger segment of the poorer population using more expeditious channels and methods that support community participation, solidarity or social investment funds have been set up in several countries of the region. According to a recent study, those funds concentrate on three types of activity: nutrition and food assistance; employment and income generation, and construction or repair of economic and social infrastructure (World Bank and IDB, 1993).

As is discussed in the chapter on women as economic actors, preliminary impact assessment shows that women have been targeted within nutrition and breastfeeding programs. They are considered to be passive recipients of aid rather than active participants (Pollack, 1993). In contrast, in other types of programs men are the main beneficiaries because of a heavy construction component in which women's participation is minimal. Although social infrastructure works represent jobs for men during the construction phase, once completed they generate new jobs for women who are traditionally trained for jobs in social and personal services.

Even if women are not direct participants in the implementation of infrastructure programs, they may still benefit from the projects if improved water sources are constructed, if better roads result in improved access to health care facilities or if a new school building is staffed.[2]

Multi-purpose Projects

Emphasis on poverty eradication as a social policy goal and on the efficiency of service provision has helped to blur rigid sectoral divisions in program design and to shift attention towards multiple-objective programs and multi-purpose measures. This has assisted in highlighting the numerous facets of women's activities, while at the same time making it easier for multiple program objectives and functions to be fulfilled.

Venezuela's Day Care Homes and Colombia's Welfare Homes are examples of this strategy. While catering to the needs of working mothers, they also provide training and income for mothers who look after households, along with equipment and repairs for their homes and a chance for the children to develop and be properly nourished.

Lima's collective meals or soup kitchens provide another example of a

---

[2]The results of these programs are not always clear cut. Possible positive and negative effects should be studied. For instance, a new road may mean that products that were previously made locally may be pushed out of the market with an inflow of new products. A school building may be built, but there may not be staff to teach children. A water system may be constructed, but if women are not trained in its maintenance, it may soon fall idle.

multi-purpose project. Women taking part receive tangible benefits. They save time, receive nutritional training and enjoy a balanced diet more cheaply than they otherwise could. The intangible benefits are also significant. Women can socialize and gain experience in participation and organization and access to other training and job opportunities. Soup kitchens have become major centers for the accumulation of resources and community information (Barrig, 1992; Yamada, 1992).

The main unforeseen consequence of this approach has been to strengthen women's position within the household by placing resources under their control. When targeting mechanisms for many of the new compensation programs were discussed, one concern was how to avoid the direct subsidies being siphoned off to satisfy non-essential needs. It was decided that using the mother as a "distribution channel" ensured that resources would be directed towards the children. Thus, the most important compensation program in Venezuela, the Food Grant, is distributed through mothers. This means that they have to produce documents to prove the identity of their children and deal with the government bureaucracy and banks. For many mothers, this represents the first contact they have had with the financial system. It also means that mothers are the ones who have to queue up to obtain the subsidy.

The Local Community as the Ideal Arena for Social Policy

When policy makers turned to decentralized processes for the delivery of social policy programs, the active role played by women in grassroots organizations and as effective channels for benefits and subsidies to the family clearly emerged. Raczynski and Serrano (1992b) state:

> There is a close link between local government action and women's participation: They are the ones to approach the municipality and ask for help, subsidies or information. They are the ones to go to the health center, or enrol their child in a kindergarten or school (p. 21).

Decentralization has therefore been identified as an appropriate mechanism to improve the implementation of government strategies. There are clear advantages to a closer connection between government and local populations. However, regional imbalances cast doubts that decentralization in and of itself will promote development and ensure equitable participation. Without complimentary policies that permit a more equal distribution of resources among regions, a clear assessment of responsibilities and improved efficiency in the management of public resources, decentralization can aggravate differences and worsen public administration. The lesson to be learned is one of selectivity and gradualism (López and Ronderos, 1994).

Community mobilization to obtain better services has put women into contact with the political system. At the same time, however, it has represented an added demand on their time (Raczynski and Serrano, 1992).[3]

The growth of interest in decentralization, community participation in the administration of social services and the role of women as community organizers has generated new evidence on how these three spheres are interrelated. Some of the experience obtained is not new, but only now does it acquire special significance.

Finally, it would be useful to analyze the local impact of the increasing transfer of powers to local governments and the role that women could play as administrators and providers of decentralized services, if they were given the relevant training.

Women's Productive Work

Women will benefit from new social policy approaches, provided that precautions are taken to diminish the larger workload they imply. The impact of the labor market is less clear. The chapter on women as economic actors explores various experiences of employment creation for women and of support for women's productive activities. Given growing critiques of income-generating projects, attention has now shifted to vocational training, support to women microentrepreneurs and credit and management support (Buvinić, 1990; Villareal, 1992). That chapter also points out that women's projects are insufficient. There is a need to take women's general interests into account in the planning and development of all labor policy and employment-related initiatives.

Moving Forward

Research has served to document that gender relations are social constructs, not something natural. The concept of a division of tasks based on women's triple role constitutes a major step forward. The increased visibility of what

[3] The chapter on political participation explores how women's participation in activities outside the home has been an invigorating personal and collective experience. It also explores the issue of women's mobilization and organization.

Box 10: Women and Community Participation

- Tovar (1992) analyzed how emergency programs have helped reinforce women's legitimacy and importance in the eyes of established institutions.
- In Argentina, Feijóo and Jelin (1987) stress that there has been an awakening among women, who have formed organizations related to a national food program (PAN) to push for basic services, water and housing. Working with these groups and strengthening them should translate into more effective state services.
- In Ciudad Guayana, Venezuela, Rakowski (1989) discovered that women's groups are interacting more frequently with local authorities. In several poor neighborhoods, they have formed groups to protect women's rights. Consumer cooperatives, child care networks, and informal employment agency services have also been created. Women's groups also cooperate with schools and health centers in special campaigns. Interviews with local officials revealed that neighborhood associations are usually directed by women. As a result, women learned how to plan, to deal with bureaucracy, to make their demands known, and to achieve their goals.
- Working in the soup kitchens has saved women leaders time they would otherwise spend on domestic chores. Above all, such work has contributed to their personal development because it enabled them to take an active part in planning the service (Barrig, 1992).

used to be invisible also constitutes an important building block in social policy. Women make contributions in different spheres, not just as mothers and wives, to the welfare of society. Delving deeper, a remarkable heterogeneity has come to light in the composition of households, women's life cycles, socio-economic levels, and different regional patterns within each country.

For development planning, as the recommendations of the Decade of Women began to have an effect, the fact that statistics and data were now available on respective positions and activities of men and women has begun to make a major difference. Data have contributed to the development of a planning approach based on recognition of the specific needs of each gender. That approach has made it possible to devise instruments ensuring that specific needs are taken into consideration in the design and execution of social and economic programs. Ideally, these programs would both assist women to do better what they are already doing and open up new doors and possibilities.

Finally, social services administrators have been able to take advantage of the experience derived from new programs–focusing on households and their members instead of workers. Thus, women's contributions and the benefits they bring in an arena in which women have long been active have been recognized. Thus, both at the local government level and in community-run programs, the part played by women may turn out to be crucial, if it is not already.

However, turning women into saviors involves a number of risks that must be avoided. It is not a question of coming up with an endless series of activities that women perform efficiently and in which their contribution is, has been and may be invaluable. Especially since they entered the labor market on a massive scale, women's chief concern is their need to balance their multiple roles as those responsible for domestic reproduction, for administering collective consumption in their communities and for earning income for their families. Such a difficult balancing act evidently has its costs.

A more efficient social policy will be one that, after recognizing women's specific contribution in each area, ensures that they have the means they need to facilitate their work. This can be done by bringing in technology to increase efficiency, introducing new services to alleviate current burdens, or helping to get rid of the stereotypes that prevent women from having access to resources that could increase their human capital significantly and prevent them from receiving just rewards.

A glance at various aspects of human development over the past three decades reveals areas in which both men and women suffer enormous deprivation. This has been due to the unequal distribution of productive assets and of the resources that the state invests to increase such assets. More equitable distribution of assets and resources obviously belongs on the social policy agenda for this decade, particularly because of its role in the struggle to overcome poverty.

The Starting Point

In all the areas studied, the behavior of men and women has differed markedly according to social stratum and the practical and socio-cultural restrictions imposed on women by the fact that they raise children. At the same time, difficulty in finding uniform data, other than general features, broken down by sex continues to impede recognition of the problems and opportunities that men and women face.

This review of the status of women and the main features of the policies affecting them makes it possible to highlight several specific needs that are not adequately taken into account today:

- Women's lack of appropriate and relevant job qualifications is one major reason why they are paid little or are excluded from the labor market.

They are frequently directed into "women's careers" and professions that turn out to be dead ends. The roots of this are a set of cultural stereotypes shared by women themselves, their families, educational institutions, and employers.

• There is a lack of suitable social security options adapted to meet the needs of working women, for whom maternity coverage is essential. This is just one aspect of the overall problem of working conditions for women. Other problems relate to the isolation, overall discrimination and level of pay that reflects their low qualifications and productivity.

• Health care is lacking to such an extent that some of the poorest countries suffer an appalling number of deaths. Malnutrition and adolescent pregnancies severely restrict women's options. These are problems that are not dealt with because of a narrow approach to women's health. Problems such as domestic violence and occupational illnesses have reached alarming proportions, without eliciting any appropriate response.

In short, the main barrier to greater participation that women still face is the tendency to assign them responsibility for the burden of reproduction as if it were a private cost. This is manifested in families in which household chores continue to be women's work even when they might also have a paid job and, above all, when fathers do not share the cost of maintaining children and society does not enforce that obligation.

The same attitude is found in the workplace. Women continue to be paid less on the assumption that their income is not the main family income and that they are secondary workers. Women are made to pay for their "unreliability" due to maternity by being given fewer job or promotion opportunities, or lower wages.

This view is also expressed in the social services mix, which presupposes that looking after the family is women's exclusive responsibility. There are few services that could make their lives easier and support their broader contributions in economic, social and political spheres outside the home.

Both the demand for social development policies and programs by families and women and the supply of such programs are conditioned by several factors that constitute hidden barriers that women still face.

The effects of socialization and women's self-exclusion condition the demands they make. Both maternity and the role that their children play in their lives determine the way women perceive themselves. Culturally and socially, an organizational pattern based on the traditional division of labor between the sexes is accepted and reinforced. That division, which relegates women to a secondary role, is not questioned despite irrefutable empirical evidence of women's decisive contributions beyond the narrow confines of the home (Flórez, 1992).

Time is still women's scarcest resource. Social programs continue to ignore women's roles as workers. Programs are not organized to save women time, nor do they consider other needs that arise out of that role, such as training for a job or occupational health care.

One of the consequences of women's limited access to public life has been that they are less informed as to their rights and the options available for solving their problems. For example, in Chile among the poor the percentage of women who knew nothing about the Complementary National Food Program, which is specifically directed towards their needs, was as high as 40 percent (Schkolnik, 1992). The conditions under which women usually labor, mostly confined to their homes or local districts, prevent them from joining trade unions or other organizations, where such information is available.

Conditions governing access to many programs need to be questioned. The newer, targeted programs consider the nature of the beneficiaries somewhat more explicitly. Many other spheres are still governed by rules for a world that does not exist: complete nuclear families receiving benefits through the male head of household, while the woman looks after the home. By disregarding differences within homes and the fact that there are different types of households—particularly those in which, de facto, a woman is in charge—such programs have only a limited chance of reaching those most in need.

As for the content of the programs, some countries have begun to attach importance to alternative forms of child care. Only rarely can one find far-reaching efforts to alleviate domestic chores. In some areas, such as caring for the sick and the elderly, there is not even awareness of the need for alternative arrangements, despite the evidence that this burden on women in the household has increased as a result of attempts to "rationalize" health systems.

Many of the above-mentioned problems could be minimized if the experience acquired by women—as those who care for other family members, as users of services and as community organizers—were to be formally incorporated in the design of programs. Yet women's roles continue to be, in many cases, to provide "voluntary labor" and otherwise be passive recipients of what a program offers. They do not participate sufficiently in the planning and execution of projects.

As mentioned, the times services are available, the way they are organized, and their location are often inconvenient for women. As a result they are under-used. The current trend towards multi-purpose and multiple care programs is more in line with women's needs and schedules. One element that is essential is the inclusion of information and training mechanisms to ensure that women are aware of both the requirements and benefits of programs.

Guidelines and Criteria for Future Policies

Given that the main barrier to a more effective contribution by women to social development is insufficient recognition of their triple role in society, then only policies attacking all three fronts simultaneously have any chance of having a significant impact on their disadvantaged position (Bonilla, Jaramillo López *et al.,* 1991). This could be accomplished through:

- labor policies that identify and address factors that cause women to be paid less at the workplace;
- socio-cultural changes in the stereotypes concerning women; and,
- social policies that explicitly address the consequences of the type, quality and form of social services for women's paid work through socializing some domestic tasks (such as looking after the children, cooking, caring for the elderly, as well as improving the home and its basic services).

Another essential criterion in the development of social policies is the need to turn the contribution that women currently make as volunteers to the proper functioning of social services into an opportunity to earn money and acquire training (Bonilla, 1991). This has been taken into consideration in the design of child care programs in several countries. In such programs, "community mothers" get not only training that might lead to permanent alternative jobs but also receive incomes.

Given the marked differences in standards of living from one country to another, and from one region to another within countries, and the fact that such differences are reflected in the situation of women, programs to meet policy objectives have to be individually tailored. In some countries it is necessary to reduce overall inequality at the same time specific inequalities are tackled. The deprivation that women have to face in many areas is often related to poverty. Programs designed to eradicate it will therefore help improve conditions for women as well as for men. As long as high levels of female illiteracy and mother and child mortality persist, effective participation by women will not be possible. In other countries in which women have benefited from a higher level of development and more extensive social networks, the most urgent step is to address directly the hidden barriers.

Women's triple role and the lack of information resulting from the isolation in which they work underscore the necessity of including special training and information components in programs in order to facilitate greater participation. However, it has to be stressed that the low degree of awareness of men's role in the reproductive sphere and the influence of stereotypes in defining the activities of both genders suggest that, in many cases, the problem is the failure to include men's points of view and contributions in programs.

From the analysis of the structure of family units and their operations, two general criteria emerge for devising actions to enhance social development:

- the need to consider not just the family unit but also its individual members since the conditions and restrictions for men and women and their use of services may be radically different; and,
- the usefulness of distinguishing different phases in the family life cycle in the targeted groups.

Policy Components

Different policy areas that could have the most impact on the situation of women are outlined below.

Project Design Phase

A pre-requisite for determining the specific needs of men and women is sex-disaggregated information on the pattern of activities, responsibilities and use of services of potential users.

Considerable progress has been made in planning from a gender perspective. Instruments to make such planning operational have been devised. Those efforts stress that incorporating a gender perspective involves respecting women's time and space, designing activities adapted to the problems they face, and adding support components such as child care to the programs directed towards them (Raczynski and Serrano, 1992).

One basic criterion is that programs expressly take into account the time women devote to a project. Time is women's scarcest resource. All social projects in which it is hoped that women will take part must incorporate evaluate this criterion.

Changing Stereotypes

Many barriers to women's participation come from cultural stereotypes, particularly the failure to include men's contributions in the reproductive sphere and the lack of awareness regarding women's ability to perform on equal terms in paid employment.

Unless efforts to incorporate women into the labor market are accompanied by activities to raise the level of awareness and information and legal reforms and greater enforcement of existing laws regarding consideration of maternity as a social cost, the present situation will not change.

Thus, there is a need to direct a set of programs at men in the area of reproduction. These could be incorporated in family planning, adolescent pregnancy, and family violence programs and would provide effective preventive measures.

Health Policy

A broader approach to health policy that takes into account the changing needs of women, as well as their patterns of activities and life cycles would ensure healthier women. Judging by the evidence available on women's state of health, health activities should first aim at reducing avoidable deaths and illnesses suffered by segments of the population living in poverty. Measures include improving breast and cervical cancer detection services, greatly extending mother-child care services and devising activities and programs to counter adolescent pregnancy and the consequences of abortion.

Second, health services need a change of approach and organizational adjustments in order to cater to the variety of health needs that women have apart from those related to reproduction. It is particularly important to analyze the incentives and obstacles to women taking part in health programs.

Third, it is important to recognize women's multiple roles and ensure that services provided respect women's need to earn a living. For example, health clinics should have extended hours of operation.

Education and Training Policy

The current issue women face in education is not how many study but what professions they choose and the quality of the education they receive. Three problems need to be tackled.

First, technical and secondary education considerably restricts women's job options, inducing them to abandon a type of education for which they cannot see the point and preventing them from getting better-paid jobs.

Second, when women start working too soon, whether in a paid job or doing household chores, educational opportunities are curtailed. It is necessary, therefore, to raise the percentage of young women who stay in the school system. De Vanzo and Haaga (1991) recommend studying the possibility of devising scholarship programs for girls in countries where there are major differences in educational statistics for boys and girls.

Third, adult education and non-formal training services need to be extended, revised and subjected to quality controls. These programs should be structured around the reality of women's lives and provide the opportunity to gain practical and relevant skills.

Social Security and Protection Policy

Recent moves to open up the economy and the resulting promotion of labor mobility lower the level of social protection. This is a particularly serious problem for women who risk maternity without any financial coverage. In the reform of social security systems, priority must be given to debating the issue of dealing with such risks. Imaginative and appropriate mechanisms must be devised to address this lack of social protection for a major part of the female population. Portability of benefits from one employer to another should be considered.

Broadening and Changing Support Programs

In order to guarantee permanent incorporation of women in the labor market, more information is necessary. Studies are urgently needed to identify institutions and channels that will ensure that there is massive expansion of support services.

Activities performed by the poorest women have such low economic and social returns that they are tantamount to unemployment and waste time that could have been used more efficiently. For this reason, the advisability of support for subsistence activities in the informal sector for the poorest women is being questioned.

Giving such support in the form of subsidies has been suggested. Such subsidies should be carefully studied to ensure that they are properly targeted. Possible mechanisms include providing a bonus for women who carry out work in support of the health sector (vaccination campaigns, instructions on how to use rehydration salts) or community canteens. In addition to the training they receive, they would get a compensatory income and would be given support while their children are young. Another option is offering scholarships for attending adult education centers or for receiving training for more profitable occupations.

Women in the Informal Sector

Frequently the informal activities that women carry out are different from those performed by men. Often women's perception of microenterprises is different from that of men. In consequence, programs should be created to attend to those particular differences or at least to take precautions to avoid standard packages being applied to cases that are not, in fact, standard. An area worth consideration is training women to produce nontraditional goods or services for export to the modern sector. Activities promoted should be based on proper feasibility studies and should include programs to assist with marketing, management, finances and training, as well as with productive aspects.

Cost Implications

There are significant fiscal and private cost implications for the above recommendations. This is certainly justifiable given the social impacts of improving women's situation. The World Bank (1994) states that improving women's productivity:

> ...can contribute to growth, efficiency and poverty reduction—primary development goals everywhere. Investing proportionally more in women than in men—in education, health, family planning, access to land, inputs, and extension—is, thus, an important part of development strategy, as well as an act of social justice. It directly reduces poverty through substantial economic and social payoffs.

Much has been achieved since women's issues were defined as a priority in 1975. To a large extent, new social policies have helped to make the role of women evident. They provide an excellent opportunity for removing the obstacles that still remain, a fact now recognized by governments and multilateral lending organizations. Greater efforts must be made to identify project effects on women and to incorporate women's contributions more effectively in activities directed towards social development.

Chapter 3

Women as Economic Actors: Retooling Employment Programs for Greater Equity

The severe economic crises and subsequent structural adjustment programs of the 1980s set Latin American and Caribbean countries back 20 years. Retrenchment and adjustment virtually wiped out the improvements in living conditions achieved in the previous two decades. Both poverty and inequality increased (Morley, 1994). According to World Bank estimates, the percentage of the population living in poverty in the region increased from 22 percent in 1985 to 25 percent in 1990 (World Bank, 1993c). A study of 13 countries in the region indicates that the poor constituted 31 percent of the population in 1989—131 million people—compared to 26 percent in 1980 (Psacharopoulos et al., 1993). By the end of the decade, more than half of those in rural areas and slightly more than one out of five urban dwellers were poor.[1]

Budget cuts in basic services, high rates of inflation, unemployment and drastic reductions in living standards have had an impact on a large proportion of the population. However, macroeconomic policies have affected men and women differently. The burden of adjustment has often fallen disproportionately on women (Cornia, Jolly, and Stewart, 1987; ECLAC, 1990; Elson 1991; Benería and Feldman 1992; Friedman 1994). First, the effect of policies has been to increase women's need to participate in paid production to provide or supplement family income. Second, the amount of time that women dedicate to unpaid work has also expanded. Women are called on to participate in

[1]Morley's (1994) findings, based on household surveys, provide evidence that inequality is almost always strongly countercyclical: rising in recession and falling in recovery. In other words, countries in recession or with sharply declining per capita income generally had rising inequality, whereas countries in a recovery phase enjoyed rising equality.

community-service programs, and more time is spent on domestic tasks (Safa, 1994; Moser, 1989; Benería, 1992a). Women's contributions to overall economic growth and the survival of households, especially poor households, have been critical.

The significant educational and health gains that women have made in the last decades have enabled them to increase their labor force participation. However, while the quality of life has improved for most women, initial marked differences within, as well as across, countries have not been erased. Substantial numbers of women in most countries are still significantly handicapped by high fertility rates, low literacy levels and the high risk of dying in childbirth.

While women are and will continue to be crucial players in economic development, their position within the labor force means that they generally hold low-productivity and poorly remunerated jobs in greater proportion than do men. Combined with other social and cultural factors, this translates into disproportionate poverty for women, especially in rural areas (Buvinić, 1994).

In the 1990s, governments and international development agencies are implementing regionwide economic and social reforms in Latin America and the Caribbean. Export-oriented strategies have replaced import substitution models, and governments are reducing programs and spending. As civil society gains strength, governments and agencies are searching for ways to reform policies and institutions so that they are more effective in reducing poverty and fostering sustained growth.

Social and economic reform strategies must build on the strong and growing economic participation of women while taking into account women's disproportionate poverty and the differences between men's and women's social, economic and political roles. Women's growing participation in the labor force (especially in the areas of agriculture, export-oriented manufacturing, the service sector and the informal sector) should be analyzed in the context of paid and unpaid activities. The experience of development interventions aimed at improving the incomes of poor women provide critical information.

Women's Economic Contributions

Women's contributions to economic growth are twofold. First, women participate in the labor force in ways that can be conventionally measured and discussed. Yet, women's unpaid activities such as subsistence production, volunteer work in the community and domestic work within the home are rarely measured and are almost never included in development plans. This type of contribution has yet to be recognized in national statistics, despite ongoing efforts by such groups as the United Nations Statistical Office and the International Labor Organization (Dixon-Mueller and Anker, 1988; Goldschmidt-Clermont, 1989; Benería, 1992b; Wainerman, 1992).

Even generally cited statistics indicate that women's economic contributions have increased since the early 1950s and that their economic participation rose even more rapidly during the 1980s. Economic activity rates for women in Latin American countries grew, on average, by 13 percent (CELADE, 1992). During the last two decades, rates of growth were 42 percent in Barbados and 67 percent in Mexico, while in Bolivia and El Salvador, rates were closer to 20 percent. Given that in many countries the severity of economic contraction has meant little or no growth in economic activity rates for men, lower levels of growth in women's participation rates are still impressive.

Much of the growth in women's economic activity over the past decade can be attributed to the increased economic participation of women in urban areas. Economic necessity combined with new opportunities has led women to take on urban employment at unprecedented levels. For many countries in Latin America, the urban economically active rate for women is over 40 percent. In contrast, national censuses and projections indicate that rural women's activity rates grew by only 9 percent on average from 1980 to 1990. According to ECLAC data, their average participation rate as of 1990 was 28 percent versus 88 percent for rural men. Yet it is widely acknowledged that in rural areas, women play significant economic roles and often have the main responsibility for the support of their households, particularly in areas of high male migration and displacement due to war. Economic contributions of women are often underestimated because of the way most population censuses document "principal activity," categorizing most rural women as housewives even though they also participate in the agricultural labor force.

Agricultural censuses better capture women's work in rural areas, often showing women's activity rates to be two or more times as high as indicated by population censuses (Dixon-Mueller, 1985). A recent study by the Inter-American Institute for Cooperation on Agriculture (IICA) and the Inter-American Development Bank (IDB) on women food producers and agricultural policy in Latin America and the Caribbean provided extensive statistical evidence on women's contributions to agricultural production. The study clearly portrays the significant undercounting that occurs in this area (see Box 1).

Two studies from Costa Rica and Ecuador also illustrate this phenomenon. In an experimental population census conducted in Costa Rica in 1983, careful re-interviewing of all rural women who would otherwise have been classified as "inactive" revealed that 41 percent of them had indeed worked for the entire year (White, Otero, and Lycette, 1986). A rural employment survey that sampled three areas in the Ecuadorian coast and three in the highlands found three times as many women working in agriculture as did the official census (Cuvi, 1992).

Women's increased labor force participation rates, combined with men's decreased participation—at least in officially recognized economic activity—has led to growth in women's share of the total labor force (see Table 4). For the region as a whole, women now constitute approximately 29 percent of the labor force (CELADE, 1992). In some Caribbean countries such as Barbados and Jamaica, women make up just under half the labor force. It is not surprising that projections based on the most recent census and demographic data put women's share of the regional labor force at 31 percent by the year 2000 (UN, 1991a). Clearly, women are major economic actors in the region.

These aggregate data mask important differences in the type of economic activities that women and men undertake. Differences exist in four main areas: sectoral concentrations, the extent of wage employment, occupational structure and wage levels.

In Latin America and the Caribbean women fill nearly half of the clerical and service jobs. These jobs account for 71 percent of the female labor force in the region (UN, 1991a). Only about 20 percent of women work in industry and transportation, mostly in manufacturing jobs in the export-processing zones of Mexico, Brazil, Jamaica, and the Dominican Republic (see Table 8).

In terms of both wage employment and self-employment, most women workers hold lower paid and less prestigious jobs (see Table 7). In the service sector, for example, women predominate in domestic services where they, with few exceptions, receive no social security or retirement benefits (Leon, 1989). While they appear to be well represented among professionals (from 37 to 60 percent in countries like Argentina, Chile, Colombia, Ecuador, Panama, Paraguay, Peru and Venezuela) professional women actually work mainly as teachers and nurses, a low-paid category of professional work. Women make up only a small proportion of lawyers, medical doctors, administrators, and managers (Conde, 1986). In industry, they tend to be employed as assembly line workers rather than as skilled workers or managers. In the informal sector, women operate the smallest, most marginal enterprises.

Still, women in Latin America have benefitted from wage employment, which is typically associated with greater stability and security. In the

Box 1: Women's Participation in Agriculture

A recent study by the Inter-American Institute for Cooperation on Agriculture, which received financial and technical assistance from the Inter-American Development Bank, provides a sense of the degree to which official statistics under-record and underestimate women's participation in agricultural activities in Latin America and the Caribbean (IICA, 1994).

Female Agricultural Economically Active Population

Country	Official Estimate	Adjusted Estimate
Costa Rica	8	27
El Salvador	12	33
Guatemala	9	26
Honduras	6	22
Nicaragua	12	22
Panama	5	27
Ecuador	42	72
Paraguay	13	82
Uruguay	9	39

1980s, 62 percent of working women earned wages versus only 56 percent of working men (UN, 1991a). Yet, women working for wages have found themselves in increasingly precarious positions as employers have withdrawn benefits and job security and have lowered wages in response to economic contraction.

Women working for wages are paid, on average, less than three-quarters of male wages, although this varies from country to country (ranging from 47 percent in Chile to 86 percent in Mexico) and within different sectors of the economy (Psacharopoulos and Tzannatos, 1992). In Brazil, for example, women in the formal and self-employed sectors earn 70 percent of the wages of their male counterparts, and in the informal sector, they earn 85 percent of the male wage (Tiefenthaler, 1992). At one level, there is room for optimism about women's potential to narrow the wage gap, given the comparable enrolment rates at the primary and secondary levels for both girls and boys in the region (Bellew, Raney, and Subbarao, 1992). The optimism wanes, however, when it is noted that women continue to be under-represented in higher education and tend to be concentrated in traditionally female fields of study. This leads to a lower proportion of women in the higher paid professions, as noted earlier.

Furthermore, in technical and vocational education programs, women are often found enrolled in courses that lead them into low-paying, low-productivity sectors such as sewing, food processing, secretarial skills and cosmetology. There is still little incentive for young women to pursue alternative technical courses designed for sectors in which they have limited prospects for employment (IDB, 1995a). In addition, working-age women in many countries are less likely to have attained as many years of schooling as their male counterparts because of previously existing educational differences. Greater effort is needed to narrow the gender gap in education.

Discrimination, in varying forms, is also a significant factor in the wage differences between men and women. Factors such as discriminatory recruitment and promotion practices of firms, self-selection of women out of higher paying occupations, and the interrupted career pattern of women due to their child-bearing role all contribute to pay inequity in the region (IDB, 1995a). The findings of a World Bank study on women's employment and pay in Latin America indicate that only one-third of the difference in men's and women's earnings could be attributed to education, labor market experience and the number of hours worked. The remaining difference, designated the "upper bound of discrimination," could not be accounted for in economic terms. The study suggests that the differences in wages of men and women in the region are small in comparison to other regions. However, the data used to measure wage differences were not sufficiently representative of women working in the informal sector and were overly representative of women working in the public sector, where they are known to have achieved higher levels of education and receive pay that is more commensurate with that of men (Psacharopoulos and Tzannatos, 1992). In addition, the fact that, for women to earn as much as men, they must have approximately four more years of formal education indicates the level of economic inefficiency that is caused by the current levels of discrimination (Krawczyk, 1993).

The difference in women's and men's earning potential has important implications for family incomes. As discussed in the chapter on women and social policy, households headed by women are increasing throughout the region. In these households, it is clear that women's economic contributions are vital. Yet there is also growing recognition of the importance of women's contributions to family incomes even when they are not the official "heads of household." In these families, women's earnings are not secondary or reserved for luxuries—they are essential for the well-being and, in many cases, the survival of families.

These insights lead to two conclusions. First, women, both those who head households and those in other family structures, require support (child care, social benefits, training, etc.) to facilitate their participation in the workforce and manage their immense workload. Second, even in situations where there is a working male partner, it should not be assumed that women have extra free time to act as volunteers in social programs. Their families depend on the income they bring in, and their time is in short supply.

A closer look at women's sectoral employment reveals the significance of their economic contributions and, in many instances, unfortunate disparities in economic benefits.

Industry Sector

The activity rate for women in the industry is only about 20 percent, a figure that has remained roughly constant for decades. This stability obscures an important phenomenon of the 1980s—the growth of export processing zones (EPZs) primarily in the garment, electronic, chemical and food processing industries. EPZs were encouraged by export-oriented economic restructuring strategies. For countries such as Brazil, Colombia, the Dominican Republic, Mexico, and Panama, employment in these zones more than tripled between 1975 and 1986 (Kreye, Heinrichs, and Frobel, 1987). The overwhelming majority of employees in the EPZs are female, and the zones provide economic opportunities not otherwise available for women. In the Caribbean, 70 to 96 percent of the workforce in EPZs is female, and in the Dominican Republic, export manufacturing now constitutes the second most important source of urban employment for women. In Jamaica, the number of women workers in EPZs rose from 200 in 1976 to 7,000 in 1986 (Massiah, 1989).

Work requirements range from basic literacy and numeracy to secondary education and typing skills (ECLAC, 1990). The level of education of EPZ workers in most parts of the world is lower than that of workers in other national industries. In Mexico, women in EPZs do not have particularly high levels of education. Electronics workers are more educated than clothing workers but are not more educated than women in the services sector (Tiano, 1986). In the Dominican Republic, however, women working in the EPZs were found to have a higher level of education than most women in the country, although it was lower than the average in the industrial sector (Joekes, 1987a). Despite the relatively low educational standards, employment in EPZs generates wages that are higher than those otherwise available to most women. Sometimes transport and even child care are provided for EPZ employees, although the latter is rare. Nonetheless, jobs in these zones are low in quality and repetitive in nature. Women are paid less than men, hours of work are long, union organization is restricted, and health and safety standards are sometimes poor (Commonwealth Secretariat, 1990). Furthermore, these jobs tend to be dead ends and fail to qualify women for better paid employment. The burnout rate is also high (Arregui and Baez, 1991)

Women's attempts to organize for better working conditions in the EPZs have not generally been successful. Although in countries such as Jamaica there have been frequent public protests against working conditions, the rate of unionization has been low. In the Dominican Republic there are no trade unions in the free trade zones, and workers are routinely fired and blacklisted for organizing activity. Government labor offices have provided little support (Safa and Antrobus, 1992).

Work in this sector can also be unstable because production requirements are vulnerable to shifts and changes in overseas markets. French (1994) cites the sudden drop in employment in Kingston's free trade zone in the late 1980s. Approximately 4,000 women lost their jobs overnight, and by 1991 the number of factories operating fell from 20 to 12.

Agriculture Sector

In the agricultural sector, a high percentage of women are unpaid family workers. Their participation thus has not been adequately captured by official census data. More accurate household surveys indicate that women's participation in small-farm agriculture has actually been rising in the past several decades as rural men have moved into wage work on large farms producing for export (Pollack, 1990). The types of activities undertaken by women are related to the economic status of their households. They include purchasing inputs, contracting laborers, preparing food for the farm workers and working the land themselves (Campaña, 1982).

On small farms in Brazil, women do about two-thirds of the agricultural work that their husbands do and carry out their household production activities as well. In Jamaica, women help to work at least 80 percent of farmland (Pollack, 1990). In Peru, one-third of women in the highlands carry out family agricultural chores with no help from their husbands, and one-fourth receive only occasional assistance (Campaña, 1982). In Chile, rural women help produce wheat, corn, beans, and potatoes. They are also responsible for winnowing grains and for the care of small farm animals (Aranda, 1982). In Ecuador, women spend up to five hours a day caring for farm animals, cultivating crops, winnowing grain, drying coffee beans and preparing other foods for sale (FAO, 1987).

A significant proportion of women in agriculture also work as wage laborers in the large farm sector. In Colombia, for example, women constitute almost 20 percent of hired employees in agriculture. In El Salvador, this figure reaches almost 30 percent; and in Barbados, it is 43 percent. These women are typically hired for non-mechanized tasks such as coffee harvesting, cotton picking, or piecework as members of migrant laborer families (Quisumbing, 1993). On agricultural plantations, women workers participate in all phases of production and harvesting. In Honduras, women supply 90 percent of the wage labor in coffee and 40 percent in tobacco (GENESYS, 1992a). In Brazil, women represent 80 percent of the seasonal labor force working on coffee plantations (Nash, 1983).

As export-oriented strategies have been implemented in the region, women's employment in agro-processing has increased considerably. Women dominate in the agro-processing labor force in Guatemala—making up virtually 100 percent of workers in processing and final packing (Kusterer, Estrada, and Cuxil, 1981), in the harvesting, processing and packing of fruit for export in Costa Rica, Mexico and Chile (Buvinić and Mehra, 1990; Arizpe and Aranda, 1986) and in flower cultivation and packing in Colombia and Ecuador (Buvinić and Lycette, 1988). Such employment has profoundly affected options for women in rural areas. Agro-processing wages have been likened to the salary paid an urban male blue collar worker and are rivalled by few other income earning opportunities for rural women (Kusterer et al., 1981).

Despite their important role in agriculture, rural women have had limited access to agricultural land. For example, in Mexico women represent about 11 percent of farm owners, and in Honduras, they represent only one percent (Quisumbing, 1993). In the Caribbean, rates of ownership are somewhat higher, but women are owners of the smallest farms (IDB, 1990). The IICA-IDB survey of women in small-scale production units in the Andean region reveals that shared ownership accounts for a significant proportion of these holdings. For the Andean region as a whole, women owners represented 24 percent; men owners, 42 percent; and shared ownership, 34 percent (IICA, 1994).

In most countries of the region, women have not benefitted from agrarian reform. In Colombia, land reform gave priority to those with more education, larger families, and farming experience and so discriminated against women who are less-educated than men and whose farming experience tends to be underreported (Quisumbing, 1993). Official statistics reveal only a small percentage of women are direct beneficiaries of agrarian reform programs in Central America—for example, in Nicaragua and El Salvador, 9 percent; in Honduras, 4 percent; and in Costa Rica 16 percent (IICA, 1994).[2]

As a result of limited land ownership and because of their small holdings and the gender-based discrimination they suffer, women have little access to agricultural credit and extension services. The IICA-IDB study also illustrated the extent to which the widespread use of inaccurate statistics on the role of women in agriculture has affected the creation and implementation of agricultural policies, as well as the agricultural extension services that have evolved out of such policies. Out of the 18 countries studied, only Colombia has created and implemented a policy for women farmers. Paraguay is currently creating a 'plan of action' for rural women. The remaining countries do not have agricultural policies specific to women or sectoral policies that integrate a gender perspective. In Central America, consideration has not been given to the role of women as agricultural producers in the formulation of agricultural and rural development policies. This has led to unequal access to both resources and services for women. The traditional division of labor and allocation of resources have been reinforced rather than challenged by existing agricultural and rural development policies (IICA, 1994).

As a direct result of such policies, women have not benefitted from the distribution and use of new agricultural technologies. Patterns in the distribution of technology have reflected assumptions surrounding the roles of men and women in rural areas. Despite the fact that, in practice, men and women often make complementary decisions about the use of tools, inputs and agricultural practices in their production processes, there is no recognition of this in the distribution of new technology. Studies indicate that extension services provided on chemical fertilizers, plant protection and animal health control are directed exclusively to men.

Furthermore, there is little, if any, emphasis on the improvement of techniques and services that would increase women's agricultural productivity. In Guatemala, for example, new technologies and farm mechanization have improved the productivity of men's labor, but women's agricultural activities have been ignored (Ferguson and Flores, 1987). In general, extension services do not include consultations with women about their need for services and

---

[2]In response to the argument that these low numbers could reflect a low demand for land by women, the IICA-IDB study points out, for example, that in Costa Rica in 1991, of the total number of women requesting land, only 28 percent received it. In contrast, 61 percent of the men who requested land received it (IICA, 1994).

technologies that would enhance productive capacities without creating additional work. In addition, while there is evidence that women farmers may more readily adopt improved farming technologies if visited by a female extension agent, women constitute only 15 percent of all extension staff in Latin America (Quisumbing, 1993). The IICA-IDB study also reports that the type of training offered to women and men differs. In Colombia, Bolivia and Peru, training for women has focused on preparing handicrafts, marketing, accounting and drying products, while men receive training in farm management, feed and grazing, seed management and in the use of machinery and inputs (IICA, 1994).

The experience women have in introducing new varieties and crops goes unrecognized by agricultural extension services, as does women's capacity to adopt and make decisions around the use of new technologies in agricultural production. Specialists involved in the IICA study suggest that the provision of labor-saving rather than labor-intensive technologies for women would enable them to be more productive. Their significant role as agricultural producers makes them logical targets for agricultural policies that are intended to improve agricultural production and alleviate rural poverty. Yet, evidence from a number of countries studied indicates that the recognition of gender roles (and power imbalances) in the introduction of a new technology is important. When these differences between women and men are ignored, women are displaced from the production process, and it is taken over by men (IICA, 1994).

Thus, while women's contributions to the agricultural sector are significant, their productivity could be greatly improved by better distribution of land ownership and by providing them with extension services and credit.

Services Sector

An expanding service sector has accounted for much of the increase in women's economic participation in Latin America and the Caribbean since the 1970s. Between 60 and 70 percent of economically active women are employed in this sector. Of these, 50 to 80 percent work in community, social, and personal services—clerical, domestic service, and catering work that may be considered to be closest to women's traditional household roles (Commonwealth Secretariat, 1990). At the professional level, it is interesting to note that women now represent between 30 and 40 percent of those employed in the finance and banking sector. However, even within the same employment category, there continues to exist a strong division between female and male occupations (CEPAL, 1994b).

The service sector provides important employment opportunities for women. It is attractive because much of it is compatible with women's household responsibilities, it can be done on a flexible or part-time basis, and it may be in a location where children can be brought along. These advantages are generally offset, however, by the relatively low pay offered for the jobs that women typically hold in the sector (UN, 1991b). In addition, women rarely climb to the highest positions within service industries (CEPAL, 1994b).

In the Caribbean, tourism is often cited as a potential source of employment and revenue. McKay's (1993) review of women's work in the tourism sector in Negril, Jamaica, demonstrates that these opportunities are often double edged. She points out that market vendors and guesthouse operators are primarily women and that these activities are thus an option for women seeking an income. She goes on to argue, however, that it is difficult for women to expand these enterprises past a minimal size. Barriers include family ties, expectations rooted in tradition and limited access to credit. Opportunities for expansion or growth of these enterprises are limited. A strategy to improve women's opportunities in this sector should take into consideration women's social roles and family obligations. These women are not fully independent economic actors, able to respond to strictly economic incentives. These ties influence a woman's room to maneuver and highlight the importance of consulting and including women themselves in decision-making roles.

Informal Sector

The informal sector—which includes unregulated workers, the self-employed (excluding professionals), and microenterprises usually not registered with government agencies—was already sizeable in many countries and grew by about 20 percent during the 1980s. Incomes in the sector declined by 41.1 percent, however, as compared to an overall decline of 17.9 percent for all sectors (PREALC, 1988). No regional data is available on women's participation in the sector, but a variety of surveys demonstrate its importance. In Bolivian cities, for example, household surveys have found that the proportion of women working on their own account reached 56 percent in 1985 and 61 percent by 1991 (Escobar de Pabon, 1993). In Mexico, women constitute between 52 and 62 percent of all informal sector workers, including domestic workers (Berger and Buvinić, 1989). In Lima, women's participation in the sector grew from 36.2 percent in 1983 to 45 percent in 1987 (Francke, 1988). Moreover, the ratio of females to males in the sector is also steadily growing throughout the region (Tochman, 1989).

Women in the informal sector are primarily involved in marketing, production of clothing and processed food, and personal services. The latter includes domestic service, which, in most countries in the region, is virtually an all-female occupation. Aside from domestic service, women operate one-person businesses more often than men, with limited capital and little access to credit or technology. For many, this means no more than piecework carried out at a worker's home on subcontract to formal sector firms. In the Caribbean many women have turned to "higgling" either as a primary source of income or as a way to supplement other earnings. Originally higglers were vendors of agricultural products. However, in recent years trade has expanded to include the selling of goods from abroad, ranging from clothing to electrical appliances (French, 1994).

The informal sector is characterized by low productivity and earnings and by a lack of job security. Nevertheless, a large percentage of women work in this sector because of its flexible work schedule, low entry and exit costs and the ability to fulfil their household obligations while earning an income. For many women these are positive advantages. Others choose the informal sector because they have few alternatives.

The informal sector constitutes an important employment haven for women and has been critical for their survival and that of their families during recent economic crises. However, while women make important contributions to the sector, they do so as the smallest business operators, generally earning incomes lower than those of men and below the minimum wage. Improving women's productivity through better access to capital and technology would increase their contribution to economic growth.

Experiences in the Region

Governments and international agencies have experimented with various programs and policy initiatives designed to increase poor women's earnings or the "productive capacity" of the poor in general. One of the primary lessons that has been learned over the last decade is that such general policy decisions are not gender neutral.

While not specifically designed to increase female employment, the opening of markets and the promotion of export-oriented agricultural and industrial growth have clearly had greater impact on women than project interventions aimed at income generation for women. Conversely, some agricultural policies and projects, as well as technological change in industries, may have also had unintentional perverse effects. The need to examine all economic policies in terms of their impact on women has been highlighted by many researchers, commentators and advocates (Bakker, 1994; Elson, 1991; Moser, 1993a).

The policies and projects reviewed below have had mixed results in providing and improving employment and income-earning opportunities for women. However, they offer useful lessons about how to incorporate a gender dimension into economic policy development and "social reforms." Investments in women's health (including reproductive health) and education are well documented as being critical for increasing women's productivity and employment options. Less understood are the far-reaching consequences of general industrial and agricultural policies for women.

Impact of Economic Policies

Focus on the Production of Tradeables

In most countries, suppressing domestic demand in the early stages of economic stabilization and of re-orienting the economy to production for export have had a significant impact on women's employment over the last decade. However, the overall effect of these processes is not straightforward. Those who produce for local consumption, and women who tend to be more involved in the production of non-tradeables, are generally most affected by lower domestic demand (Howden, 1993). However, as production for export has increased, firms in industry and agribusiness have provided both wage and self-employment for women.

Opportunities for self-employment often stem from subcontracting arrangements between informal sector firms that produce for export firms in the formal sector, or between small independent farmers and processing plants in "satellite farming" ventures. There is evidence of the positive impact of this work on women's economic and social opportunities (Joekes and Moayedi, 1987). In Guatemala, for instance, women employed in a frozen vegetable processing plant earned 150 to 300 percent more than what they would otherwise have earned in domestic service or informal sector enterprises (Kusterer et al., 1981). In Mexico, while the EPZ jobs pay low wages, they provide women with work that is substantially better paid than the alternatives commonly available to them in farm labor, domestic service, and market vending (Joekes and Moayedi, 1987).

However, there is also documentation of exploitation of women wage workers in EPZs, of women microproducers in workshops, and of seasonal workers in agriculture, especially by less affluent national firms. In the case of subcontracting, women workers can easily be exploited through low pay and minimal job security. However, the presence of women-based intermediary agencies can help ensure that contractors get quality and timely products and that women producers gain access to credit, technical assistance and organizational skills to operate efficient contracting arrangements with large firms.

The promotion of tradeables in agriculture can also have unintended adverse effects on women's income-earning opportunities. Women's unpaid family labor contributions to the production of cash crops might be increased at the expense of time spent on tending crops for household consumption or other independent off-farm activities from which the income accrues to women directly (Joekes et al., 1988). The emphasis on export production may also result in a reduction of the amount of land available to women for their own productive activities. For example, in the highlands of Guatemala, subcontracting with male farmers to grow snowpeas and cauliflower for export resulted, in some instances, in women substituting unpaid labor on the family farm for their previous income-producing marketing activities. Women increased their workload while losing their only source of independent income (von Braun, Hotchkiss, and Immink, 1989).

Evidence suggests that the shifts in the allocation of women's work, brought about unintentionally by this effort, may have a long-term detrimental effect on child well-being due to the reduction in the income and resources under women's control (Katz, cited in Quisumbing, 1993). A feasible solution to this situation would be to ensure that women are contracted, and paid, directly for their work.

The greater demand for women's labor in new sectors of the economy is beginning to have an impact on sectors traditionally dominated by women. Women tend to express strong preferences for work in factories or processing plants over domestic service work, which pays less and carries a heavy social stigma. Work in export firms and agribusiness is helping to upgrade the conditions of domestic service work in some instances. The increased demand for female seasonal wage labor in harvest operations and agricultural processing plants in Chile has likely resulted in substantial improvements in wages and working conditions in domestic service employment. Likewise, in the Dominican Republic, there is evidence of reduction in the number of women entering domestic service and of an increase in salaries (Arregui and Baez, 1991).

Women, Trade Liberalization and Technological Change

Technological change and the accompanying reorganization of production brought about by economic restructuring processes and global competition have also had different impacts on women's employment. Trade liberalization and technological change have been shown to be factors in reducing women's employment in firms in Argentina and Mexico (Roldán, 1991; De la O-Martinez, 1994).

Pearson (1993) points out that there are significant variations in women's employment across industries. She is more optimistic about the potential for women in data-entry enterprises compared to the more limited outlook for garment manufacturing and electronic assembly. Looking specifically at the case of Jamaica, she highlights specific characteristics of this sector (the involvement of local capital, the training offered employees, and its physical location outside of the free trade zone) that distinguish it from industries typically associated with EPZs. Given these differences, this type of industry has the potential to support a highly skilled, flexible and innovative information services sector that could provide a higher quality of work opportunity than either the garment or electronics industries.

Yet there is a risk that this potential will remain unrealized. Pearson argues that the dominance of women in this sector (by 1989 approximately 90 percent of the 2,500 employees in the data entry-data processing sector in Jamaica were women) has led employers to underestimate the skills and potential of this workforce.[3]

Although more work needs to be done, the evidence suggests that trade liberalization is not gender neutral. A study of the impact of trade liberalization on women in Mexico examined four sectors of the economy that collectively employ 80 percent of female labor—agriculture, textile, the maquiladora industry, and services. This study presented a series of hypotheses on the impact of the North American Free Trade Agreement (NAFTA) on women's participation in these sectors (Cardero, 1993). The sector that will experience the

[3] "It is a damning reflection on the evaluation of women's skills that workers who have been able to adapt to considerable pressures at work, who have shown flexibility of response to frequently changing programmes on an ad hoc basis and have organized speedy through-put of data entry at a guaranteed level of accuracy and quality should be considered no more qualified than school leavers with basic typing skills. Instead of being channelled towards managerial or information technology training courses and employment, both the women themselves and their past and potential employers are content to allow them to proceed to secretarial training and employment, where their skills and talents will remain unrecognized, unrewarded and under-utilized" (Pearson, 1993: 294).

Box 2: Women and MERCOSUR

Given the significant increase in women's participation in the workforce, FLACSO-Brazil is involved in a research and training project that will analyze the potential impact on women's situation in the labor markets of Brazil, Argentina, Paraguay and Uruguay of the formation of the Southern Common Market or MERCOSUR. Materials on women's situation in the four member countries, on women's participation in the labor market and on the factors that influence their participation (including laws and labor regulations) will be prepared. Representatives from government planning ministries, unions, business organizations and NGOs that work with women are targeted for educational efforts. The project aims both to raise awareness and to support the development of concrete proposals to ensure that greater economic opportunities for both women and men result from the creation of MERCOSUR (IDB, 1994).

most change as a result of trade liberalization is agriculture, where one-fourth of the economically active population in Mexico is employed. From 1987 to 1992, this sector was stagnant largely because of agricultural trade liberalization, the reduction of the price-support system, and increased costs for agricultural inputs. Farmers will be forced to search for new opportunities and, Cardero argues, migration will increase the competition between men and women for jobs in the urban areas.

Cardero speculates that the textile and garment industry, three-quarters of which is made up of female labor, will not be negatively affected by NAFTA. In fact, if textile production improves as expected as a result of trade liberalization, women are most likely to benefit in terms of increased employment in this sector. The maquiladoras industry employs approximately 4 percent of the female labor force. Sixty percent of this sector is comprised of female labor. The service industry, which grew throughout the 1980s, will also likely experience expansion, particularly as uncompetitive manufacturing companies close down and as farmers migrate to urban centers. This sector will be affected by trade liberalization in areas such as financial services and telecommunications. Given that women's skill levels in these areas are not competitive with men's, they are unlikely to benefit from any growth in this sector. In the face of increased competition from men, more women will move into the lower-paid informal sector (Cardero, 1993).

Trade liberalization and technological change will affect women's employment in all of these sectors positively and negatively. However, women's ability to respond quickly to changing market signals and to compete effectively in a world of rapid economic changes will depend on the continued existence of barriers to women's access to resources such as land, training and credit and of rigidities and discrimination in the labor market. This is an area that requires significant further consideration and research.

Project Initiatives

Income Generation and Microenterprise

Despite their frequent failure, income-generation projects have been preferred by most development agencies as the strategy to increase women's incomes (Buvinić, 1986; Villarreal, 1992). Generally, this type of project aims to teach a new skill or to upgrade skills women already have and to provide some of the resources needed to use the skills in the production of marketable goods or services (Buvinić, 1986). Project features often include group organization and group production; training in awareness raising and gender solidarity; skills development in traditionally female tasks; subsidized credit or other inputs; and attempts at marketing the group product. There are two questionable underlying premises to this strategy. The first is that group functioning and participatory styles are effective vehicles for women's enterprises. Second, it is assumed that these projects will promote gender awareness and solidarity. Projects are implemented by government agencies and women-only organizations in the non-governmental organization (NGO) sector, and the participants and implementors often volunteer their time. Income-generating projects generally fail to improve the economic situation of women for several reasons:

- Multiple objectives often call for complexities in project implementation that are beyond the capabilities of implementors and the time participants can offer to the project.
- The preferred participatory style of management projects is not conducive to effective economic performance (Tendler, 1982). Group-based production can be effective but group-based decision making for production usually is not.
- Income-generation skills taught are most often the so-called traditional "female skills" such as food preparation, baking and sewing with patterns. In reality, these skills are often not familiar to many women, are sometimes difficult to teach, require background knowledge that most poor women do not have, and usually result in low-quality products that have little, if any, market demand.

Box 3: Generating Income

Typical examples of income-generating projects include 15 projects for poor women in the outskirts of San José, Costa Rica. Eleven were sewing groups, where five to 25 women produced school uniforms and other children's clothing for sale to local factories. According to a review of the projects, only two of the 15 projects earned "some income," and only one had "satisfactory" income (Yudelman, 1987). Another example was a fruit-growing project in a depressed rural area in the same country that sought to generate income for women by growing fruit for sale. The project's cost was almost six times greater than the income generated by the sale of the fruit (Villarreal, 1992).

- General business skills (management, marketing, and accounting) are rarely taught or included in the project development, or when they are taught, the information is rarely put into practice.
- Poor women cannot afford the voluntarism required in these projects and so leave them, while somewhat better-off women stay on. Using female volunteers, while cost-saving in the short term, is not viable in the long run.
- The lack of technically competent personnel is also frequently a significant element in project failure.

As the problems with income-generation projects became more widely understood, other options emerged. One of the primary changes was the move away from support for groups brought together by project officers or other outsiders to support for the self-started activities of women. Drawing on the lessons learned from the experiences of the income-generating projects, new projects tended to place much greater focus on the marketability of the product to be produced and to offer optional training programs.

The best-known evolution of the income-generating project is support for "minimalist" microenterprise projects. These projects deliver credit and, sometimes, training and technical assistance to individuals who already operate microenterprises in the informal sector, mostly in commerce and services. Their objectives are largely economic—to improve the economic performance of microenterprises, to generate employment, and to "graduate" informal sector producers to the formal sector. Some projects include a gender-specific objective (i.e., to increase women's incomes), and some target only women clients. These projects have a narrower set of objectives when compared with income-generation ones. Thus, it is easier to achieve project goals. The success of these efforts varies according to how they deliver credit. Microenterprise-support activities have taken two principal forms. NGOs run some programs. More recently, formal financial institutions such as banks and credit unions have increased their services to the poor, especially women.

Many poor microentrepreneurs, especially women, have found it difficult to access credit through formal lending institutions. For example, in the early 1980s, the government-owned Industrial Bank of Peru established a credit line for urban microenterprises in Lima and secondary cities. While one of the explicit policies of the credit line was to reach female clients, only 16 percent of the loan portfolio had been disbursed to women by the end of the second year of operation. The characteristic features of formal sector lending discouraged potential women clients from applying for loans. Fixed loans were preferred over working capital loans, focusing on longer grace and loan periods and larger loan amounts. Loans favored manufacturing over the commerce and petty trading in which most women's enterprises engage. In addition, the credit line had tough collateral and documentation requirements that proved to be quite restrictive in practice (Buvinić and Berger, 1990).

As a response to this type of situation, many NGOs throughout the region have developed credit schemes that replicate lending in the informal sector. NGO initiatives that have emerged generally lend small initial amounts at market interest rates, segment the market into microproducers and microvendors, develop solidarity groups for microvendors, and have few collateral requirements and little paper work. The NGO programs that have produced the best results have had technically qualified, paid staffs and are often set up specifically to run the credit program. These program features respond to the main factors that have inhibited women's demand for credit from formal institutions. Therefore, these schemes are "women-friendly." The results are viable projects for male-run and female-run microenterprises, at least in the short term.

Most of the empirical evidence on the impact of these NGO-run minimalist microenterprise projects on business incomes is favorable. It shows growth in women's business income in the short term. Increases in the profits of women-operated enterprises range from 25 percent in some programs and for some categories of women-based enterprises to 50–100 percent in others (Guzmán and Castro, 1989; Otero, 1989; Reichmann, 1984).

These minimalist NGO credit programs are not, however, without disadvantages. They provide moderate coverage, and have questionable long-term financial viability since they do not function entirely as formal financial

Box 4: Support for Microproduction

While women often comprise more than half of the recipients of loans for commercial activities in NGO credit programs, they tend to be less well represented in the loans given to microproducers. In Quito, Ecuador, the NGO Prodem overcame this pattern by obtaining technical assistance on gender issues, disaggregating information by sex of borrower and setting up a special earmarked fund of $50,000 to be disbursed to women. Two years later, women accounted for 65 percent of microvendor group borrowers and 35 percent of individual borrowers in microproduction (Buvinić , Berger and Jaramillo, 1989).

intermediaries and do not have deposits or savings. They have limited capacity to graduate clients into the formal banking sector. They have not been very successful at transforming enterprises—especially women's enterprises, which are the smallest and least productive—from subsistence level production to activities that can be more competitive in national and international markets. Another issue that requires further research is how frequently a woman borrower becomes a "front" for a man. More successful programs run the risk of attracting men who then want to take over the program. At times, women take on the credit risk but do not directly benefit from the use of the credit.

Currently, discussion on microenterprise development centers around the issue of long-term sustainability of financial services to this sector. In past years, some institutions involved in microenterprise finance have reached viable operational levels, with several NGOs evolving into banks, such as BANCOSOL in Bolivia. This evolution allows an increasing number of women microentrepreneurs to access credit and improves the financial viability of the institution. A growing group of institutions—including banks, credit unions and NGOs—are also starting to provide savings services for the poor.

Some formal financial institutions, such as the Caja Social in Colombia, are providing a variety of financial services to low-income neighborhoods and are adopting lending criteria that make their services accessible to low-income women. However, many of these programs remain concentrated in capital cities. The challenge is to expand services to women in rural areas as well as to other urban centers. The evolution of a division of labor between the services to microenterprises that the formal financial institutions and NGOs provide, which builds on the strengths of both types of organizations, represents another interesting possibility. Within this framework, financial institutions provide the credit while NGOs play a "social mediation role," with a focus on providing other enterprise-support services (Bennett and Goldberg, 1993).

Training Programs for Women: Reinforcing Traditional Roles?

A CINTERFOR and ILO (1991) assessment of major vocational training institutions in Latin America and the Caribbean, prompted by the urgent need to train the work force to compete in international markets, found that women constituted approximately 42 percent of trainees in 13 vocational education institutions in 1987. This would seem to indicate that the region's experience with vocational training for women has been quite positive. Unfortunately, this is far from the case. Most female trainees have been enrolled in courses oriented to traditionally female-dominated, low-wage occupations in trade and services that often have low market demand.

Thus, rather than opening up new employment and earning possibilities for women, training is actually perpetuating female-male differences in economic opportunities. The problem in the region, therefore, is not one of female access to vocational training but of access to quality, non-stereotypical training that would, among other things, prepare women for the requirements of an increasingly high-technology work place.

Until recently, experience in providing non-traditional training to women in Latin America and the Caribbean has centered around small, isolated projects. In an effort to expand the benefits of these projects, and building on the lessons that have been learned, a more comprehensive strategy has been designed for national training institutes in nine Latin American countries. The purpose is to address women's specific training needs. New strategies mirror project-specific efforts such as encouraging females toward training in marketable skill areas, revising training materials and course curricula to upgrade quality and respond to women's educational needs, forming links with the private sector as well as with internships and placement activities that target women, providing gender training for program staff, and offering alternative child care arrangements for women with small children. The significance of such a comprehensive strategy is underscored by the transformations taking place in institutions as they try to address the social and occupational needs of women trainees. These institutions train as many as 2.5 million students per year.

New strategies, if successfully implemented, have long-term implications for the training of women in the region because of the continuity that the

Box 5: Inter-Institutional Coordination in Training

The United Women's Woodworking and Welding project in Jamaica, in which the Women's Bureau and the Vocational Training Division of the Ministry of Youth were involved, provides an excellent example of inter-institutional coordination. Implemented in the late 1970s and early 1980s, the project provided training in non-traditional skills such as carpentry and welding to low-income women in Kingston. The Women's Bureau designed, coordinated and administered the program, taking into account the target women participants' particular characteristics, such as low levels of literacy. The bureau also conducted gender awareness training for the administrators and faculty of the Vocational Training Division, which provided the training services. Since the division had prior experience in providing training in the required areas, the instructors and training materials were of high quality, and the training was technically sound (Antrobus and Rogers, 1988).

major training institutions can offer, the legitimacy and credibility of the institutions, and the quality of the facilities and resources available for both training and research (IDB, 1995a). The implementation of a comprehensive strategy also allows for the possibility of inter-institutional coordination between women's organizations and vocational training institutes to ensure the effective and appropriate training of women (see Box 5).

A national program in Chile is currently providing short-term training and internships for new entrants to the labor market, with support from the Inter-American Development Bank. One unique aspect of this program is the links that are established with private sector firms that need skilled labor, which sponsor the internships and provide on-the-job skills training to participants in the program. The program has targeted women's participation by presenting female as well as male trainees in a non-stereotypical manner in advertising campaigns and by integrating gender-specific activities into the program. These have included providing child care options and gender awareness training for project staff, encouraging internship placements for women in the private sector, developing demonstration projects to provide training for women in non-traditional occupations, and implementing outreach programs to ensure the effective participation of women (IDB, 1995a).

A new large-scale training program in Argentina has also been designed to facilitate women's participation in skills training. Assistance for child care costs is provided through modest stipends to women with children under the age of five (IDB, 1995a). This initiative not only enables their participation but also provides women with the opportunity to make their own arrangements for child care. With such arrangements in place, following their training these women should find it easier to conduct job searches and to start working.

Compensatory Interventions

Since the late 1970s Latin American and Caribbean governments have implemented a series of compensatory interventions or programs to mitigate the political costs of adjustment and to provide employment and transfer income to the poor. Throughout the region, different structures and mechanisms were put into place, with later initiatives often building on the lessons of earlier programs. Some programs, such as Bolivia's Social Emergency Fund (FSE) and Chile's Social Solidarity and Investment Fund (FOSIS), were demand-driven. Both private and non-profit agencies developed proposals requesting funding and executed the projects. Other programs were supply-driven, top-down interventions, financed and run by the central government, such as the emergency employment programs in Chile and Peru.[4] Following on the success of the FSE, as of 1992 there were 15 such funds in operation in Latin America and the Caribbean (Wurgaft, 1992).

In general, the ability of compensatory interventions to have a positive impact on women's lives has been mixed. The primary benefits for women have been through welfare-oriented programs that provide foodstuffs and help women meet the needs generated through their roles as mothers. There have been few longer-term gains for women through employment creation or skills development (Pollack, 1993). In other words, women participated in food programs where the flow of benefits lasted as long as the program, while men were the primary beneficiaries of employment programs that offered the potential for longer-term spin-offs (Moser et al., 1993). For example, in programs that aimed to provide short-term employment to cushion the dislocation that results from adjustment measures there were attempts to provide on-the-job training, although this was often minimal given the unskilled nature of most of the work. Women have found it difficult to take advantage of these programs, especially in industries that do not traditionally employ them (Moser et al., 1993).

---

[4] Other differences among programs include institutional structures (some programs are administered by existing government ministries, while in other cases, new organizations are established); source of financing (internal, external or both); different degrees of geographic targeting; and, sector focus or cross-sectoral focus (Moser, Herbert, and Makonnen, 1993).

Factors that appear to have had an impact on benefits for women in compensatory interventions include:

- an explicit targeting of women;
- an explicit recognition of women's multiple roles (especially women's need to earn an income); and
- an active participation (or the potential for participation) by women in implementing agencies.

Compensatory programs have reached women when they have sought to do so. Women have often been identified as beneficiaries in food subsidies and feeding programs. This type of intervention aims to support the nutrition of individuals and households at risk in times of price changes. Examples include the Jamaican Food Stamp Program, a food coupon program in Honduras, and the HCBI *(Programa de Hogares Comunitarios de Bienestar Familiar)* in Colombia. Moser et al. (1993) argue that this type of program can provide temporary relief to the intended beneficiaries—including women. They caution that there are important prerequisites for success that vary from case to case, which include administrative coordination, appropriate targeting mechanisms, the compensation of low-income women for their work in the program and an appropriate delivery mechanism. Box 6 offers an example of one program that reached women through careful targeting.

The Bolivian FSE is an example of one social fund without a policy on women. It had four main components: employment generation to build economic or social infrastructure, social assistance or welfare, credit for production and technical assistance. Approximately 82 percent of the FSE funds went to infrastructure. The main beneficiaries were thus male construction workers. Women mostly received social assistance (Zuckerman, 1990; Buxell, 1991).

Some women reportedly worked in employment projects. Yet, given the absence of a policy and instructions to differentiate between men's and women's participation, information on women workers did not usually get registered. In the case of a food-for-work program implemented by Caritas in Potosí, it was found that between April 1988 and March 1991 there were 3,291 workers in the project, of which 42.5 percent were women (Buxell, 1991). Castaños et al. (1988) observe that when women worked in FSE-supported projects, they worked in exploitative conditions and were paid less. In addition, Pollack (1993) reports that researchers visiting project sites often found large numbers of women and children at work substituting for men as "unpaid family workers."

Box 6: Peru's Temporary Income Support Program (PAIT)

Between October 1985 and June 1987, PAIT provided work for about 374,000 temporary workers in six work campaigns with an approximate investment of $100 million. PAIT workers were paid the equivalent of a minimum wage for an eight-hour work day. In real terms, the minimum wage was about half of that needed to satisfy the basic needs of poor families (Wurgaft, 1988). A majority of these workers were women. They were poorer and less educated than the male participants and were more often heads of household with responsibilities for children (Vigier, 1986).

The program effectively reached women in part because it adopted an explicit goal that 30 percent of jobs would go to them. In addition, it was designed and promoted as a community development activity and was implemented by a community development organization, thus reaching women because they were volunteer workers in community development activities. The PAIT enabled poor women to substitute paid for unpaid work in community participation. The program did not require prior training, allowed flexible work hours, recruited workers from nearby neighborhoods so that there were no transportation costs, and allowed women to bring their children to work. These features made it an attractive work option for poor women, who organized community child care centers to accommodate their market and home responsibilities. By 1986, 84 percent of the workers were women, and about 4,000 children attended PAIT-organized child care centers. Sixty-five percent of the workers improved their income, and half of these cut back on their work hours. Men's rejection of the program, probably due to low wages and the stigma associated with poverty programs, may have contributed to such a high percentage of female workers (Vigier, 1988).

While it lasted, the PAIT appears to have been an effective anti-poverty intervention for women. The major problem was the temporary nature of both the work and the program, which may have been terminated in part because its clients, poor urban women, did not have enough political clout to keep alive a transfer program targeted to them.

For programs to succeed, program designers and administrators must understand women's multiple roles. A study of Guyana's Social Impact Amelioration Program points out that its supplementary feeding programs were grounded on questionable tenets. They often assumed that women were willing to provide long-term voluntary labor or were prepared to work for modest stipends. Failure to recognize women's need to earn a viable income constitutes a significant flaw in program design (Sollis and MacDonald, 1994).

Women's participation (and the eventual flow of benefits to women) has also been influenced by the nature of the implementation agencies. For example, poor women's access to the employment generated by the Bolivian FSE was constrained both by the lack of a specific policy toward women and the nature of the implementing agencies (i.e., the construction companies that were not structured to hire women workers). If implementing agencies are those that usually work with women, such as the Bolivian church-based organizations that implement food-for-work programs, it is more likely that a social fund will respond to poor women's practical or strategic needs.[5] Male-dominated organizations such as labor unions and traditional cooperatives, as well as private construction companies, will generally submit projects for funding that do not include women.

A study of the comparatively smaller Chilean Social Solidarity and Investment Fund (FOSIS) shows how poor women's needs are affected by the capacity of executing agencies. The fund has no specific policy towards women. Its responsiveness to the needs of poor women is left entirely to the interest, capacity and orientation of the agencies that apply to or compete for FOSIS funds. A cursory review of projects financed through August 1992 suggests that women's strategic needs are better addressed by the fund in Santiago, where non-governmental and women-based organizations predominate, as compared with the smaller secondary cities, where the presence and capacity of this sector is much reduced. In Santiago, FOSIS benefits women by financing microenterprise interventions and skills-training programs for adolescent mothers and poor women heads of households. In the smaller, more isolated cities across the country, FOSIS finances welfare-oriented projects for poor women presented by the municipalities, church groups, and neighborhood associations (Buvinic, forthcoming).

How Can Women's Job Opportunities Improve?

It is now becoming clear that policies and compensatory strategies that were not specifically designed to benefit women or to address gender issues have, in fact, affected women's employment options more than projects explicitly directed to them. This is in part because many of the projects aimed at women were limited in financial resources and scope or were poorly conceived. In contrast, given women's entry into labor markets and the fact that women operate in the same economies as do men (although, as discussed, not always under the same conditions), general policies have had a tremendous impact on their lives and work.

---

[5] These two concepts are explored in the opening chapter on the differences and similarities among women.

First, policies that affect employment and income are not gender neutral but have different effects on men and women. Second, the policy environment also influences the success of projects aimed at expanding women's economic opportunities. The implications of a gender analysis of major policy directions should be clearly understood before initiatives are undertaken.

What Must Be Done

Study Economic Restructuring and Women's Employment

As indicated throughout this chapter, major changes at the macro level generally have clear gender implications, and yet, much more research is needed to understand these implications. There is a need to develop the capacity to understand and systematically document policy and project impact by gender. In particular, trade liberalization policies and technological change resulting from economic restructuring processes need to be analyzed to determine their impact on women's employment. Governments, donor agencies and research institutes alike should undertake these analyses.

Increase Access to Services

Women's employment opportunities are generally limited by the availability of child care and other supports that help them meet domestic obligations. A successful employment policy must be linked to other policies. The recommendations that follow must be combined with increased access of the poor to basic services (water, sanitation, and transportation) and with investments in women's health (including a minimum reproductive health package) and education. These are central elements in a social reform package that targets women —both to foster growth and to reduce poverty and inequality in the region.

Improve Working Conditions

Governments that are in the process of promoting export-oriented, labor-intensive industrial growth, either by setting up export-processing zones or by providing other incentives to domestic and multinational corporations, need to ensure quality employment for workers (the majority of whom are women) and promote worker rights in the context of highly competitive markets that can easily displace or substitute women workers.

Quality employment for women implies providing decent wages, adhering to specific health and safety regulations, providing on-the-job skills training, offering access to on-the-job or community child care and health services, and forming women-based worker's associations.

The promotion of quality employment for women should involve various actors and strategies. Governments can finance the dissemination of information on women's employment conditions and economic contributions. Employers, largely male-dominated trade associations and the women workers themselves need to be informed about the critical connection between women's economic participation and family welfare and about the importance of women workers' rights. Social security legislation needs to be reformed on the basis of gender as well as pro-poor criteria. Governments need to set up and enforce environmental standards in industry and promote appropriate policies in the industrial sector that encourage the development of productive home-based industries and small firms.

Finally, governments and development agencies should promote and finance the creation of intermediary, non-profit agencies whose function is to bridge the gap between large employers and low-income women producers, as well as between women and credit and training institutions. These intermediaries can provide employers with quality production and women producers with credit, technical assistance, and the organizational skills needed to operate efficient contracting arrangements with large firms.

Provide More and Better Education and Training

The quality of women's educational and training opportunities needs to be improved. First, efforts should be made to narrow the gap in fields of study in higher education by encouraging more girls to enter into non-traditional fields. Second, most governments in the region should take steps to revamp state-run vocational and skills training programs and to press for changes in private sector programs. This would ensure that women receive training in non-traditional, profitable skills that respond to the requirements of an increasingly high-technology workplace.

Training institutions should be provided with the knowledge and the incentives to increase the proportion of women receiving such training. Scholarships and vocational guidance for potential women trainees can complement outreach programs, quotas, and other affirmative action policies established by training institutions.

Support Women Farmers

Women's contributions in the agricultural sector should be made visible and should be supported. For example, export-oriented agricultural policies should be complemented by mechanisms that facilitate women's access to child care and to the productive resources they need to improve their earnings in agribusiness and the productivity of their work in food production for domestic and export markets.

This can be done by directing policies, institutions, and projects to provide women farmers with secure access to land and land titles, credit, skills training and new agricultural technologies and agricultural inputs that will improve yields. Complementary assistance includes providing basic rural infrastructure and processing technologies that can increase the efficiency of women's home production activities. This will not be easy

The emphasis on large rather than small farmer agriculture, on production rather than processing, and on the male family farmer as the recipient of agricultural services for the family farm has built strong biases in agricultural institutions against women farmers. Undercounting women farm workers does not help. These biases are present in most agricultural organizations, from those that undertake research to those that deliver extension services. Especially in those countries where women's participation in the farm sector is and historically has been high, national agricultural policies, institutions, and projects need to be overhauled.

Agricultural research must be undertaken that emphasizes crops that women grow, that yields technological improvements in pre- and post-harvest activities that women undertake, that integrates vegetables and small ruminants into the farming system, that investigates the preferences of women farmers and uses them to test farm technologies, and that includes nutrition in setting research priorities. Policies should also be put in place to ensure that small farmers, including women, are provided with the incentives and the resources (land, credit, and technology) to adopt agricultural innovations. Institutional changes should give women access to training and extension services.

Promote Women's Enterprises

Projects should be promoted that provide minimalist credit to microenterprises since these are generally effective in increasing women's income in the short-term. Evidence suggests that the indirect benefits to women from these projects (i.e., saving time) may even be greater than their direct effects (increasing profits). They should be preferred over group-based income-generation projects targeted specifically to women, and over credit-plus interventions. An issue that must be addressed for most of these projects, including the more successful minimalist interventions, is their long-term viability. Most projects have limited coverage and do not serve to transform women's enterprises from subsistence-level production to activities that can be more competitive in national and international markets.

Gender-friendly policies are needed to foster women's enterprises and ensure long-term project viability. These include:

- donor and national commitment to providing non-traditional skills training to women and financing start-up costs of direct assistance programs for women's microenterprises;
- revision of regulatory and legal frameworks with special emphasis on removing the constraints that female microentrepreneurs face in setting up businesses and having access to productive resources (especially legislation that keeps married women from having independent access to property and resources and to the requirements and permits needed to set up and operate businesses);
- industrial policies that favor the development of small-scale enterprises; and
- promotion of the institutional growth and professionalization of NGOs for women and the capacity of government agencies to address gender issues.

Recognize Women as Important Wage Earners

Compensatory programs such as social investment funds and emergency employment programs need to include gender-sensitive objectives, not only to promote the employment of women but also to support their participation in the identification and planning of projects to be funded.

The compensatory programs reviewed capture poor women's need for employment and income in economic downturns and show how program design, to a large extent, determines the extent of women's participation.

Governments can design emergency employment programs that either promote or discourage women's participation and either reinforce or challenge sex discrimination and sex stereotypes in the labor market. A gender-aware design would:

- provide a sufficiently varied range of employment options and executing agencies to include women but not completely feminize the program (feminization results in higher stigma and risk of closure);
- consider using women-based intermediaries and work options that include home-based production;
- provide work close to the home, set flexible hours, and include options for child care;
- define an explicit policy to reach women;

• back this policy with adequate human resources and gather statistics disaggregated by sex;

• provide skills training; and

• avoid setting different wage structures for men and women or, worse, separate programs for them.

Policy makers should also review accepted notions that women are secondary workers, earn complementary wages, and undertake work that is less productive than men's work.

The capacity of the implementing organizations is the key to making demand-driven social funds responsive to the strategic needs of poor women. Because the capacity of organizations in the public and non-governmental sectors to address the needs of poor women is limited, these institutions need to allow for and encourage charging overhead to cover capacity-building costs.

Understand Women's Diverse Roles

Public information and education campaigns on the important and diverse economic roles and contributions of women are especially important in the region, where the gap between myth and reality is wide. There is a need to understand the types of campaigns that will best work in specific circumstances.

Experience shows that it is extremely difficult to incorporate a gender perspective within projects given the lack of recognition of the contribution of women and an almost exclusive focus on their reproductive role. But in Latin America and the Caribbean today, women are a vital resource the region cannot afford to waste.

Chapter 4

Changing Politics: Women and Democratization

Women in Latin America and the Caribbean are more active in politics than ever before. They participate as community organizers, human rights advocates, feminists, mothers, environmentalists, peasants and unionists. To a lesser degree, women also take part as parliamentarians, government ministers, judges and state officials. While they are leading actors in civil society, women still tend to play minor parts on the national stage. These roles are, however, being recast.

Dramatic political and economic changes over the last two decades have created new opportunities and challenges for women in the region. After years of authoritarian rule, many Latin American countries began the transition to democracy a decade ago. Democratization promotes and has been promoted by women's participation. The mobilization of women challenging political repression and economic hardship during the 1970s and 1980s was a catalyst for the transition to democracy. The involvement of women changed, and continues to change, the form and content of political systems throughout the region.

Democratization gives women and other groups formerly excluded from the political process greater opportunity to participate. It opens space for women in governance, within both state and civil institutions. It also increases interchange between these two spheres, as women's organizations play a greater role in lobbying, consensus building, policy making and implementation. Democratization includes growing public demands for transparency in political institutions and processes. With the decentralization of the state and a changing view of its primary role (from an interventionist state to one that promotes an "enabling environment"), functions are being transferred to local actors. Civil society is thus gaining a greater role in governance.

Women were particularly hard hit by structural adjustment policies, which worsened inequity and poverty in the region (CEPAL, 1994b). By the early 1990s, 200 million people, or nearly half of all Latin Americans, were unable to meet their basic needs, while a quarter lived in extreme poverty (CEPAL, 1994a). Driven by necessity, women in thousands of poor communities formed self-help groups to provide their families with food and shelter.

The UN Women's Decade (1975–1985) led to increased recognition of women's rights worldwide. Most countries in Latin America and the Caribbean created special offices or ministries to promote gender equity. Many areas of discriminatory legislation have been changed, including family and labor laws. There has been a burgeoning of women's organizations and networks at the local, national, regional and international levels.

Even with these steps forward, women in the region still have a long way to go to attain equality with men. The fledgling democracies there are far from pluralistic or representative. While significant numbers of women take part in local affairs, they are still excluded from high-level posts in national governments, parliaments and political parties. Despite their alleged equality, in practice women remain second-class citizens.

To understand women's political role, it is first necessary to examine how, when and why women do and do not participate and what difference their involvement makes. Analyzing women's roles in governance through both the state and civil society reveals ways to strengthen the democratic participation of women at various levels of public life, from community organizations to national legislatures.

Overview of Women's Participation

Opening Thoughts

Before exploring women's political participation, three general themes arise. What is meant by women's political participation? What is the relationship between changes in public, formal political structures and changes within the household? Is it possible to generalize across a region as varied and diverse as Latin America and the Caribbean?

Although a thorough discussion of each of these themes is beyond the scope of this overview, these questions are found interwoven (both explicitly and implicitly) throughout the growing discussions of women, social movements, feminism, democratization, civil society, and governance in the Caribbean and Latin America.

Some authors have characterized women's social movements as a new form of doing or engaging in politics (una nueva forma de hacer polītica; Safa, 1990; Cañadell, 1993). Many women within Latin America have wrestled with the challenge of working within structures while trying to change them. The influential Chilean feminist Julieta Kirkwood pointed out that the issue is not simply one of incorporating women into a male-defined world, but of transforming this world to do away with the hierarchies of class, gender, race, and ethnicity that have subordinated many Latin Americans, men as well as women (Kirkwood, 1986).

Yet this challenge is not straightforward. Women's political participation is not uniform, nor do all women share the same ultimate objectives. It is not just poor, urban women or campesinas who have participated in political movements for social change. Women have mobilized around other causes or interests. Waylen (1992) looks at women's organizations to preserve the status quo. There are also notable examples of women's involvement in political parties from across the spectrum, not just the left or progressive social movements.

Women's organizations have also struggled to create new organizations and styles of organizing. Young (1990) reviews the debate around women's organizations, highlighting struggles around hierarchy, leadership and styles of decision making. She cites Yudelman's (1987) conclusion that women seem to have difficulty in creating and maintaining organizations that are "participatory, conflict-free and functional." Vargas (1992) also questions the assertion that women automatically do politics differently from men. She outlines other "myths" feminists mistakenly drew on during the 1980s.[1]

A second major theme involves the relationship between women's domestic responsibility and identity, political participation and changes within the household. Just as women's position in organizations and public political life is changing, so is women's role within the household. The popular Chilean slogan urging democracia en el país y en la casa (democracy in the country and in the home) neatly conveyed women's concerns for change within the very public sphere of national politics and within, until recently, the private sphere of domestic relations. In the last decade, change within these two spheres has become interrelated.

[1] These myths include: Feminists are not interested in power; feminists do politics in a different way; all feminists are equal; there is a natural unity in just being women; any small group is representative of the movement; women's spaces in themselves guarantee positive processes; because I as a woman feel something, it's valid; the personal is automatically political; consensus is democracy.

There are two sub-elements to this second major theme. First, the politicization of mothers has become almost an inevitable topic in any discussion of the women's movement in Latin America. The section below on women's organizations briefly reviews this issue, but it is worth highlighting here as well. Many Latin American women have entered the sphere of the "political" through their role as mothers—to find missing children who were "disappeared" by military regimes or to lobby for improved domestic services. Although there has been much debate on whether or not this mobilization of women through their domestic responsibilities holds the promise for greater social change, many now argue that this potential does exist. "The politicization of motherhood breaks down the rigid boundary between public and private, which has kept women in the home and denied them their place as political subjects" (Jaquette, 1994: 224).[2]

The second sub-element is the increased profile of intra-household dynamics. In contrast to traditional economics and social analysis, which stopped at the family's doorstep, the case is now being made that the relationships within the family are important variables and should be understood if benefits and resources are to reach all members (Blumberg, 1991; Roldán, 1988; Sen, 1990).

The third major theme is the importance of remembering that although generalizations around the lives of women and men in Latin America and the Caribbean can be made, they should be made with caution. The vastly different economic situations of individual people combine with diverse political systems, races, cultures, and religious affiliations to produce a heterogeneous mix. This chapter attempts to avoid the dangers of over-generalization on the one hand and an inability to synthesize and identify general trends on the other.

Historical Context

The political participation of women in Latin America and the Caribbean has changed significantly from precolonial times to the present. In the last century alone, women have come to play more prominent roles on the national political stage. By the turn of the century, women were fighting for their "emancipa-

[2] Or as Safa (1990: 361) argues: "The collectivization of private tasks, such as food preparation and child care, is transforming women's roles, even though they are not undertaken as conscious challenges to gender subordination. These women never reject their domestic role but use it as a base to give them strength and legitimacy in their demands on the state. In moving their domestic concerns into the public arena, they are redefining the meaning associated with domesticity to include participation and struggle rather than obedience and passivity."

tion," which included their right to vote, attend school, have paid employment and get divorced. Beginning in 1900, feminist organizations were formed in numerous countries including Argentina, Chile, Venezuela, Colombia, Mexico and Peru (Portugal, 1986; Sefchovich, 1980).

Women's suffrage movements gained strength in the 1930s. By the 1950s, most Latin American and Caribbean women were voting in national elections. Uruguayan women were among the earliest voters in 1932, while women in the Bahamas had to wait until 1962 to cast their first ballots in national elections (IPU, 1992). Having obtained the right to vote, many women's suffrage movements dissipated, rather than going on to seek broader political and civil rights.

During the first half of this century, some women also took part in political parties, trade unions, student associations and even armed rebellions. These movements were usually led and controlled by men. General interests (often class-based) subsumed any gender-specific concerns that women members might have had. Women were considered part of the broader struggles (Murguialday, 1989).

Since the mid-1970s, women's political participation has increased in numbers and quality. Many more women have become involved in a broader range of issues and organizations. Latin American women became more vocal and visible political actors for several reasons. Under military regimes, women from all classes mobilized to defend human rights. In a break with past patterns, this form of political organizing was often easier for women than for men. Given the increasing economic crisis, lower-class urban women formed community organizations to provide basic services as well. Many women were prompted to participate in these forms of political protest and organization through their role as mothers.

A "second wave" of women's mobilization, following the suffrage movement decades earlier, began sweeping Latin America and the Caribbean in the late 1970s. It was propelled by the growing international recognition of women's rights, especially during the UN Women's Decade (1975-1985). Some Latin American women were exposed to feminism during their political exile. Others became politicized by fighting dictatorships and economic hardships at home. By the end of the 1980s, the feminist movement was dynamic and diverse, comprising millions of women in community organizations, political parties, trade unions, NGOs, campesino federations and government offices.

Current Situation

Currently, women are prominent activists within civil society in Latin America and the Caribbean. Community, environmental and human rights groups often have majority female membership. Thousands of women oriented NGOs seek economic, political and legal rights. Women are most evident within non-institutional politics, or social movements, at the local level.

Despite these changes, women remain marginal in formal politics. Relatively few women occupy leadership positions in government, political parties or trade unions. These political institutions are still dominated by men. Thus, women have little impact on policy making or implementation. The situation of women varies from country to country, however, there are common elements to consider when assessing women's potential political role. Several factors condition or influence women's participation, including existing political traditions, institutions and cultures; ethnic origin; and social conditions and support systems.

The Anglophone Caribbean has a long parliamentary tradition, yet the legacy of British colonialism hinders the political involvement of women there. The colonial approach promoted dependency and created an elitist state that inhibited popular participation. State structures were generally inflexible and resistant to change, while bureaucrats were trained to maintain the status quo (Jones, 1992; Anderson-Manley, 1994).

The corporatist tradition in Latin America affects the political options available to women's organizations. Under corporatism, the state directly or indirectly supports major groups in society. "Corporatism has reinforced the hierarchical, personalist and repressive practices of the ruling elites. Such practices perpetuate race, class and gender barriers, creating subjects rather than citizens. There are signs that the state has tried to incorporate women's groups in a variety of ways. In some cases, governments have used women's organizations as delivery mechanisms for emergency aid, which is...provided in exchange for political support" (Jaquette, 1994: 231).

The influence of the traditional Catholic Church varies across the region. It has less impact in the Anglophone Caribbean, where Protestant and Evangelical churches are gaining popularity, than in parts of Latin America. Conventional Catholicism extols the role of women as wives and mothers, while denying them reproductive or economic rights that would allow them to participate more fully outside the home. However, another church-based movement helped mobilize women. The grassroots, progressive Catholic Church that evolved during the 1960s and 1970s turned towards the poor and against military regimes. With the Church's protection, many women formed community or human rights groups to demand political and economic change (Alvarez, 1994). Machado (1993) notes how the Brazilian popular church provided women with a space for discussion, which eventually led to increased organization and politization.

The military has been a strong force inhibiting women's participation. The association of the public sphere with the military is a major factor in explaining women's exclusion from formal politics in Latin America (Bourque, 1989). Some analysts connect the recurrence of military dictatorships with the prevalence of authoritarian relations in society as a whole, and in the family in particular (Chuchryk, 1994). The military and the traditional Catholic Church are still male-dominated institutions, as are political parties in the region. Parties might mobilize groups of women in their struggle to win state power, but women rarely hold leadership positions. Men control political culture and activity (Kusterer, 1993).

These institutions reflect and reinforce machismo and marianismo, two visions or stereotypes that influence the socialization of men and women in the region. Machismo is generally seen as a cult of virility whereby men enjoy special privileges within society and the family and are considered superior to women. Men are thus expected to rule the public domain and the household. Machismo is considered more prevalent in mestizo (mixed Spanish and Indian descent) than indigenous communities, which are said to have greater degrees of egalitarianism between the sexes. Marianismo, the cult of the Virgin Mary, glorifies motherhood and female sacrifice. It assigns women a subordinate position in society and relegates them to the private world of housework and child rearing (Portugal, 1986; Brydon and Chant, 1989).

Cultural bias usually portrays women as being too emotional or parochial to be effective political actors. Clichés abound, such as "women can't understand politics;" "women and politics don't mix;" "women are already represented by their husbands;" "politics is for men" (FLACSO, 1992-93). These and other stereotypes of women are perpetuated through the mass media, thus reinforcing cultural barriers to gender equity.

Ethnic origin or identification can influence women's participation. Indigenous women face many of the same economic obstacles other women do, plus unique social and cultural barriers. They are generally less educated and literate than the overall female population and than their male counterparts and are subjected to racial discrimination outside their communities (Radcliffe, 1993; Hernández and Murguialday, 1992).

The economic condition of women also affects their political role.

Women work a triple day at home, on the job and in the community. Female heads of households are among the poorest people. While struggling for their family's survival, women have little time or energy left for civic participation. Since the days of slavery, Caribbean women have played much the same role as men in economic production. This has given them a somewhat greater degree of social and economic autonomy than their Latin American counterparts (Mathurin Mair, 1975; Ellis, 1986).

Social factors can also impede women's equal access to politics. The lack of daycare and other services makes it more difficult for women to get involved outside the home. Women on average still have less formal education and training than men, although gender gaps are gradually closing. But even as women attain comparable levels of education, they do not become as politically aware and active as their male counterparts. Studies have shown that education does not increase women's political participation to the same degree as it does men's, in part because of cultural biases that women do not belong in the public domain of politics (GENESYS, 1992b; Ellis, 1986).

Strengthening Democracy: More Women in Politics

There are several reasons why having more women in politics would strengthen the democratic process. First, a government that excludes half its citizens is not democratic. Women and their specific demands must be fairly represented on the national political agenda. Having more gender-sensitive women and men in legislative offices would facilitate needed changes in areas including female poverty, labor equity, reproductive rights, family law and domestic violence.

Second, women tend to pursue more of a social justice agenda than their male counterparts. Most Latin American women in politics have shown genuine concern for the neediest members of society. These public activists have been dubbed "supermothers" (Chaney, 1977) for, like good mothers, they are concerned with family welfare issues such as education, housing and health.

Third, some analysts contend that women bring to political participation unique skills, insights, values, interests and ways of working into the political arena. There are studies indicating that women "do politics" differently from men. Women are characterized as being less aggressive and competitive and more conciliatory and cooperative than their male counterparts (Rivera-Cira, 1993). Some have argued that rather than seeking strong individual leaders, women's groups prefer a teamwork approach in which everyone has a voice. Resisting hierarchical, bureaucratic structures, women create horizontal, flexible associations. Women's organizations are helping to change the way politics will be done in the future (CEPAL, 1994b). Critics reject this argument, pointing to the difficulties that many women's organizations have encountered while trying to build alternative structures (Young, 1990; Yudelman, 1987).

Fourth, preliminary studies suggest that greater female participation may make government institutions more ethical, honest, compassionate and equitable. A few scholars go so far as to claim that "What is good for women is also good for the society at large" (GENESYS, 1992b). Given that there are still relatively few female decision makers, however, some analysts reserve judgement on the impact of women on political institutions. Will they begin "behaving like men" once they enter public office, or will they seek to transform that domain (Jelin, 1990)?

Fifth, most Latin American women have motives for entering politics different from men's. Women are perceived as having a stronger sense of duty than men. Driven more by altruism than calculated self-interest, women pursue dignity or justice, not material gain. According to public opinion polls, women politicians are considered less "corruptible" than their male colleagues (Chaney, 1977; Milicic and Cereceda, 1992; Rivera-Cira, 1993). Given that endemic corruption remains a serious problem in many Latin American countries, having more women in office could help restore public trust and strengthen democracy.

Women's Participation in the State

Political Parties

Since gaining the franchise, women have voted less often than men, even in countries where voting is "mandatory." It is often difficult for women to register as voters because they lack the requisite proof of citizenship. A large number of rural women are currently not registered and are therefore ineligible to vote.

According to electoral studies, women vote more conservatively than men and more to the right than the left. Well-off, educated women working outside the home are most likely to vote. Female constituents are concerned mainly about public order and security issues (GENESYS, 1992b; Lago Cruz, 1990).

Women have long participated in political parties in Latin America and the Caribbean, even before they had the right to vote. Many autonomous feminist organizations were born within the same political parties they now challenge. For the past two decades, there has been an ongoing debate between female party militants and feminists as to whether gender interests are best promoted within party structures or from outside through independent women's organizations. At times, these two camps have collaborated; at others, collided. Feminist or women's political parties have not thrived in Latin America.

Most Latin American parties now include women's issues in their programs and electoral platforms; however, these issues rarely assume prominence during the campaign. Notable exceptions to this general statement were the Colombian, Costa Rican and Chilean elections in the early 1990s, in which the women's agenda was a crucial component of the presidential platform. The impact of Chilean women on party platforms is seen in Box 1.

Despite the role of Latin American women as political party activists and organizers, very few hold leadership positions. Discrimination and cultural prejudice make it difficult to break men's traditional stronghold on top posts. Furthermore, women often lack the financial resources necessary to launch political careers. Given their need to combine family responsibilities with paying work, women generally lack the time needed to establish political networks and the required support base. Women can also feel excluded from the male-oriented language and form of party politics and cannot always identify with the goals and strategies of male partisans.[3]

Recruiting women has not been a traditional priority for the majority of political parties across the political spectrum. In the current transition to electoral politics in Latin America, parties are more concerned about developing new structures, models and agendas (CEPAL, 1994b). However, some political parties in the region have recognized the need to incorporate more women, especially into leadership positions (see Table 9).

The Electoral System

As candidates, Latin American women are often less informed about electoral politics and less interested in taking part than are men (Lazarte Rojas, 1991). Women comprise a very small percentage of the total candidates, and few women contenders are elected (see Table 10).

---

[3] For example, Safa (1990: 359) writes, "Latin American political parties traditionally have been dominated by men and have been seen as engaged in struggles for power in which the poor are essentially clients. Poor people's loyalty to the party is exchanged for favors, such as paving a road, providing state services guaranteeing title to land, or getting jobs."

Box 1: Making Political Parties Listen

Chilean women from all walks of life helped win the 1988 plebiscite to restore democratic rule. Following that victory, the National Coalition of Women For Democracy was formed to prepare for the 1989 presidential and parliamentary elections. It launched the most concerted, sustained mobilization of women in Chilean history.

The coalition sought to take part in the electoral campaigns, encourage women candidates, put women's issues on the national political agenda and formulate a gender program for the new government. The proposed program included the allocation of 30 percent of decision-making positions to women, the creation of a national women's ministry and the elimination of sexism in education and advertising.

When the democratic opposition won the elections, it did not meet all the women's demands. Women were still underrepresented in political decision-making positions. Only 10 of 167 parliamentarians elected and 1 of 15 mayors appointed were women. President Aylwin did create the national women's office (SERNAM) in 1990 and made its director a cabinet minister. The women's coalition also succeeded in putting its demands on the agenda of all Chilean political parties. Even right-wing parties were forced to develop an official position on women's rights (Chuchryk, 1994).

Jamaican women have been more involved in electoral politics than many of their neighbors, but the case illustrates some general trends in the region. A woman first won a parliamentary seat in 1946. Two years later a woman became chairperson of a political party. The percentage of female candidates running in local government elections doubled during the 1970s, to reach 12.7 percent in 1981. At the national level, female candidacy increased from 2.6 percent in 1962 to 12.1 percent in 1983. The number of female electoral candidates has been growing, even though the relative percentage remains low (Anderson-Manley, 1994).

To increase the number of women in office, several countries in the region have been debating affirmative action, or "positive discrimination" measures. These range from appointment mechanisms to quotas. Appointment enabled women to enter parliament for the first time in Dominica, Mexico and Saint Lucia, among other countries in the world. Anglophone Caribbean countries appoint their entire upper house, while Chile and Belize also fill a specific number of seats through appointment. This could provide one route for more women to enter parliament (IPU, 1992).

Another route is through elections, with the help of quota systems.

Box 2: Quota Laws: An Electoral Experiment

Argentina was one of the first Latin American countries to hold a widespread debate on affirmative action for women. In 1991, the legislature passed a law requiring political parties to present women as at least 30 percent of their candidates for all elective posts. Any candidate list failing to meet the quota will not be officially registered. Similar legislation is currently under consideration in Uruguay.

Analysts disagree about the effectiveness of Argentina's quota law. Some credit the law with paving the way for 26 new women deputies, which was five times the previous number. Sceptics, including many female political partisans and feminists, either oppose the principle of quotas or contend that the law has not been enforced since it was passed (Feijoó and Nari, 1994; Rodríguez, 1993).

Compulsory quotas, through which a certain percentage of seats are reserved for women, work best in countries with a proportional representation list system. There are two types of quota: one defining the percentage of women candidates in an election and the other establishing the number of seats that must be occupied by women following the vote (IPU, 1992).

For seats in parliament or the national assembly, quotas can either be legislated (through the Constitution or electoral law) or introduced by a political party. Argentina is one of the few countries in the world to have legislated quotas for women in parliament, as Box 2 shows.

Quotas established by political parties can be either compulsory or merely guidelines. Political parties are far more likely to establish gender quotas within their internal structures than for legislative elections. This is the case with political party quotas in Venezuela and Colombia, for example. Quota systems have received mixed reviews. Proponents claim that quotas ensure a critical mass of women in legislative bodies, increase recruitment, give women more political experience and overcome skepticism about women's competency to hold public office.

Critics allege that in the Latin American context, quotas may actually make it easier to isolate women as a special sector. "Women will be expected to take care of women's issues, leaving the rest to men. And men can deny any responsibility for women's issues on the grounds that they have already met their obligations by giving women guaranteed representation" (Jaquette, 1994: 232). Quotas could also be used to promote women who would not "rock the boat" rather than more independent candidates. Some politicians in the region warn that quotas would reduce the quality of representation by limiting the choice of potential candidates. Others contend that women should win their seats on the basis of their merit, not their gender (IPU, 1992).

Specific examples from outside the region can be cited to either support or refute the case for quotas. In the early 1990s, women in Germany held 56.8 percent of the parliamentary seats for the Green Party, after it adopted quotas that women must comprise at least one-half of party posts and electoral candidates. There are no quotas in Finland, yet in 1991 it had the highest proportion of women parliamentarians in the world (38.5 percent) (IPU, 1992). Even if quotas have been effective in some European countries, they would not necessarily work in either the Latin American or Caribbean gender-cultural contexts. Thus, further study is needed to determine whether quotas and other "positive discrimination" measures would increase the number and impact of women in political office.

Women have been elected to relatively few high-level government positions in the region. Dominica is the only Caribbean country to have elected a woman president. Women served short, interim presidential terms in Argentina and Bolivia, while Nicaragua is the only Latin American country to elect a female head of state. Two of these women presidents, Nicaragua's Violeta Chamorro and Argentina's María Estela Martínez de Perón, first achieved prominence in national politics through the legacy of their deceased husbands.

Having a female head of state does not automatically open the door for other women to enter parliament. With the election of a female president in Nicaragua, the percentage of women legislators rose only slightly (from 13.5 percent to 16.3 percent) and remained unchanged in Dominica (at 12.9 percent; CEPAL, 1994b).

On average, women held just under 8 percent of the region's parliamentary seats in 1993 (CEPAL, 1994b). Women occupied nearly a quarter of the lower chamber seats in Cuba, followed by Guyana with 20 percent. The highest proportion of women senators was 36 percent in Saint Lucia. However, the upper house is appointed in the Anglophone Caribbean. In Latin American countries with bicameral congresses, women tend to be better represented in the House of Deputies than in the Senate (see Table 11).

The number of women holding national elected office has not necessarily risen over the years. After Southern Cone countries returned to constitutional rule in the 1980s, some elected fewer women to office than before the dictatorships. In Argentina's 1991 elections, women made up only 3 percent of the members of Congress, compared with 12 percent in 1983 and 22 per-

Box 3: Local Power with a Gender Perspective

After 17 years of dictatorship in Chile, a democratically elected government took office in 1990. President Aylwin appointed María Antonieta Saa as the first woman mayor of Conchalí, the country's largest municipality. Most of Conchalí's 400,000 residents were poor. Ms. Saa started a new kind of municipal government in which all local groups could participate in community decisions and programs.

Seventy women were trained through a six-month leadership course. A center was established to provide legal and psychological advice about domestic violence. Special training in this area was provided for police officers. Conchalí's mothers' centers all began working together through their new community association (Isis et al., 1993).

Ms. Saa served as mayor for two years, until she was elected to Congress. During her tenure, the situation of women and general living conditions in Conchalí improved significantly. In the 1992 municipal elections, women comprised 11.5 percent of elected councillors, which was double the rate of female representatives elected nationally (Fisher, 1993).

cent in 1951 (when women first voted). Declines in the number of women elected were also seen in Chile and Uruguay during the 1980s. Analysts explain that with the return of democracy, political parties regained control of national politics and men took back the leadership posts they had held before the dictatorships. Being marginalized in political parties, women could not or did not choose to compete in electoral races (Fisher, 1993). In other Latin American and Caribbean countries, however, the number of women elected to office has grown over the past few decades.

Throughout the region, more women candidates have run in local elections than in national ones. Despite the growing number of female candidates, local government is still monopolized by men. The percentage of women in local governments regionwide does not exceed 20 percent and is often less than half that figure (FLACSO, 1992-93; Isis, IULA, and CELCADEL, 1993b; see Table 12).

Some 15,000 local governments operate throughout Latin America. These structures had little power in the past, given the highly centralized nature of government. In many Latin American countries, state and municipal authorities are still relegated to a relatively insignificant position vis-à-vis the federal or national government. At times, local authorities are not even considered legitimate partners in national governance. In other countries, however, municipalities are gaining strength. Democratization, fiscal pressures on central governments and decentralization of the state result in the transfer of decision-making power and administrative tasks to local governments.

There is great potential for increasing women's participation in local government. Being the closest to community issues such as health, housing or sanitation, women are local experts who can provide invaluable leadership in tackling these problems. Women generally encounter fewer cultural or social obstacles to taking part in local affairs than they would at higher levels. Working closer to home also solves some practical problems because many women cannot afford the cost or time to travel. Municipal government can serve as a training ground to prepare women to later play a more active role in national politics (Hirshmann, 1993; Isis et al., 1993; Anderson, 1990). It has already done that for some women (Box 3).

Government Institutions and Policies

In 1992, 4 percent of ministerial posts in Latin America and the Caribbean were held by women, as compared to 9 percent in Western industrialized countries (Navarro, 1992). Despite the relatively small percentage of women decision makers currently in government, there has been a steady increase over the past 20 years.

Anglophone Caribbean states tend to have more women in top government posts than their Latin American neighbors (Anderson-Manley, 1994). The Bahamas and Haiti were the only countries in the region where women held at least 20 percent of ministerial level positions in 1994. Women held one-third or more of the sub-ministerial positions in Antigua and Barbuda (43.8), Dominica (37.8) and Bahamas (34.5). In nearly half of the countries in the region, women comprise less than 10 percent of high-level government officials (see Table 11).

Even where women are appointed to top government positions, they are usually in areas such as health, education or social welfare. There are few female decision-makers in higher profile ministries such as finance or defense. According to the UN (1991b), this "ghettoization" prolongs women's ineligibility for traditionally male preserves. Most of the relatively few women to be appointed as ministers are not given cabinet rank. If they are, they may receive a symbolic cabinet seat without having any real power.

Many governments in the region are working to strengthen the role of women as political and economic decision makers. They plan to hold periodic meetings of women ministers and government officials in charge of women's issues. The first of these was scheduled for June 1995, in preparation for the Heads of State Summit in Argentina. This, and future meetings, will allow women ministers and other officials to exchange experiences and develop strategies to strengthen women's participation in government.

Electing or appointing more female leaders does not, in and of itself, guarantee that gender issues will become more prominent on the national agenda. Even the election of a female head of state does not automatically provide "trickle-down" benefits for other women. Once they attain political power, women often assimilate the male-dominated system and priorities (CEPAL, 1994b). They are co-opted or transformed by the state, rather than transforming it from within. Thus, in addition to having more female representatives, governments require integrated, gender-specific policies and effective mechanisms through which to implement such policies.

Central government policies traditionally did not specifically address women's problems. For example, social development was aimed at disadvantaged regions or low-income sectors, without assessing the gender impact of such programs. One Peruvian study warned that rather than benefitting the female population, some of these broad programs actually used women to serve other government goals (CENTRO, 1993).

In response to international treaties and domestic lobbying in the late 1970s, most governments in the region established national offices, institutes or ministries to deal with women's issues. To date, these national machineries for women have received mixed reviews.

Case studies in the Caribbean highlighted the common problems facing women's bureaus. Marginalized within the bureaucracy, national offices are not given the authority and resources to implement their assigned functions. They lack trained staff, policy direction and adequate funding, often depending on international donor agencies. Women's bureaus move from one department to another, following the few women ministers as they change portfolios. In some Caribbean countries, women's bureaus are headed by men (Commonwealth Secretariat, 1983 and 1985).

These constraints are not unique to Latin America and the Caribbean. Staudt (1990) notes that "of seventy-nine countries, machineries were found to be limited by small budgets and staff, by attitudes that legitimize female subordination and by mandates that focus on welfare." She notes further that "in the case of the World Bank [and presumably other international financial agencies] a women's unit operates uneasily amid technical units."

The Caribbean women's bureaus often produce vague national policy statements. Some countries lack the means or the political will to implement policy goals. Critics warn that the special bureaus could institutionalize or co-opt the women's movement. In many cases, however, the national offices have collaborated with women's NGOs to change discriminatory laws and develop training and education programs.

In Latin America, gender-specific ministries can reinforce the corporatist tradition by treating women as a single sector whose demands must be channelled through a single access point in the system. Creating separate women's departments in political institutions (government, political parties, trade unions) can sometimes remove gender issues from the mainstream, or "malestream" political agenda (Corcoran-Nantes, 1993).

Measures to strengthen national machineries include the development of a clear mandate for the bureau that focuses on influencing policy across the entire government to promote the incorporation of a gender analysis. Rather than implementing small marginal projects, the resources of these offices would be better spent developing a policy framework that promotes increased understanding of the rationale behind and the development of gender-sensitive policies and programs. Staff in these offices should see their role as "catalytic" and seek to improve relationships with policy makers in other crucial ministries. Efforts should also be made to strengthen relationships with women's organizations and encourage the development of national lobbies that can pressure politicians and hold them accountable for promises made during elections on women's issues.

Legal Status

The UN Convention on the Elimination of All Forms of Discrimination Against Women (CEDAW) is the most important international legislation promoting women's rights. Under the Convention, a state should pass national laws to eradicate discrimination, take temporary affirmative action measures to accelerate de facto gender equality, and act to change sociocultural patterns that perpetuate discrimination (CEPAL, 1994a). All Caribbean and Latin American countries have signed, ratified or acceded to the CEDAW and other important international treaties, as well as enshrining the political rights of women in their national constitutions.[4]

[4] This chapter presents a brief introduction to the extensive issue of legal, regulatory and legislative reform. Further references include Allen and Wall, 1987; CLADEM, 1994; Corvalán, Rivarola, and Zarza, 1987; Facio, 1993; Navarro, 1992; Palacio, 1993; Rivera, 1991; Silva, 1992; Tamayo, 1989.

Box 4: Changing Legislation: Two Success Stories

The Women and Development Unit (WAND) in Barbados promotes WID programs throughout the region. WAND has raised awareness of women's rights among policy makers, linked government agencies and NGOs and strengthened women's organizations. WAND has helped change legislation in Barbados and other Caribbean countries on issues including equal pay, family and reproductive rights and domestic violence (CEPAL, 1994b; Yudelman, 1987).

The Comité Latinoamericano para la Defensa de los Derechos de la Mujer (CLADEM) is a regional network with offices in 15 countries. CLADEM seeks to protect gender rights, promote women's political participation, provide legal education and change discriminatory legislation. To date, CLADEM's advocacy has led to major legislative reform in Peru and a few other countries. In addition to its national programs, CLADEM works locally with community legal educators and participates in regional and international campaigns. CLADEM has contributed to the drafting of UN and OAS conventions on women's rights.

The legal status of women varies from country to country. In general, however, there are still major obstacles to women's full and equal participation in all spheres of national life. Even where appropriate legislation exists, governments often lack the mechanisms, resources or political will to monitor and enforce these laws.

Labor law is one example of the disparity between principle and practice. Many countries in the region have legislation guaranteeing women equal opportunity and equal pay for equal work. Recent studies have shown, however, that women still face significant discrimination in terms of access to better jobs and fair wages (CEDAW, 1993). Data from Colombia indicates that women constitute the majority of unemployed workers (Ramírez, 1988). Female labor in Latin America is concentrated in the least productive jobs or in the informal sector (see the chapter on women as economic actors). Thus, the majority of women are not even eligible for the maternity benefits provided to full-time employees. These benefits deter some employers from hiring "more expensive" women workers. Efforts are underway in some countries to get the state to pay at least part of the cost of maternity benefits.

Women's organizations in Latin America and the Caribbean have focused on two priorities for legal reform: family law and domestic violence. Family codes are gradually adjusting to economic realities and pressures for greater democracy. Many countries have eliminated the most archaic family

Box 5: Cuba's Family Code

Following widespread debate in neighborhood committees and workplaces, the Cuban government passed a new Family Code in 1975. This ground-breaking legislation stipulated that men and women were to share equally the tasks related to the household and child rearing. It also guarantees women equal rights over the family's assets and participation in the country's economic and political activities. In tandem with the Family Code, the Cuban state implemented policies to provide women with birth control, daycare, education and job training.

According to some analysts, the Family Code contributed to a significant increase in the number of women in the workforce. Between 1970 and 1979, the workforce participation rate for married women rose from 16.3 to 36.7 percent. For women in common-law unions the figure jumped from 9.2 percent to 24.8 percent. The Family Code is also credited with eroding machismo over the past 20 years (Larguia and Dumoulin, 1986).

Critics claim that the Family Code is ineffectual and empty. The provision concerning shared housework lacks any sanctions or mechanisms for implementation. In areas where legal sanctions exist, such as child support, individual women must take their husbands to court. Most could not afford to hire a private lawyer. There is no collective support to enforce the Family Code (Osmond, 1993).

structures such as obedience to the husband or his complete control over the family. Recent laws include recognition of single mothers and de facto unions, divorce and equal rights for children born out of wedlock (Palacio, 1993). Female heads of households are gaining legal recourse concerning their access to property and credit. In terms of reproductive rights, access to abortion remains an important issue. Half the deaths of pregnant women in Latin America are estimated to result from illegal abortions (Cartaya, 1994). Abortion laws range from very or relatively strict in two dozen countries to liberal in Uruguay and Cuba (IPPF, 1993).

Domestic violence in Latin America and the Caribbean is another major obstacle to improving democratic rights and participation, and to eliminating discrimination against women. Although there are no definitive statistics showing the extent of violence against women, it is considered one of the worst social problems in the region. It affects women of all socioeconomic classes and ethnic origins (CENDOC, 1991; CLADEM, 1994; Isis, 1990; Schuler, 1992).

Most countries in the region ratified the UN's 1993 Declaration on the Elimination of Violence Against Women, which resulted from work done

Box 6: Women's Police Stations

The state women's council in São Paulo, Brazil started the first women's police station in 1985. Since then, 170 such posts have opened across the country. Peru, Colombia, Bolivia and Costa Rica have also established family police stations, where women can go to report crimes of violence against them or their children. Their reports are handled by specially trained female officers.

This police program has helped improve women's relations with the judicial system and other state structures. The presence of the local stations acts as a deterrent, thus protecting women. It is hoped that in the future these stations will provide more comprehensive services, including psychological and legal support to victims. The systematization of this experience will help bring about the legal reforms needed to curb violence against women.

by governmental and women's organizations worldwide. This was followed by a regional pact, the Inter-American Convention on the Prevention, Punishment and Eradication of Violence Against Women (known as the Convention of Belēm Do Parā), which was adopted by the Organization of American States (OAS) in June 1994. These international treaties hold the potential to be important instruments, provided there is a constituency in each country to lobby the government for change and to monitor progress.

To date, national responses to the problem of violence against women have generally been isolated and inadequate. Argentina, Brazil, Colombia and Chile have passed laws sanctioning domestic violence. Government agencies and women's groups have collaborated to create a new model of law enforcement to protect women, as described in Box 6.

Several non-governmental agencies now provide legal education and services for women who traditionally would not have had access to the judicial system. These agencies raise awareness about women's rights, assist in legal cases and lobby for legislative reform. In Peru and elsewhere, women from poor neighborhoods have been trained as legal promoters. They counsel their neighbors and handle cases at the local level, while acquiring practical leadership training.

Judicial System

Only seven women throughout Latin America are Supreme Court magistrates (CEPAL, 1994b). Women are far more visible in the lower courts. In the Dominican Republic, for example, 31 percent of appeal court judges are women.

Box 7: Strengthening Justice through International Links

The International Association of Women Judges (IAWJ) has over 2,000 members in all levels of the court system in 55 countries, including 16 in Latin America. The IAWJ coordinates action among women judges worldwide, aimed at tackling the legal and judicial problems impeding the equality of all people. It also seeks to increase the number of female judges so that legal-judicial systems promote women's rights and interests. Female judges have worked to enact laws sanctioning domestic violence and have sponsored workshops on this subject for judges, lawyers, social workers and law enforcement agents.

The IAWJ is starting a program to train men and women judges on how to apply international and regional human rights conventions to cases affecting women within their national courts. One of the pilot sites of this program is Costa Rica, where judges from Central America will be trained.

Female legal professionals also participate in the Women's Rights Committee (WRC) of the Inter-American Bar Association (IABA). The WRC comprises lawyers, judges, law professors and other legal professionals working on women's rights. It seeks to provide a channel to exchange information, discuss judicial options and make recommendations to bar associations, women's organizations and governmental agencies.

Nearly half of Guatemala's justices of the peace are women. Women comprise over 40 percent of municipal and circuit court judges in Panama. Four out of five judges in Chile's juvenile courts are women (FLACSO, 1992-93).

Increased participation by women at all levels of the judicial system could help improve the equality of justice. Studies done in the United States have shown that female jurists are more pro-woman than their male counterparts. Women supreme court justices tend to support measures aimed at redressing gender-related societal imbalance. This agenda includes issues such as sex discrimination, sexual assault, alimony, property settlements and child-parent relationships. Female justices hold to their beliefs, even when the majority of the court opposes an expansion of women's rights. While female judges uniformly supported women's rights, however, they were divided when dealing with criminal rights and economic liberties. In these areas, women justices represented both extremes. They were either more conservative or more liberal than their male colleagues (Allen and Wall, 1987).

Female judges, lawyers and other legal professionals are taking part in regional and international institutions to promote women's rights. Two of these institutions are described in Box 7.

Women's Participation in Civil Society

Women's participation in civil society is often divided into several categories. There are women's organizations working on human rights, community affairs and feminist issues. Women also are active in politics within "mixed" associations (e.g., unions, indigenous or campesino) where they advocate either general social goals or the adoption of gender-specific demands within these organizations. Waylen (1992) rightly points out that these are not mutually exclusive categories. There are links between them (she cites the arpillera workshops that combined protest against human rights abuses with women's need to earn an income). Women may participate in more than one organization.

Women's Organizations

Women as Human Rights Activists

A broad spectrum of female activists organized to defend human rights under military regimes. The Argentine Mothers of the Plaza de Mayo demanded the return of their children, who were "disappeared" by the military junta. Trapped by the women's declaration of the sanctity of motherhood, military leaders did not know how to handle groups of mothers and grandmothers. At first the juntas allowed women's meetings, which were often held under the church's protection, while banning those organized by men. When the military finally began repressing women, the Madres risked their lives to continue to speak out.

These women had not been politically active before. Politicized as mothers, they developed new forms of protest that challenged the legitimacy of military rule. The Madres became the best-known of several women's organizations that defended human rights against authoritarian regimes in the region (Feijoó and Nari, 1994).

Women as Community Organizers

The economic pressures of the 1970s, which deepened with the debt crisis of the 1980s, also mobilized women as mothers. Structural adjustment policies hit the urban poor, especially women, very hard. "Lower-class urban women (mujeres populares) organized to demand relief from the state, supply the basic services that the state could no longer provide, or feed their families collectively when it was no longer possible to do so individually" (Jaquette, 1994: 3).

Women formed neighborhood self-help groups to obtain adequate food,

Box 8: Communal Kitchens in Lima, Peru

Formed during the economic crisis of the late 1970s, communal kitchens became one of the most successful types of collective consumption organizations. By the early 1990s, they were serving a million meals daily to shantytown residents who comprised nearly one-third of Lima's population. The kitchens grew in number and strength despite facing significant opposition. Several women in the self-help groups were threatened or killed by *Sendero Luminoso* (Shining Path) during the 1980s. Others made enemies or friends within the government, to the point that the organizations became an important part of local politics in Peru.

Many of the kitchens sprang up spontaneously. Others were started or at least supported by the church or the state. They currently receive food aid from international donors, as well as assistance from the municipal government or other local agencies. Each communal kitchen serves from 15 to 50 households. The food is bought and prepared collectively, with each family paying according to the number of meals consumed.

Through the communal kitchens, many women have learned to speak about and tackle their problems at home and in the community. They have acquired new management and organizing skills that can help them enter the workforce. Following their experience in self-help groups in Lima, some women have been elected to municipal government.

Sceptics claim that communal kitchens have solved immediate food shortages while ignoring the underlying cause of the problem—unequal distribution of resources and government inefficiency. Participation in self-help groups has not generally raised awareness about gender identity or increased women's political power in the community. Some analysts contend that for self-help groups to have any long-term impact, they need to develop closer ties with the state and political parties (Barrig, 1994b; Safa, 1990).

water, housing, child care centers, health clinics, and so on. These local initiatives spread throughout the region. By 1991 there were 5,329 communal kitchens and 9,739 Glass of Milk committees in Peru alone (FLACSO, 1992-93).

There has been much debate around these "collective consumption" organizations (Safa, 1990; Moser, 1993a). Some critics claim that "survival organizations" like communal kitchens take pressure off the state to provide services and redistribute resources. Others cite cases where groups co-opted by the state defended, rather than challenged, the status quo. For example, mothers' clubs sponsored by the Pinochet regime reinforced traditional values and depoliticized lower-class women. Some feminists have warned that by participating as mothers, rather than as citizens in their own right, women perpetuate conventional gender roles. According to this view, "practical" gender demands for food or shelter bring "welfarist" responses, thus reinforcing the patronage and clientelism that have long been employed by political parties and the state (Chuchryk, 1994; Barrig, 1994b).

Advocates reply that women should organize as community mothers in political cultures where the concepts of community and motherhood are valued. "The rhetoric of political motherhood is rational and powerful for women, a 'collective action frame' that avoids the costs of a frontal attack on traditional values while leaving considerable room to maneuver in the public sphere" (Jaquette, 1994: 228). Given that many Latin American women become active citizens through motherhood, their political participation takes a form different from that of women in advanced industrialized countries.

By politicizing the issues of survival and of everyday life, the community organizations enable women to confront political and economic repression. "Latin American women...think that their roles as wives and mothers legitimize their sense of injustice and outrage, since they are protesting their inability to effectively carry out these roles, as military governments take away their children or the rising cost of living prevents them from feeding their families adequately" (Safa, 1990: 355). Joining organizations raises women's consciousness by allowing them to see the connections between their personal concerns and broader political issues, and by forcing them to challenge the gender biases that kept them from entering the public sphere.

Through their community work, many women develop organizational and leadership skills that then allow them to expand into other areas of public life, within broader social movements (e.g., environmental or consumers) or in governmental positions at the local or national level.

Participation transforms and empowers women, boosting their new self-esteem and allowing them to question traditional family relations. While studying a Quito neighborhood, Rodríguez (1994) found that as women got involved in neighborhood organizations, they began challenging power relations within and outside their households. Women demanded a greater say in household decision making. By breaking domestic "rules," family relations were strained or even broken.

Women-oriented NGOs and Feminist Organizations

The UN Women's Decade helped generate greater international and national awareness of gender issues. This, combined with women's greater access to education and integration into the workforce, led to a proliferation of "women-oriented" NGOs. Some of these organizations focused on what have been called strategic gender issues, such as reproductive rights, domestic violence and employment equity.[5] They lobbied for legislative change, as well as providing legal services and education for women of all social strata.

While opposing military rule, NGO women often formed a common front with their counterparts in community, church and partisan associations. This strategic alliance weakened as the transition to democracy advanced. Feminist organizations, comprised mainly of middle-class, professional women, often disagreed with community groups over collective goals and strategies. Divided by class, race, and politics, the women's movement was far from homogeneous or unified during the 1980s.

Women-oriented NGOs in the region have grown too numerous to count. Chile alone has 120 NGOs with women's programs and another 38 specializing in gender issues. Ecuador has 45 and 20 respectively (FLACSO, 1992-93). International donors have funded both women-oriented NGOs and governmental agencies throughout the hemisphere. At times, external support has meant the survival of small women's organizations. Their relationships, however, have been rocky at times and are a topic of increasing discussion and analysis (Ford-Smith, 1989; Barrig and Wehkamp, 1994; Yudelman, 1987).

Local women's organizations have often joined to form national federations or umbrella groups, which can have different forms and functions. For example, the coordinating body in Bolivia (Coordinadora de la Mujer) is a loose network that includes women's organizations and other NGOs working with women. Joining together can make local organizations more effective and powerful. Many national associations then unite in regional and international women's networks, such as the Caribbean Association for Feminist Research and Action (CAFRA) or Isis International. These networks allow women to exchange information and experiences with counterparts around the world, coordinate public education and advocacy campaigns, and increase their policy impact at all levels.

Many of the women-oriented NGOs, as well as the community organizations mentioned above, describe themselves as "feminist." That means different things to different people in Latin America. "Feminism" can be broadly defined as a belief that it is necessary to combat the oppression of women. There are, however, varying views on the nature of that oppression and the appropriate strategies to overcome it. For example, middle-class feminists might

---

5 There is considerable debate around the terms of practical and strategic gender needs and interests, which is briefly reviewed in the overview chapter of this book.

Box 9: A Global Women's Network

Isis International is one of the most extensive women's networks in Latin America, as well as being part of a worldwide association of over 50,000 individuals and groups in 150 countries. Its Latin American program is headquartered in Santiago, Chile. Through Isis, women in Latin America and the Caribbean can exchange information and experiences with their counterparts in Asia and Africa, as well as in developed countries.

Isis promotes communication and cooperation among rural and urban groups seeking women's empowerment and full participation in sustainable development. It coordinates regional campaigns to end violence against women, as well as providing women's health programs. The Isis database and resource center contain materials on a wide range of women's issues.

fight discrimination or sexual harassment in the workplace, while working-class mothers tackle poverty by forming neighborhood kitchens (Waylen, 1992; Schild, 1994).

Many female community leaders initially resisted the label "feminist," which they equated with the self-indulgent demands of rich women. During the 1980s, however, many low-income women began developing their own, working-class variant of feminism. This variant shared some views with other feminist perspectives, yet deviated on others (Schild, 1994). Several analysts now refer to the many types of feminism, or feminisms, that exist in the region. These currents are divided by factors such as class, race, political affiliation and sexual orientation (Vargas, 1992). They have been coming together, however, through periodic meetings (see Box 10).

Women's Participation in Mixed Organizations

In addition to participating in women-specific groups, women have played an important role, along with men, in gender-mixed organizations in civil society. Women mobilize as consumers, squatters, environmentalists and indigenous activists, to name just a few areas. In the economic sphere, women participate as unionists, campesinas, academics, entrepreneurs, and professionals including journalists, lawyers and physicians. Women who are activists in gender-mixed organizations such as political parties and in the autonomous women's movement are said to have a doble militancia, or double militancy (Vargas, 1992).

Mixed organizations have diverse policies and programs promoting the participation of female members. According to Schild (1994), "in the course of acquiring a sense of personal and political efficacy, women who choose to participate in advocacy groups with men face the greatest challenges" (p. 72). Rather than work according to their own styles and in a way that respects their other responsibilities, women have to conform to the structures and organizational cultures of male-dominated organizations. Within organizations, women have used various strategies, including the formation of women's caucuses and women's units, and have attempted to change organizations so that they respect, respond to and reflect the gender-specific demands of their membership (ICAE, 1989).

The varying progress and problems of women within mixed groups are illustrated through a brief discussion of campesino organizations in Peru and Nicaragua and indigenous organizations in the region.

Women in Campesino Organizations

The situation of women in campesino organizations varies from country to country. In Nicaragua during the 1980s, comparisons can be made between the profiles, of women's issues in the Nicaraguan Association of Rural Workers (ATC - Asociación de Trabajadores del Campo) and the ranchers and farmers (UNAG - Unión Nacional de Agricultores y Ganaderos) during the 1980s. Given the feminization of its membership, the ATC's women's secretariat first undertook an extensive participatory research project to document the concerns of rural women workers. They then devised a campaign aimed at convincing the union to adopt women's demands into their overall program (ICAE, 1989). In contrast, efforts to have UNAG consider the needs and interests of its female membership were less successful. Women active in this sector were unable to develop a strategy to convince the leadership that their concerns warranted specific attention (Pérez Alemán, 1990).

Women's participation in mixed organizations takes on another dimension when the issue of race is also interwoven. In her study of Peru, Radcliffe (1993) found that campesinas suffer from a "triple oppression" as female peasants in a Third World country. Another dimension is added for many campesinas who are also indigenous Quechua or Aymara people. Given their high rates of illiteracy and mortality and their undervalued role in agriculture, campesinas were traditionally ignored by the state. Within peasant communities, public political space and authority were usually held by men.

As Peruvian campesinas became better educated and learned Spanish, allowing them to understand the radio and media, they got more involved in

Box 10: Latin American and Caribbean Feminist Encounters

Since 1981, women from Latin America and the Caribbean have been holding biannual encuentros or encounters. These meetings went from 200 participants when they started to nearly 3,000 a decade later. The encuentros help gauge the evolution, strengths and limitations of the women's movement in the region.

- In 1981 in ***Bogotá, Colombia,*** 230 participants gathered. The feminists wanted their political practice to be kept outside political parties, while party militants advocated the "double militancy" of feminism and class struggle.
- In 1983 in ***Lima, Peru,*** there were 650 participants. Party militants and feminists were joined by women from the community organizations in an analysis of patriarchy.
- In 1985 nearly 1,000 participants came to ***Bertioga, Brazil.*** Race and sexual preference were on the agenda, as participants began considering how to incorporate the unique concerns of indigenous and black women. Tensions arose when women from the shantytowns were not allowed in without paying.
- In 1987 1,500 participants, many from Central America and the Caribbean, were brought together in ***Taxco, Mexico.*** Women came from new sectors such as government ministries, NGOs and Catholic feminism. Class, generational and regional divisions surfaced. South American feminists wanted to leave practical demands like urban services and communal kitchens to the neighborhood women, while they would handle strategic gender issues.
- In 1990 in ***San Bernardo, Argentina,*** the gathering of nearly 3,000 participants was the most diverse ever, bringing together Christians, ecologists, pacifists, lesbians, unionists, squatters, indigenous and black women, parliamentarians and political party militants. This *encuentro* led to the formation of new women's networks and the coordination of regional campaigns on issues including abortion rights and gender images in media.
- In 1993 in ***Costa del Sol, El Salvador,*** the encuentro of 1,300 participants was almost moved to another country because of death threats against the organizers and other security risks. Issues covered included human rights violations, women's rights, electoral quotas, and problems of discrimination and racism within the women's movement. The encounter improved the integration of Central American women into the broader regional network (Fempress, 1993; Vargas, 1992).

politics. Continued lack of state support and marginalization drove more women into the informal labor force. This further broadened their experience and awareness. Peruvian campesinas grew less willing to allow men to speak and act on their behalf. Over the last 10 years, campesinas have become more active in political protest by participating in land invasions, forming local defense and income-generating groups, and lobbying government. Their involvement has helped change the form and content of peasant demands.

Campesinas are also playing a greater role in union work and leadership. By 1989, women sat on the national executive committees of Peru's two largest peasant confederations. While the majority of female leaders stress their non-gendered agenda as peasants, some have introduced women's issues and even formed separate affiliate organizations for campesinas. The majority of campesinas, however, still reject feminism as a position for urban, wealthier women only (Radcliffe, 1993).

Women in Indigenous Organizations

Many campesinas are indigenous women. As such, they often face unique challenges to political participation. In addition to the triple workday and lack of access to services, they confront cultural and educational barriers. With the assimilation of Western culture, many indigenous women became more isolated and marginalized. They lost some of their say in family decisions as men became the intermediaries between indigenous communities and the outside world. Fewer indigenous women than men speak Spanish. With public education almost always offered only in Spanish, 90 percent of Guatemala's indigenous women are illiterate. Lack of education or training limits women's participation (Hernández and Murguialday, 1992).

Indigenous organizations in Latin America have been debating the role of women. They have taken three basic approaches—denying that indigenous women have specific demands, advocating a return to precolonial gender relations, and creating special women's groups within or outside mixed organizations.

In the first approach, many organizations consider that indigenous women are in basically the same situation as their male counterparts. That means women should not organize separately or make gender-specific demands. These organizations are usually led by men. Even some female leaders, including Rigoberta Menchú, have clearly stated their opposition to the formation of women's groups within the indigenous movement.

The second "return to the past" approach recognizes that women face marginalization and discrimination, and attributes this to the machismo imposed by the conquistadors and the destruction of indigenous culture. These organizations claim that in precolonial gender relations, men and women had equal rights and authority in society. Therefore, contemporary women will be free only when indigenous people return to the ways of their ancestors. Critics warn that this nostalgic view idealizes traditional cultures and overlooks the gender hierarchy that really existed.

The third response is for women to create their own groups, within or outside indigenous organizations, as they have been doing for the past decade.

These groups may differ in terms of their autonomy, structure and objectives, but they all concur that as indigenous women, they also have to change oppressive gender relations. For example, a Colombian association of indigenous and peasant women (ANMUCIC) with 20,000 members got a law passed ensuring that all land titles include women's names and that lots could be assigned to female heads of households (Hernandez and Murguialday, 1992).

The majority of indigenous women in any type of organization claim that "Western feminism" has nothing to do with their reality. However, some of the indigenous women who participate in the broader women's movement now recognize that they share some feminist demands and concerns. Indigenous women are increasingly involved, along with feminists, community organizers and partisan activists, in biannual continental conferences (see Box 10).

Strengthening Women's Role in Governance

The mobilization of women in Latin America and the Caribbean has increased significantly during times of economic and political crisis. This is the opposite of what happened with men, who tended to be demobilized during the dictatorships, relative to their previous level of activity. Since the crises have subsided, however, women have tended to return to their private lives, retreating into the shadows.

Now that formal democracy has been restored, national machineries have been created to handle women's issues and many political parties have gender platforms, there is a concern that the majority of women will once again be demobilized. Civil organizations in the region are currently seeking ways to maintain or even heighten the level of female involvement by converting short-term demands into a long-term campaign for greater integration into the political system (Jelin, 1990).

Over the last 20 years, women have developed new modes of political action. According to Jaquette (1994), however, what worked during the transition to democracy will not necessarily work in this period of consolidation. In order to evolve from opposition politics to participatory politics, women must innovate new methods and agendas for the 21st century.

There is a need to fortify women's role in civil society, both in gender-specific and mixed organizations. A strong, autonomous women's movement can contribute to the creation of a responsive and responsible state. Through lobbying, constituency-building and consultation with elected representatives, women's organizations can help change government policy and legislation. Future relations between civil society and the state will be based more on cooperation than on confrontation, as in the past. Modern democracy tends toward a bottom-up approach that starts with civil society and passes through a receptive state before returning to civil society.

In order to make two-way democracy effective, there should be more women in power within state structures. Women's leadership and direct participation in decision making will help keep gender issues at the top of the national political agenda.

Women Must Be More Involved

Many of the democracies in Latin America are still fragile. Women's full participation is needed to consolidate democracy in the region, while a stable political climate is required for economic development.

Women have made considerable political progress over the past two decades. International conventions have raised awareness and recognition of women's rights. National offices, policies and laws have helped put women's issues on the political agenda. More women are involved in a broader range of activities than ever before. However, this participation is mainly through civil society, at the community level. Women are still not adequately represented in the formal political process, including political parties, elections and national decision-making bodies.

In order to optimize women's political participation, many cultural, economic, social and legal barriers must be overcome. Good intentions alone do not bring about change. Concrete measures are needed to convert rhetoric into reality. Women's groups, national governments and donor agencies all need to take steps to optimize women's participation.

Promoting Women's Political Participation

Comply with international conventions and agreements. Each country should establish mechanisms to monitor and enforce compliance with international conventions on women. These mechanisms could be determined jointly by the state and representative women's organizations. For example, each state should revise and amend all domestic legislation to ensure it meets the provisions of the Convention on the Elimination of all Forms of Discrimination against Women.

Make women's offices (national machineries) more effective and pow-

erful. Women's offices need specially trained staff and increased funding. They should be inter-sectoral, with high-level decision-making powers, and national in scope so they can support women in decentralized positions or local government. Alongside the women's bureaus, gender desks should be created within planning agencies, to coordinate with the bureaus.

Appoint women to senior executive and judicial posts. There is a dire shortage of women in top decision-making bodies of government. As an interim solution, some of the region's highly qualified women should be appointed to strategic posts.

Implement electoral reform. Electoral laws must be amended to facilitate the equitable representation of women. Voter lists should be updated to include the large number of rural women who are currently not registered and are therefore unable to vote. Comparative studies should be done to determine the efficacy of anti-discriminatory practices such as quotas that currently exist in developed and developing countries. If these measures have proven effective, targets should be set for institutions, including political parties, to ensure that women comprise a certain proportion of leaders, candidates and elected representatives.

Ensure legal reform. This is an essential component of an integrated strategy to achieve gender equity. Major changes are required in the civil, labor and criminal codes in order to reduce the obstacles impeding women from being more active in decision making. Women's organizations should actively participate in the formulation of new laws.

Develop inter-sectoral policies. Governments should develop integrated, inter-sectoral policies (health, education, agriculture, labor, etc.) to eliminate barriers to women's participation across the board. Currently, affirmative policy in one sector is often undermined or contradicted by inappropriate policies in other areas. Each state sector should draw up equality plans to ensure that public spending takes women's needs into account. These plans must be periodically assessed and should incorporate the gender perspective at all stages of execution.

Remove social and economic barriers to participation. Given that women still face a triple work day, they require access to daycare facilities, education, shelter, food, and health care to be able to devote more time and energy to politics.

Conduct public awareness and gender-sensitivity campaigns. Putting more females into office will not in and of itself guarantee more sensitivity to gender issues or ensure their presence on the national agenda. Female and male leaders alike need gender education, as does the whole society. Machismo is predominant among many men and women in the region. A significant cultural change will be required to confront gender inequality. The state could sponsor campaigns through schools, the media and government offices to change the attitudes and values that currently limit the political participation of women.

Improve collaboration between governments and women's organizations. States could be better informed about the wealth of human resources available in their societies and build upon those strengths. As knowledgeable and capable actors in the community, women's groups could effectively deliver municipal and other local programs. Given that women's organizations have developed unique skills, insights and methods, they should be integrated into policy making and implementation, especially concerning gender issues. Better coordination between civil society and the state is needed at the local, national, regional and international levels. States and donor agencies should give more recognition to civil society's growing contribution to governance.

Provide gender education and training for women. This training will promote women's increased participation at all levels. Building on the work already undertaken by feminist organizations, the state should support legal education and counselling programs. Civic training for men and women could include gender-perspective courses on electoral participation and local government. Women of all ages should be actively encouraged to take part in politics.

Build capacity of women's organizations. Develop their political skills in areas such as lobbying; formulating legislative and policy demands; public education and advocacy; coalition building; consensus politics; negotiation and mediation. Women's organizations could be trained to make more effective use of the media and public opinion polls to define their political priorities and maximize their impact.

Improve coordination among women's organizations and broaden their support base. Women's groups must continue working to overcome the infighting that currently divides them and unite around specific, realizable goals and objectives. They should address the state and the rest of civil society in a coherent and cohesive voice. Gender initiatives could be strengthened by including potential allies that are currently outside the network such as high-profile women, or agencies working with women that are not specifically considered as "women's organizations." By broadening its support base, the women's movement would heighten its overall impact and effectiveness.

Chapter 5

Gender and the Environment: Women as Managers and Consumers

Women have a vital role in environmental management and development. Their full participation is therefore essential to achieve sustainable development.

Principle 20, Rio Declaration on Environment and Development, United Nations Conference on Environment and Development (1992).

Although it has been recognized internationally that women play a critical role in managing the environment, their profile in the sustainable development debate remains marginal and "women's initiatives" and "environmental initiatives" are all too often seen as competing for scarce resources rather than as being complementary. Yet there is a growing understanding of the importance of women's participation in environmental programs and of the specific constraints that women face.

As Latin America and the Caribbean near the next century, there is growing awareness that emerging social and economic models of development must be intimately linked to sustainable use of the region's natural resources (IDB-UNDP, 1990). The region lays claim to 23 percent of the earth's potentially arable land, 12 percent of the soil under cultivation, 17 percent of the grazing land, 23 percent of the forests (46 percent of the tropical forest) and 31 percent of the available surface water. The region also contains 3 percent of the proven reserves of fossil fuels and 19.5 percent of the world's available hydroelectric potential (IDB-UNDP, 1990).

The region is home to an impressive diversity of forest species. It is estimated that more than 90,000 of the planet's 250,000 higher plant species live in these forests, most of which are tropical. Ten percent of these are believed to be medicinal species, 10 percent have industrial uses and 15 percent are edible, which means more than 31,000 species have economic value for future development (IDB-UNDP, 1990).

As is now widely known, the natural heritage of Latin America and the Caribbean has been degraded because past development undervalued the sustainable use of natural resources and maintenance of a healthy and safe environment. Deforestation is one of the most critical environmental problems in Latin America. With an estimated 966 million hectares of forest, the region has the highest deforestation rate in the developing world, losing 1.3 percent of its forest each year (WRI, 1990). If the present rate continues, Jamaica will have no forests left in 30 years (Wiltshire, 1993). Current projections for the region as a whole indicate that by the year 2000, Latin America may lose between 30,000 to 100,000 tropical species due to loss of habitats (IDB UNDP, 1990). Ninety-eight percent of the tropical dry forest along the Pacific Coast of Central America has already disappeared (WRI, 1992).

Caribbean island states are particularly vulnerable to environmental degradation. For example, the increasing pollution of the seas and oceans threatens the coral reefs, which form an essential part of the region's ecosystem. These coral beds are rich sources of biodiversity and play a major role in reducing global warming. They are also a major tourist attraction (Wiltshire, 1993).

The region's environmental problems are not limited to rural areas and the depletion of natural resources. In fact, equally severe environmental problems confront urban populations. At the root of urban problems are major demographic changes associated with rural-urban migration and the inability of cities to provide healthy and sanitary environments due to lack of appropriate policies and financial and technical resources. Recent estimates show that between 1960 and 1990, 94 percent of the region's population increase was in urban areas. During this same period, the share of urban population in the region shifted from 49.4 percent in 1960 to 71.2 percent by 1990 (CEPAL-CELADE, 1993), which makes Latin America and the Caribbean the region with the largest proportion of urban dwellers in the developing world.

Continued rapid growth of cities brings a host of environmental problems. These include overcrowding, congestion, pollution, lack of sanitation, in adequate housing services and water supply, and waste disposal problems. The growing urban population will generate 370,000 tons of solid waste per day by the turn of the century (Campbell, 1989). A recent study found that in Brazil nine of the country's biggest metropolises produced 25,000 tons of inadequately treated garbage every day (IBGE, 1990).

To protect its natural heritage and reverse past economic, social and demographic trends that have led to urban and rural environmental degradation, Latin America and the Caribbean will need to marshall the active participation of their people. Only with more participatory models of development can social and economic policies be both appropriate to the needs of the people and respectful of sustaining valuable resources and maintaining the quality of the environment. In formulating policies and programs that promote the involvement of individuals—both women and men—in the management and protection of their own environment. It is imperative to consider the importance of gender in structuring the relationships individuals maintain with the environment and in creating opportunities and overcoming constraints to their involvement in sustainable development initiatives.

How should gender issues be taken into account in an environmental context? This is a somewhat difficult task. Both gender and the environment are generally considered cross-cutting themes in development planning. What happens when two cross cutting themes cross cut each other? The challenge is both to identify areas where these two themes support each other and to minimize conflicts. This challenge is made even greater because the environment has also become a programming sector, generating its own series of programs and policy issues.

There are ways in which a gender analysis can produce a more effective understanding of how both men and women relate to natural resources. Such an analysis therefore provides a clearer basis from which to design initiatives. Various roles women play in relation to the environment throughout the region are important, as are constraints that should be addressed to build sustainable development alternatives.

Three Blind Alleys

Until recently, much of the discussion within development circles about women and the environment has focused primarily on two conditions of women's lives—fertility and poverty. These two approaches have been questioned extensively, and their usefulness is now in doubt. A third approach, flowing from the ecofeminist perspective that argued that women had a special affinity with nature, has also been challenged. Although this last line of argument may have raised the profile of the issue, its contribution to policy development is somewhat dubious.

Women, Population and Environment

The focus on population or fertility with regard to women and the environment is based on concerns about the impact of population growth on the environment and natural resources. That population growth is directly linked to environmental degradation in the developing countries, including those in Latin America and the Caribbean, has been widely promoted by a number of population planning and environmental groups. It has had an impact on public opinion and official policy on the importance of limiting global population. These groups do not necessarily represent the mainstream of the population or environmentalist communities, many of which see their approach as too simplistic and narrow (Lohmann, 1990; Erikson, 1990) and too often expressed in terms that characterize women in developing countries as mere instruments of fertility reduction (Sen, 1994).

Environmental scientists and economists have begun to explore the more complex link between environmental change and social and economic institutions. It is now increasingly well accepted that, while population growth and density are certainly factors that can exacerbate environmental degradation, they are not the main cause of degradation in the developing countries (World Bank, 1992). A more complex relationship between a country's particular configuration of natural resources and its economic and social policies, rather than population growth per se, determines whether and to what extent degradation occurs.

Questions have also been raised around the assumed interrelationship between poverty, the environment and population programs that have been based on the facile equation of these issues. Green (1994) argues that development agencies have been too quick to adopt this scenario and questions the assumptions behind the conclusion that "all it takes is the adoption of a series of 'win-win' policies (plus a variety of targeted environmental policies), which if implemented concurrently will provide solutions simultaneously across the poverty, population and environment imbroglio."

In the population planning community, many have begun to assess critically past strategies for fertility reduction, recognizing that the establishment of demographic targets can lead to abuses against women and, ironically, to ineffective population programs. In Mexico and Colombia, for example, family planning programs combining intensive persuasion, and, in some cases, small-scale incentives schemes have raised charges that some women have been coerced into accepting contraception or sterilization. In Brazil and Puerto Rico, feminists have questioned the ethics of contraceptive testing programs, especially hormonal methods used among low-income women. Such approaches have made some women suspicious of family planning services.

In fact, the high proportion of women who wish to limit fertility yet fail to use modern contraception or resort to dangerous abortion is now seen as reflecting the inadequacy of traditional family planning programs. Moreover, the impact of family planning per se has not been well demonstrated. With few exceptions, even strong family planning efforts have produced only moderate declines in birth rates where development levels are low. Birth rates decline more rapidly only when development is advanced and family planning efforts are strong (World Bank, 1984; Kabeer, 1992; Dixon-Mueller, 1993).

Emphasis on the quality of care provided through family planning programs has now gained substantial support, as has the adoption of a broader reproductive health approach under which comprehensive reproductive and sexual health services are provided (Bruce, 1989; IWHC, 1993). Greater attention is also being paid to improvements in women's status that are associated with fertility reduction—including educational attainment and employment opportunities (Mason, 1984; Lloyd, 1991; UNFPA, 1989).

Women, Poverty and Environment

Another approach to women and the environment has focused on the links between women, poverty and the environment. There is legitimate concern that it is the poor who are disproportionately affected by environmental degradation. It is argued that the poor, operating from a very limited resource base (including marginal and fragile lands and little or no access to improved and sustainable production techniques) are forced to adopt survival strategies that put short-term gain ahead of conservation for the long term. This situation, ironically, further undermines the resource base of the poor (World Bank, 1992; Paolisso and Yudelman, 1991). Women's disproportionate poverty and their responsibility for providing household water, fuel and other subsistence needs provide the basis for linking poor women and environmental degradation.

It is, in fact, true that about half the world's poor live in rural areas that are environmentally fragile. The poor in urban areas typically live in crowded settlements with very limited access to sanitation services and safe water. They depend heavily on resources that they do not own and over which they have little control or legal right. Because their limited economic resources and poorly defined property rights can limit their ability or incentive to invest in the conservation of the resources upon which they rely, poverty can become linked with environmental degradation.[1] Thus, emphasizing poverty alleviation as an environmental management strategy may be justified.

On the other hand, a focus on women's poverty and household responsibilities that depend on natural resources may seem to imply that poor women are substantially responsible for environmental degradation. This draws attention away from the much more well-established links between environmental degradation, higher standards of living, agribusiness and industrial production. As incomes increase, changes in consumption patterns contribute to larger scale exploitation of natural resources. For poor women, on the other hand, virtually all resources are scarce and must be conserved accordingly. Even when constrained from making long-term investments in environmental maintenance, poor women are not the main contributors to environmental degradation.

Women's Affinity with Nature?

Another line of analysis, albeit with a very different pedigree, sees both women and nature as oppressed and subjugated, the joint victims of patriarchal power structures (Braidotti et al., 1993). This school of thought, often characterized as ecofeminism, emphasizes women's affinity with nature and suggests that women's relationship with the environment is somehow special (Shiva, 1988). Women are seen as natural conservationists. For example, a spokesperson for Women's Environment Network writes, "women's priorities are usually oriented towards the good of the community thus placing more emphasis on the protection of the environment and the resources within it" (quoted in Jackson, 1993: 1950).

Critics of this approach outline a number of flaws. First, it does not present clear evidence for its basic assertions, rather it takes its position as self-evident. The proof of this "special relationship" is often based on the same examples (Jackson, 1993). Second, women are generally conceived of as a homogeneous category, and the differences among women are glossed over. The fact that women may have opposing interests based on different class positions, race or age is almost always absent from this analysis.

---

[1]Property rights here refer to security of continued use or ownership and the justified expectation that any benefits from investment in the conservation of a resource will accrue to all individuals who make such investments. Secure property rights, in this broad sense, can readily be attained through systems of communal ownership and do not require systems of private ownership to be effective.

A third criticism of this position is that it ignores the fact that women relate to natural resources within a broader context—how they earn their living, where they live, their stage in a life cycle, their relationships with the men in their lives, and so on. In reality, each case yields different relationships, making generalizations difficult. Women's relationships with natural resources reflect the variations among women mentioned above, as well as gender relations and the dynamics of political economies and agroecosystems (Jackson, 1993).

Ecofeminism leads to the assumption that women form a "natural" constituency to be mobilized in defense of the environment. Thus, in addition to the general heavy workload that the vast majority of women already carry, development agencies are encouraged to add environmental conservation. In the words of one critic, "ecofeminism gives women responsibility for 'saving the environment' with no attention to whether they have the resources to do so" (Leach, 1991: 15).

Gender and the Environment: Emerging Alternatives

The criticisms of the three approaches outlined above highlight elements of an emerging alternative analysis for women and environment and sustainable development. This framework includes two primary elements, a gender analysis and the recognition of market and policy failures.

Contributions of a Gender Analysis

The growing arguments in favor of a gender analysis within development circles in general have been well documented (Moser, 1993b; Kabeer, 1994; Østergaard, 1992a, Guzman, Portocarrero and Vargas, 1991). Analysts have increasingly looked specifically at the contributions of this approach to the fields of the environment and sustainable development at both the theoretical level and at the level of project and program planning (ECOGEN: Thomas-Slayter, Esser, and Shields, 1993; ECOGEN: Thomas-Slayter and Rocheleau, 1993; Leach, 1991; Jackson, 1993; Wiltshire, 1993; Caro and Stormer, 1994; Rojas, 1994).

In general, the incorporation of a gender analysis into the environmental field involves gaining an understanding of the divisions and relations of labor and the varying rights, responsibilities and interests between men and women in each specific setting. A gender analysis also broadens the scope to include productive activities, work within the household and mobilization and action at the community level. A focus on women's specific activities outside the general context of gender relations and the broader cultural, social and political processes is of limited value.

In gender analysis of environmental initiatives, Leach (1991) suggests starting with the specific resource-use situation and process (for example, the use of trees, urban sewage or cotton production). It is important to look at the differences and divisions work, responsibility, knowledge and the rights to use and decide the use of resources and products—between different social groups, including women and men. The next step is to understand how these divided interests and activities come together in relations between people and between the different aspects of production and resource use, such as the sequence of tasks required to produce a product or the links between land ownership and the decisions about pesticide use. The use of this analysis, Leach argues, yields an understanding of "resource-using processes" involving gendered interests and opportunities.

A similar approach has been developed within the ECOGEN project. It offers a concrete methodology for gender analysis within the natural resource management sector. This approach focuses on the interconnected aspects of gender and class relations with an emphasis on how different categories or groups of people cooperate, complement, coexist, compete and conflict with one another. The ECOGEN framework analyzes the interactive processes in gender, resource and environmental issues; the links between micro and macro structures in social and ecological systems; the diversity of ecosystems and communities; the relevance of strong viable local institutions and organizations; and the ways in which local organizations and their resource management activities are structured by gender (ECOGEN: Thomas-Slayter and Rocheleau, 1993).

In a gender analysis, there may be tradeoffs between environmental initiatives and women's interests. Green (1994) points to the example of replacing heavy pesticide use with integrated pest management systems that rely on precise and timely spraying of crops, crop rotations and the introduction of natural predators. Although this series of measures would appear to make eminent environmental sense, it is also important to consider the impact of these measures on gender interests. The extent and manner that women will be affected by these proposals depends on the division of labor within the specific farming system. If there is a reliance on unpaid or limited female labor for pesticide application, this could constitute an additional task in women's already overloaded work schedules.

Market and Policy Failure

Women are economic actors, agriculturalists and consumers of resources. They are affected by market and policy failures closely linked to inefficient use and mismanagement of natural resources. The functioning of markets and policy is important for both women and men. The particular situations that these factors create are gender-specific, however, they are conditioned by the particular roles and responsibilities of women and the specific economic constraints they face.

Market failure. Market failure occurs when imperfect markets generate prices that do not reflect the social costs and benefits associated with goods, leading to their inefficient allocation. The conditions that lead to market failure are especially common in the natural resources sector (Panayotou, 1993). They include poorly defined property rights, absence of markets (or unpriced resources), extensive externalities, public goods, and lack of full information. Insecure, poorly defined or unenforceable rights discourage payment for, investment in, and conservation of resources. Individuals have no assurance that they can cover the costs involved in management of the resource. Farmers with insecure tenure are less likely to invest in planting tree crops, for example, because it is unclear whether they will be able to recover the costs of that investment.

An absence of resource pricing or markets also discourages conservation because individuals are not aware of the scarcity of the resource. An example of the absence of a market is the unregulated use of the environment for waste disposal typical in many Latin American and other countries worldwide. Air pollution, essentially a dumping of waste into the air, is also in this category. In São Paulo, Brazil, for example, a concentration of heavy industry and reliance on automobiles for transportation without pricing for the right to produce emissions has led to levels of air pollution well above maximum "acceptable" standards. Recently, both the federal and state governments have attempted to set emission standards for different sources of pollution. Licensing and zoning efforts are also underway to control existing and potential new sources of emission (Panayotou, 1993).

Extensive externalities associated with natural resources also contribute to inefficient use, as when an individual's actions or investment decisions have effects on others. These effects are not taken into account in an individual's decision to use or invest in resources. For example, farmers use pesticides that ultimately harm fish through chemical runoff into marine estuaries.

Many environmental resources such as air, wilderness or biodiversity are not managed efficiently because they are public goods. The free market will not provide such goods. Since they benefit all individuals, no one individual or group of individuals is willing to pay for them. Instead, they must be provided by governments, and their production may depend on the interests of pressure groups rather than on the preferences of all consumers.

Finally, lack of full information about costs and benefits of resource use can lead to the mismanagement of resources. Without accurate information on the benefits of maintaining a multiple-use forest, for example, logging it today may appear to be a more profitable investment (World Bank, 1993c; Panayotou, 1993).

Policy failure. When markets fail in the efficient allocation and use of natural resources, it may be appropriate for governments to intervene. Government interventions have the potential to improve market outcomes, and the benefits of intervention should outweigh the costs. But, in reality, governments intervene in markets to achieve a variety of social and political objectives. These often have unintended side effects on the environment. Fertilizer subsidies to encourage adoption of new high-yield crop varieties, for example, have typically led to overuse and the contamination of off-site water resources due to runoff. Road construction has, in some instances, encouraged large influxes of population to the newly serviced areas and, without well-defined property rights, deforestation has often resulted.

Four types of policy failure occur in natural resources management:

- distortions of otherwise well-functioning markets through taxes, subsidies, regulations, or public projects with net negative impacts;
- failure to take account of significant environmental effects of policy interventions that are otherwise warranted;
- intervention to correct a market failure that instead leads to an outcome that is worse; and,
- lack of action when intervention is required to improve the functioning of a failing market (Panayotou, 1993).

In the case of the Brazilian Amazon region, mentioned above, policy failure played a major role in deforestation. In the 1960s, the Brazilian government decided to encourage the development of the Amazon. Tax and credit incentives were put in place to encourage ranching and the conversion of forest to pasture land. During the 1970s, close to 10,000 square kilometers of forest were cleared annually by wealthy investors. This rapid conversion of forest land was unrelated to population growth or poverty. In fact, it occurred as Brazil's population growth rate fell, and the incentive programs actually discriminated against the poor because of the rise in land prices caused by the programs (Panayotou, 1993).

Policy failures have contributed to environmental degradation in other countries. In Costa Rica, for example, where 70 percent of total land area is suitable only for forests (whether plantation, managed or protected), some 45 percent of the land area had been converted to annual crops, permanent crops or pasture by 1987. Most forest losses were due to increases in pasture land. Between 1950 and 1984, 1 million hectares, or roughly 20 percent of total land area, was converted from forest to pasture because government policy provided for subsidized credit to cattle ranchers and allowed high delinquency rates among those who received it, thus encouraging the use of land for ranching when it would otherwise have been unprofitable (Cruz, Meyer, Repetto, et al., 1992).

Similarly, in Honduras, perverse incentives have encouraged the expansion of pasture for livestock and precipitous declines in fallow land and the amount of land in forests. Ironically, land reform programs that allowed expropriation of unused fallow and forest land actually encouraged landowners to fence land and plant it as pasture as a way of establishing use of the land without increasing labor inputs (DeWalt and DeWalt, 1982; Jarvis, 1986). This and other policy and market failures have led to patterns of production that jeopardize sustainability and generate immediate profits at the expense of wasteful mining of natural resources. According to DeWalt, Stonich and Hamilton (1993), none of these changes has resulted, even indirectly, from population pressure.

Exploring Women's Environmental Roles

Throughout Latin America and the Caribbean, women—as individuals and through organizations—are responsible for a wide range of activities intimately linked to the environment, and to the creation of sustainable development. As do men, women have a stake in the promotion of the sustainable use of the environment. Men and women vary, however, in the roles they play and constraints they face. It is critical that development initiatives understand these differences.

When women and the environment are linked, the discussion often focuses only on poor women within the agricultural sector. Yet it is important to recast the discussion in a broader context and look at the diversity of women's situations. In addition, it is important to consider complex interweaving of environmental concerns that consider women's productive activities in both urban and rural settings and women's roles as mothers, consumers, and protagonists in the development of their economies and societies.

Women as Environmental Activists

Throughout Latin America and the Caribbean, women have been active in organizations that have called for changes in the way natural resources are used and that have worked to develop alternatives at the micro (within neighborhoods and communities), national (through policy work and advocacy efforts) and international (networking and participation in international conferences such as UNCED) levels (Häusler, 1994). Women have formed their own organizations and have worked within environmental organizations. Yet, just as women are not a homogeneous category, these organizations do not always present a united front (Braidotti et al., 1994).

There has been a marked increase in women's environmental organizations and women's activism on environmental issues through the hemisphere. The growing link between women's issues and environmental issues has prompted the leader of one Venezuelan organization to observe "today, all women's groups in Venezuela are environmentalist, regardless of whether they know what environment means" (García Guadilla, 1993: 75).

Women's organizations working in the environment are generally involved in a wide range of activities. A study of 35 Brazilian women's NGOs grouped their activities into several areas—sensitization of women to the quality of environment as a citizenship right and to the links between poverty, environment and women; popular education and the development of an information center on women and environmental issues; environmental education in the schools; research on topics such as technological alternatives, women and ecosystem management, reproductive health and contraceptive technologies, and population issues; community-based activities to assist women in the management and trading of natural resources; and advocacy around legislation (Pitanguy and Herculano, 1993).

In addition to a wide range of activities and objectives, women's organizations concerned with environmental issues also involve women from different classes and social sectors. Middle-class, educated women often head up urban NGOs that aim to provide community services or work at the level of policy and advocacy (García Guadilla, 1993). Women from poor communities have organized to improve their basic living conditions.

Interestingly, women's involvement in environmental NGOs has not been matched by women's involvement in either elected governments or within bureaucracies. There are few women making policy and programming decisions about the environment within the state structures. The chapter on women's political participation explores this issue in greater detail.

Women as Consumers

Women represent a significant group of consumers because they purchase goods and services for themselves and their families. Women are generally the major purchasers of food stuffs, cooking fuel, cleaning products, clothing and other domestic items. There is a growing recognition of both the rights of consumers to know about the environmental antecedents of their purchases, and the responsibilities of consumers to understand the environmental consequences of their purchases.

Although the issue of consumers and the environment is generally seen as a concern for northern countries, there is a growing awareness of these issues around the world. The International Organization of Consumer Unions (IOCU) Regional Office for Latin America and the Caribbean established a program on women and consumer issues, which looks at the need to understand the relationships of women with consumer responsibility in the environmental context (Rodda, 1991).

Women Farmers, Gardeners and Agricultural Wage Laborers

As noted in the chapter on women and economic policy, in Latin America and the Caribbean, agriculture has been viewed traditionally as a male-dominated sector. This perspective has been supported by national level censuses and surveys that report low levels of participation of women in the agricultural sector (UN, 1991a). Consistent with low reported participation rates, a cultural stereotype of rural women as homemakers has reinforced the perspective in the region that women do not make important contributions to agriculture (IDB, 1990).

As is discussed in the chapter on women and economics, there is mounting evidence to support a revised perspective on the importance of women to agricultural production in Latin America and the Caribbean. Household surveys indicate that women's participation in small-farm agriculture has actually been increasing in the past several decades as rural men have moved into wage work on large farms producing for export (Pollack, 1990). This means

Box 1: Women and Environmentally Sound Agriculture

The Consejo para el Desarrollo Integral de la Mujer Campesina (CODIMCA) is a peasant women's organization with 3,600 members in 300-400 groups in nine departments in Honduras. Most members are single mothers. Organic gardening (in one department 90 percent of the members have their own gardens), cultivation of medicinal plants, compost pits, soil conservation techniques, and nurseries for coffee seedlings form part of a comprehensive program to assist poor women farmers in using sustainable agricultural practices. The program includes literacy training, Lorena stoves, and sanitation. When women have access to land (rented or borrowed, seldom owned), they grow soybeans and black beans collectively for the market. The organization has trained 20 women in alternative agricultural techniques, and they, in turn, help other women (Paolisso and Yudelman, 1991).

that women's contributions to food production are greater than what was previously believed.

In addition to producing food primarily for home consumption, many women throughout the region actively participate in commercial agriculture, both as producers on family-run farms and as wage laborers. A study of the Amazon basin shows, for example, that small and poor frontier farms rely on women to process, store, and market commodities such as rubber and pepper (GENESYS, 1992a). In Honduras, in addition to food crops, 50 percent of all rural women also help plant cash crops (White et al., 1986). In parts of the Andean region in Colombia, Ecuador, Peru and Bolivia, a significant proportion of rural women manage all farm operations for at least part of the year as a result of seasonal male migration (GENESYS, 1992a). A study of female-headed farm households in one community in the Caribbean shows that women typically manage all daily farm activities, although they may receive assistance from male relatives for cash crop production (Chase, 1988).

Women also earn agricultural income through wage labor on large farms producing both traditional and non-traditional crops. In Honduras, women supply 90 percent and 40 percent of the wage labor for coffee and tobacco production, respectively (White, Otero, Lycette, et al., 1986). In Costa Rica (Buvinić and Mehra, 1990) and Mexico (Arizpe and Aranda, 1986; Arizpe, 1988; Barrón, 1990; Lara and Maria, 1988) export fruit and vegetable companies rely almost exclusively on female labor to meet harvesting, processing, and packing requirements. In Brazil, women represent 80 to 90 percent of the seasonal labor on coffee plantations (Nash, 1983).

Finally, in the region many women typically maintain a home garden where they plant a range of food crops, condiments and medicinal plants. Although not large, these gardens are an important source of important food items and income for women and their families (Gliessman, 1990). In Santiago, Chile, for example, home gardens maintained by women are a low-cost source of supplemental food for the family and income for women, who sell surplus produce in local markets. The food produced and income earned are particularly important during seasonal lulls in women's other income-earning activities (Ortuzar, 1992).

Men remain the primary agricultural producers in Latin America and the Caribbean. Throughout the region, however, women agriculturalists are critically dependent on the environment. Given their expanding involvement in production tasks and roles as farm managers, they can play an important part in sustainable management of land and other resources. Box 1 offers one example of how women have been targeted with sustainable agricultural techniques.

Women and Coastal Zone Management

Women also work in coastal areas where employment opportunities can be affected by coastal zone management plans. It is important to understand the work that women do to both enable women to benefit from interventions and to ensure that coastal zone management programs target the right people.

There is a growing recognition of women's participation in fisheries and other coastal activities. In many fishing communities, women have responsibility for pre- and post-harvest fisheries activities. These may include preparation of fishing gear and bait, unloading boats and nets, processing the catch, and marketing. Development initiatives often fail to recognize this gender division of labor or to support women's work in this area (FAO, 1988). Modernization and technological shifts can also have implications for women different from those for men, given the division of labor. Women's labor may become redundant or be replaced by men's labor. For example, in situations where women carry fish to market on foot or by public transportation, the introduction of refrigerated trucks could displace women (CIDA, 1993).

Women are also involved in the coastal tourism industry. In many Caribbean island states, women have traditionally operated small guest houses that are gradually being replaced by large, high-rise hotels on the beach. This trend has also had implications for local agricultural markets (where some food crops are primarily produced by women) due to a growing substitution of imported foods for local foods. "From an ecological perspective it also shifted the industry to a type of tourism that has had severe consequences for beach erosion, pollution, and destruction of the coral reefs" (Wiltshire, 1993).

Women's Multiple Uses of Forest Resources

In many countries, women collect and process timber and non-timber forest products to help meet home consumption and income needs. In many poor rural households, fuelwood gathered from forest areas continues to be the dominant form of household energy for cooking and heating. It is estimated that 80 million poor people in Latin America depend on fuelwood for cooking purposes (IDB-UNDP, 1990), a household responsibility predominantly undertaken by women. For example, women are often the household members most responsible for collecting fuelwood, which in turn can be used to produce charcoal for home use and sale (Flora and Santos, 1986; GENESYS, 1992a).

In a recent study of eight villages in Mexico, 91 percent of the households were dependent on fuelwood as their prime source of energy. Although fuelwood was collected by all members of these households, it was women who were primarily responsible for ensuring that adequate supplies were obtained (Arizpe, Paz and Velãzquez, 1993). Among indigenous societies of South America, women typically spend significant amounts of time collecting fuelwood. Among the Tatuyo of Colombia and the Nambicuara of Brazil, who are foragers and agriculturalists, women spend six to eight hours per day collecting fuelwood and other forest products (Aspelin, 1975; Dufour, 1984).

Women also collect wild foods, raw materials and medicinal plants from forests for home consumption and sale in local markets. In Mexico, forests provide women and their families with resin, honey, mushrooms, fruits, medicines, and wood, which is used in making tables, instruments, utensils and brooms. Women barter forest products for goods that, in turn, can be sold to earn needed cash (Arizpe, et al., 1993). A case study of the Dominican sierra shows that women collect palm fronds to weave mats, bags, and to use in light construction (Flora and Santos, 1986). In St. Lucia, some women use various timber species for broom making, an important income-earning activity for poor women (Watson and Drayton, 1990). Women in Jamaica represent a third of the owners of small-scale enterprises processing forest products, while in Honduras women own 10 percent of all enterprises based on forest products (Fisseh, 1985).

The collection, processing and sale of forest products is an important source of essential household materials and income for rural women and un-

Box 2: Agroforestry: Balancing Women's Immediate Needs with Longer-term Natural Resource Conservation

In 1988, CARE-Guatemala initiated an 18-month women in development initiative to increase women's participation in CARE's agroforestry and integrated aquaculture projects. According to a diagnostic survey conducted at the outset, women were most interested in short-term activities yielding either income or food for household consumption. Their priorities are understandable when one considers their role in the day-to-day subsistence of the household: 66 percent of women interviewed contributed up to half of their household's (cash and noncash) budget; 13 percent were their family's sole support. While miscellaneous activities such as crafts and domestic work were of some significance, agriculture was the chief source of income for 79 percent of the women surveyed.

In the agroforestry project, the WID initiative assisted staff to develop activities combining short- and medium-term benefits such as soil conservation, composting, vegetable gardening (higher-value crops) and nursery production of forestry and fruit species, flowers, and ornamentals. CARE hoped that, although initially motivated by short-term objectives, women would become engaged in activities that would generate longer-term improvements in their social and economic situation.

An evaluation survey later discovered that women dramatically increased their participation in both agroforestry and aquaculture activities. In March 1988, the agroforestry project had 1,647 female participants, equivalent to 11 percent of total project participants. Ninety-one agroforestry groups (or 25 percent of total project groups) included women. By January 1990, the number of women rose to 2,505. More significant, perhaps, is that the number of agroforestry groups that included women rose to 139 (Johnson and Castillo, 1990).

derscores the importance of policies that encourage the multiple use of forests on a sustained basis.

Women Working for a Healthy Community Environment

With the increasing pollution and contamination found in most Latin American cities, women in urban and peri-urban communities, many of whom are extremely poor, are responding by strengthening their efforts to protect their family's and community's health from environmental hazards. As is true worldwide, a primary household responsibility for women in Latin America is maintaining a clean and sanitary household and immediate community environment (Melo, 1991). Securing safe drinking water, preparing and storing foods in a hygienic manner, removing organic and inorganic wastes, and educating children about the importance of sanitation and hygiene are home responsibilities either undertaken directly or supervised by women.

Box 3: Managing Appropriate Technology for Household Waste Removal

In two communities in the Valle de México and Mérida in the Yucatan, women play a crucial role in managing the waste recycling system known as the Integrated System for Recycling Organic Wastes (SIRDO). The SIRDO drainage system was designed and installed by the Grupo de Tecnología Alternativa (GTA), an NGO, in a block of houses. Grey water (kitchen, bathroom, and laundry water) is discharged through one pipe to a filtering system in which 80 percent is recycled for use as irrigation water for green areas and gardens. Black water (toilet water) proceeds through a second pipe to a tank where the solid waste is separated. The waste is placed into an aerobic chamber where it is combined with other solid household waste and dried to make fertilizer. Water filtered from the black water is treated and reused to water household gardens and for fish ponds.

After the first few years, GTA delegated all maintenance responsibilities to a cooperative headed by a woman and composed predominantly of women. The cooperative, formed to sell the fertilizer, undertakes daily maintenance of the system. Maintenance responsibility is rotated among the women. An additional outcome of women's involvement has been their organization of other community environmental activities. Women started a program to collect inorganic waste (plastics, glass, metal) to sell for recycling and constructed a small playground for the community's children (Schmink, 1984).

As noted in a regionwide survey, there is a broad range of environmental activities carried out by women, such as removing trash and waste; recycling organic and inorganic materials; planting trees, bushes, and flowers to create green areas; and encouraging activism against local industries that pollute or contaminate community environments (Paolisso and Yudelman, 1991). For example, peri-urban women's groups in the Dominican Republic are constructing dry latrines (Yudelman, 1989). In shantytowns and urban slums in Brazil and Peru, women have formed groups to secure government assistance for community sewerage, improved drainage around public water taps, and regular garbage disposal (Anderson, 1989; Chauhan et al., 1983).

In a peri-urban community of Mexico City affected by high levels of water and air pollution, women are perceived as the "environmental risk managers." Despite monetary or time costs, women are increasingly adopting practices such as boiling water to reduce water-borne health problems (Joekes, Heyzer, Oniango'o, et al., 1993). In Buenos Aires and La Paz, some women recycle organic household garbage to prepare compost and mulch to use in growing vegetables and medicinal plants for sale or home consumption.

The environmental activities of poor women in urban and peri-urban areas also include efforts to improve the community landscape. Women are

Box 4: Confronting Urban Air Pollution

In two neighborhoods of São Paulo, Brazil, women have formed groups to protest against local industries whose pollutants are threatening their families' health. In the neighborhood of Agua Funda, the Grupo de Mulheres do Movimento Contra a Poluição da Agua Funda was formed because of women's concern that air pollution from a local steel factory was causing increased respiratory problems, particularly among children. After several years of protest, city administrators finally required the factory to install filters to reduce substance emissions into the air. Air pollution was reduced, and the number of respiratory problems declined.

The success of the women's group in Agua Funda inspired others. Women in the Santo Andre neighborhood, an industrialized area of São Paulo, formed the Grupo Ecológico Consciencia. Women were concerned that an increase in asthma, bronchitis, allergies, and other health problems in the neighborhood was due to the air pollution ("black powder") from nearby tire factories. The group petitioned the city department for environmental sanitation, requesting that the factories install devices to reduce smoke emissions. The group also protested in front of the tire factories and planted trees around the factories as symbolic acts to draw attention to their problems and inspire other women (Paolisso and Yudelman, 1991).

working to create green areas or recreational space through such activities as planting trees, bushes, grasses, and flowers. Women's work in creating and maintaining these areas can help to reduce erosion and gullying due to rainfall runoff. Such work also has aesthetic and symbolic importance.

Given the high population densities of poor urban and peri-urban areas and the overall absence of public parks, even small areas planted in grasses, flowers, and trees are important. In providing shade and a pleasant atmosphere in which to relax and hold meetings or for children to play in, they improve the "liveability" of urban habitats. Parks and green areas can also be important symbols of a community's commitment to and awareness of the need to improve the quality of the environment.

Women are also taking steps to increase their understanding of environmental and sustainable development issues, which they see as a prerequisite to educating their children and other family and community members. In Argentina, Bolivia, Brazil, and Colombia women are major participants in environmental education projects. In Buenos Aires, for example, women participate in seminars to learn more about health problems related to inadequate sanitation and hygiene. In Paraguay and Uruguay, women are working with NGOs to collect information on environmental problems confronting their communities and to develop informal education programs (Paolisso and Yudelman, 1991).

Finally, in one community in Costa Rica women have successfully integrated a number of environmental activities into a program that forms the center of their community development program. Located outside San José, the Guararí Community Development Project is a model project for housing low-income families in ways compatible with raising the standard of living of local people, encouraging the acceptance of smaller families, and protecting and restoring the natural environment.

Women, many of whom are single heads of households, are leaders in the community's environmental activities. Respect for and protection of the environment are fully integrated into the community's development strategies. Natural flora are being conserved as much as possible. The community's symbol is a large shade tree, and each house is required to have a garden. Children are involved in campaigns to plant trees. Residents grow and propagate medicinal plants for home use and have established nurseries to grow tree seedlings for local markets. Plans are in place to remove litter and garbage, in part through the purchase of waste containers with money made from raffles and sales. Guararí also has an ambitious plan to rehabilitate the surrounding watershed that will include recreational facilities, nature walks, and lectures (Dennis and Castleton, 1989).

In efforts to ensure healthy and sanitary household and community environments, women's roles can be pivotal. Throughout the region, as part of their household responsibilities, women are performing community-level sanitation, recycling, waste removal, and environmental advocacy and education activities. These endeavors must be recognized and supported as critical community development and environment activities, and not seen only as part of women's domestic work.

Sustaining Biological Diversity

With the increase in the number and quality of case studies on women's agricultural, livestock and forestry roles, better information is emerging on roles women play in using and conserving the region's rich biological diversity. In the Paraná State of Brazil, research has revealed that women have an in-depth knowledge of medicinal plants and make use of more than 60 such plants. In the Maya Biosphere region of Guatemala, women have extensive knowledge of the varieties and properties of a large number of tree species, which they use to produce tree products for sale (Schmink, 1990). Throughout Central America,

Box 5: Women's Use and Conservation of Forest Products

In the state of Maranhão, Brazil, the babassu palm, grown in maintained stands of secondary forest, provides poor women with raw materials for producing an array of household and market goods, such as baskets, fish traps, bird cages, animal feed, planting medium, palm wine, oil, and soap. In addition, fruit husks can be made into charcoal. In one area of Maranhão, babassu charcoal was the principal cooking fuel in 96 percent of surveyed households (Anderson and Anderson, 1983). Use of babassu charcoal protects forests from excessive fuelwood harvesting.

The kernel of the babassu fruit provides rural households with an important source of income. An estimated 400,000 rural workers in Maranhão make a living extracting kernels from the babassu palm. Women predominate (up to 86 percent in one sample) in collecting and processing the oil-rich kernels for sale to local industries for producing lauric vegetable oil for soap manufacture, other industrial uses, and feed cakes. The sale of kernels is an important source of income in the period between crop harvests. The kernels can be stored, and since extraction can be done at home, it does not compete with domestic tasks such as cooking and child care (Hecht, Anderson, and May 1988).

The expansion of cattle ranching and rice cultivation and the privatization of babassu forests by large landowners has resulted in reduced access by poor families to this important natural resource. Moreover, increased mechanization of kernel extraction has resulted in loss of income-earning opportunities for women. The Associação em Areas de Assentamento no Estado do Maranhão (ASSEMA) is helping groups of women learn more about the conservation laws related to babassu areas and how to lobby government officials for reforms that would ensure their continued access to babassu forests. ASSEMA is also helping women secure membership in rural unions and teaching them about sustainable natural resource use.

women's home gardens, which contain a wide range of traditional cultigens and introduced cultivars, are potentially valuable stores of diverse plant genetic materials (GENESYS, 1992a; Solís and Trejos, 1990).

In a community in Costa Rica, women raise 60 to 70 plant species in their gardens, including food crops, trees, herbaceous and ornamental plants. Many of these serve multiple purposes as food, fuel, medicine, and raw materials for handicrafts (Gliessman, 1990). In a Ucayali river community in Peru, women collect and grow species of herbs for food and medicine on raft gardens. Routinely washed away by floods, these raft gardens help to redistribute species along the length of the river (Padoch and Pinedo-Vāsquez, 1991). In the highlands of Peru, genetic diversity is also maintained in the flocks of rustic sheep and native camelids that women traditionally maintain, and women are rescuing ancestral knowledge on native birds (GENESYS, 1992a; Paolisso and Yudelman, 1991).

Lastly, in many Latin American and Caribbean countries, some women take care of tree nurseries for community reforestation or agroforestry projects. Thus they are in a pivotal position to share their knowledge of forest species and contribute to forestry efforts that maintain species diversity (Paolisso and Yudelman, 1991).

Women in Latin America also can play an important role in integrated conservation and development (ICDP) projects supported by national and international conservation organizations (Mehra, 1993). These projects seek to protect biological diversity by promoting economic development in communities located near biologically rich areas that are at risk of degradation and overexploitation. To date, most ICDPs have not recognized the importance of considering gender in their efforts to support communities' sustainable development and stewardship of biologically diverse areas (Mehra, 1993). However, this appears to be changing. Many ICDPs in Latin America and the Caribbean offer excellent opportunities to engage women in community efforts to manage biologically diverse areas.

Women's role as information sources and managers of the region's rich biological diversity is beginning to be recognized. While women have a vested interest in preserving biological diversity, their current efforts will need appropriate program and policy support if they are to make significant contributions.

Constraints in Managing the Environment

Women face a number of difficulties in managing and protecting the environment. Although specific constraints vary from case to case and from sector to sector, the issue of women's status is of overriding significance.

Status of Women and Women's Involvement in Decision Making

Chapter 24 of the UNCED document, *Agenda 21,* clearly acknowledged that women's ability to play a pivotal role in sustainable development depends, to a significant degree, on improvements in their status. Governments are called on to implement the Nairobi Forward Looking Strategies for the Advancement of Women by increasing the proportion of women decision makers, planners, technical advisors, managers, and extension workers in environment and development fields.

Although women and women's organizations have played significant and courageous roles throughout the Americas, the marginalization of women continues to inhibit their ability to join fully in policy debate and the construction of viable alternatives (INSTRAW, 1993). In addition, policy makers discussing macro issues such as energy policies and industrial promotion strategies generally assume that these policies will have the same impact on men and women. This assumption has been proven false over and over again.

Women, Work, Production and the Environment

Land Ownership. Most women farmers in Latin America and the Caribbean do not hold title to the lands they farm because land reform schemes have either failed to recognize their traditional rights or because of legal restrictions on inheritance (IDB, 1990). With the exception of Nicaragua, in all countries in the region where agrarian reform has taken place, women have been generally excluded from receiving lands. Even in countries such as Bolivia, Colombia, Honduras, Mexico, and the Dominican Republic, where legislation has specifically recognized women, only a small percentage of the rural female population has gained access to land (IDB, 1990).

In many cases, women's lack of agrarian rights is due to cultural factors. Most agrarian and inheritance laws state that land should be given to the family household head, which is assumed to be a man. In the case of land inheritance, it is assumed that men will work the land, while women will marry men with land. The lack of land ownership, together with cultural values that place women in a subordinated economic position, result in women being excluded from participating in decision making about adopting sustainable agricultural practices.

Even when women do have access or title to land, they usually only have relatively small plots (IDB, 1990). Even small plots can require large amounts of women's time and labor. Evidence from Peru suggests that women's agricultural labor and time commitments are greater for farms that are smaller and poorer, farms where women are most likely to have sole responsibility for the management of the land (Deere and León, 1982). With little land available and the need to cultivate it intensively, women are left with few options for adopting new technologies, which while beneficial in terms of long-term sustainability, are immediately more labor intensive and not without risk to short-term production levels.

Without title to land, women may be excluded from participating in agricultural assistance programs since they often require that participants have secure and titled lands. Moreover, women may have little incentive to make investments in terracing or other labor-intensive soil conservation practices. They have no guarantee of continued access to the land (Mehra, 1993).

Access to Credit. Women's more limited access to credit in agriculture makes it difficult for them to purchase the farm inputs that can lead to resource conservation and sustainable yields. With access to affordable credit, women are better positioned to purchase fuel—efficient stoves, appropriate technology for home- and community-based recycling and waste-management projects, and improved tools and technology that allow them to adopt new cultivation practices without large increases in their labor time. Credit can be used to purchase better quality land, freeing women from cultivating marginal land prone to environmental degradation. In arid areas, credit can be used to purchase pumps or tubing to channel irrigation water.

In urban areas, women's limited access to credit can curtail the possible environmental activities of entrepreneurs. If women's enterprises are struggling to survive, it is unlikely that attention will be paid to urban environmental concerns such as recycling, garbage disposal, waste resulting from specific production processes and environmentally friendly energy inputs.

Access to Extension Services. Women farmers also have limited access to information and technologies for improving the sustainability of agricultural lands because, in most developing countries, agricultural extension services often do not reach them (Berger, DeLancey and Mellencamp, 1984). As a result, women have fewer options available to maintain production as resources are degraded.

Farm households headed or managed by women are particularly vulnerable to difficulties caused by restricted access to extension services. Female-headed farms often depend primarily on family labor. Typically these women cannot afford to hire wage laborers. Without access to labor-saving extension techniques, such households must grow food crops with relatively low labor requirements and shorter growing cycles. This leads to more rapid depletion of soils and ultimately, degradation and lower productivity of this land (GENESYS, 1992a).

Without equal access to agricultural, fishing and forestry extension services, women are less informed about technological inputs for improving sustainable use of natural resources. Moreover, without direct access to extension services, women receive secondhand information that may be inaccurate and fail to contribute to improved agricultural, forestry and conservation outcomes.

Lack of Information

Women may also face limitations in acquiring information on how to maintain and improve the environment. Illiteracy rates among poor rural and urban women are relatively high compared to those of men (World Bank, 1993c).

In addition to constraints related to illiteracy, in countries such as Peru, Ecuador, Guatemala, Bolivia and Mexico, large numbers of rural women speak only their indigenous languages (Hernández and Murguialday, 1992). For example, in Ecuador, 95 percent of the rural Indian women speak only their indigenous language, while 60 percent of men are bilingual.

Low educational attainment among rural and poor urban women is a major factor contributing to low participation in community- and local-level meetings and decision making. For example, in forest communities in Mexico, a recent study found that only 34 percent of the women interviewed attended community meetings, although 64 percent thought that it was important to participate. Eighty-five percent of the men interviewed participated in meetings (Arizpe, et al., 1993).

Illiteracy, lack of fluency in the national language, and low levels of education make it more difficult for women to receive information about harmful forest product collection techniques, fast growing tree crops as an alternative to fuelwood collection, and other innovative and sustainable methods for meeting their needs while maintaining environmental resources.

Lack of Time

Finally, the ability of women to participate in environmental activities or programs is constrained by a lack of discretionary time. As is the case for women in developing countries worldwide, women's dual household and market production roles in the region leave them with little free time. Resource scarcity and depletion also stretch women's work days. Thus, even if women want to participate in environmental or conservation activities, they may not be able to do so without cutting back on the time they spend on other activities (productive or household) vital for survival (Mehra, 1993).

Supporting Women in Sustainable Development

The effectiveness of policies that promote the sustainable use of the environment could be significantly enhanced if it were recognized that women and men have different needs and interests and different access and control over resources, and if support for the involvement and participation of women were reinforced. Through their household and market roles, women use, manage and are knowledgeable about natural resources and their environment.

However, women face a number of constraints that make it difficult for them to contribute to management and conservation of the environment. If future sustainable development policies are to benefit fully from the environmental contributions women can make, the issue of women's status and the engendering of macro policies must be addressed.

Women's limited access to property, financial support, extension services, new technologies, and information are also critical issues. These constraints negatively affect women's participation in a number of sectors. For the Latin American and Caribbean region, policies and program changes in important sectors such as agriculture, environment and public health, energy and education, and science and technology are required if sustainable development efforts are to benefit fully from the contribution of women.

Improvements in Women's Status and the Engendering of Macro Policies

Women's ability to participate effectively in environmental initiatives is linked to their general decision-making power and status. Unless women are included as both a resource and target group in the policy-making process, the future of sustainable development is dubious (Wiltshire, 1993). Although this argument has been accepted at the formal level in documents such as *Agenda 21,* much work remains to be done to implement these agreements.

One key to the process is strengthening women's NGOs. Future research (and action) on women's environmental roles would benefit greatly from collaborations with the rapidly increasing number of organizations in the region that have begun to address women and environment issues. A recent study identified 94 organizations in the region that, to varying degrees, focus on women's environmental roles in their programs. These organizations included national and international NGOs, government ministries, multilateral and bilateral aid agencies, and community groups. The specific women and environment activities these organizations support include organic gardening, agroforestry, reforestation, cultivation of medicinal plants, waste management, sanitation and hygiene, creation of urban "green areas," and environmental education and dissemination (Paolisso and Yudelman, 1991).

These institutions, many of which are members of regional and international environmental networks, represent invaluable partners in future research and action on women's environmental roles and contributions to sustainable development. They can help bridge the micro- and macro-level discussions of women and the environment, serve as critical nodes both in disseminating information and technologies to women and in channelling information from women back to policy makers and program implementors, collaborate in applied research studies of the resources that women use in their home and market work, and help link efforts in the region to the growing international women and environment movement.

It is also important that, when policy is being formulated, the potential impact of policies on both women and men be considered. For example, in the energy sector, as governments develop policies and devise strategies, women and women's organizations should be involved in the discussions. Often decisions such as whether to opt for large-scale hydroelectric production or geothermal power generation could have an impact on women through the eventual price and reliability of domestic electricity and power for small enterprises run by women. Women are also affected by pricing decisions for fuels used in cooking and, where common, home heating. There is also a potential to create employment for women, as well as for men, in infrastructure construction for energy projects.

Environment and Public Health

In both urban and rural areas, women in Latin America and the Caribbean are making valuable contributions to maintaining the quality of the environment. These efforts can be better supported by:

- *Formulating property and using rights policies that protect women's access to resources that are held in common or are state owned.* Women's responsibilities in managing the use of biomass energies, obtaining water, and collecting forest products typically require access to forests or water sources that are either held in common or are state owned. As communities, local level organizations and government institutions develop sustainable use plans and legislation for these public areas. Consideration must be given to ensuring that women will continue to have access to the land and resources they need to fulfil their home and market activities. Secure access and, thus, the expectation of continued benefits, are the best incentives for sustainable use of resources.
- *Developing policies that promote multiple-use management of forests.* The importance of non-timber products such as wild food crops, medicinal plants, construction materials and fuelwood, both for women and national

economies overall, must be included in forestry sector assessments. Policies that promote the sustainable harvest and marketing of these resources and ensure that local populations will have continued access to them need to be developed.

• *Establishing water rights and water users associations that include women.* In both rural semi-arid areas and in poor, peri-urban municipalities, women are usually excluded from participating in decisions about water allocations and measures to ensure water quality. Given women's knowledge of the household level demand for this essential resource and their expertise in managing its collection, storage and use, their contributions can be critical to conservation efforts by water users associations.

• *Design and implement reforestation and agroforestry programs in ways that improve women's participation.* In a number of countries, women have been included in reforestation activities, although their participation has been typically restricted to working in nurseries and fuelwood plantations. Here, as an extension of their domestic responsibilities, women's involvement is primarily limited to only the care and watering of seedlings. Women's involvement should be expanded to include participation in decisions regarding species selection, location of plantings, and the marketing and use of harvested timber and non-timber products. As has been shown in Mexico, Costa Rica, and Honduras, incorporating women's needs and expertise is essential to the success of fuelwood plantations, which can be sources of income-generation for women (Velázquez, 1993).

Agriculture

For women to participate in efforts to make agriculture more sustainable, policies and programs must:

• *Increase women's access to land.* Land registration and reform schemes that tie land title or usufruct rights to an individual's responsibility for decisions on production and land management must be developed. In implementing such schemes, the important and diverse roles of women farmers in the region must be recognized. Accordingly, deed titles should be in the names of women who are farm managers and should legally recognize women's rights to the land that they farm along with their husbands and other family members, particularly in the case of indigenous women agriculturalists.

• *Improve the ability of extension services to provide women with environmental information and new technologies.* Women farmers should be included in agronomic and biotechnological programs that are introducing integrated rural production systems (farming, animal husbandry, forestry exploitation, and aquaculture); providing information on using conventional technologies such as agrochemicals, irrigation and mechanization in an environmentally safe manner; and new techniques for organic agriculture and integrated pest management. The knowledge and experience of women farmers should also be used in projects that focus on working with farmers to rehabilitate deteriorated or altered ecosystems so that they provide a productive base for sustainable cultivation.

Extension services must be structured to provide incentives (or at least not disincentives) for extensionists to work with women farmers, who generally will have the smallest farms. More channels for informing and involving women farmers must be used, including women's groups, non-governmental organizations, and programs for women in related development activities. Efforts must also be made to enhance the technical farming skills and the market expertise of young girls from farming families, including training them to be extension workers.

- *Make agricultural credit available to women farmers.* In adopting sustainable production and soil conservation technologies and, generally, making long-term investments in the lands they farm, women will need access to credit. Because so little agricultural credit has gone to women in the region, special efforts and lending features may need to be used to reach them. As with microentrepreneurs, women farmers may need to borrow in smaller amounts than men. They will not benefit as much from credit made available through producers' cooperatives because of their limited membership in such organizations. Educational disadvantages and the lack of documentation of civil status and land ownership means that minimal application procedures should be required of women. Many of these alternative lending features have been used quite successfully in reaching women entrepreneurs in the region (Berger and Buvinić, 1989; White et al., 1986). It is likely that they would be equally successful in reaching women agriculturalists.

Energy

It is important to *involve women (as policy makers and NGO activists) and include a consideration of women's interests in discussions on energy policy and uses.* Macro energy policy issues, such as the building of a hydroelectric dam, do have gender implications. At a minimum, decision makers should ensure that their programs are not detrimental to women.

There are also considerations at a more sub-sector level. In Latin America and the Caribbean, just under 20 percent of all energy consumed comes from fuelwood and dung. It is estimated that some 80 million people in the region still cook with fuelwood, using technologies that are extremely energy inefficient (IDB-UNDP, 1990). In the immediate future, large numbers of women and their families will continue to rely on fuelwood stoves for cooking, heating, and home-based processing of market products.

Women should be surveyed and consulted about the design and use of energy-efficient stoves. Lack of fuelwood stove efficiency reduces the productivity of poor women's domestic labor and market work in home-based enterprises that require fuelwood for processing market products. In recent years, fuelwood-efficient stoves have become more acceptable (World Bank, 1993c). To ensure greater success, women's knowledge of the time and energy constraints to cooking with fuelwood, the burning qualities of different woods, the effects of different stove designs on cultural preferences in food preparation and taste, and the consequences in terms of indoor smoke pollution of different stove designs are all factors that should be incorporated into program design.

As biomass energy programs promoting efficient fuelwood stoves become more successful, the demand for fuelwood from forested areas already under pressure will be reduced. Also, increased efficiency could make it possible for small fuelwood plantations to meet the energy needs of poor women. Efficient use of planted fuelwood trees can also lead to a reduction in the use of dung and crop by-products as fuel, thereby increasing their availability for use as organic fertilizer and mulch.

Education, Science and Technology

An improved dialogue between women and the practitioners and researchers working to make development sustainable can improve the effectiveness with which environmental information is used and can strengthen the understanding of women's actual and potential environmental roles. To accomplish this, a number of strategies are proposed:

- *Improve women's access to environmental information by supporting new channels of communication.* Efforts to educate women about environmental sustainability and improving their families' home environments must take account of the disparities between male and female educational attainment and basic literacy in Latin America. Environmental and development NGOs need to collaborate in developing literacy programs for women that include practical information about safe pesticide use, environmental health and sanitation, and better management of natural resources. With the assistance of popular organizations and community groups, environmental and women's organizations need to develop nonformal environmental education projects that reach women. These projects should seek women's active involvement in developing materials and should explore alternative means of mass communication.

- *Elicit and use women's knowledge of environmental resources in developing projects to improve sustainable management of the environment.* Because of their dependence on natural resources and responsibility for protecting their families from environmental hazards, women are often important sources of knowledge about conservation techniques and strategies for maintaining healthy and hygienic communities. To date, most sustainable development projects in the region have not benefitted to any significant degree from this knowledge. As more research findings on women's environmental roles become available, this information needs to be integrated into the design, implementation and evaluation of sustainable development policies and programs. The information collected should also be used to present, in public education campaigns, a more gender-balanced view of how women and men use the environment and contribute to conservation efforts. Like men, women are concerned about their environment and struggle with skewed resource prices and incentives that subvert their efforts to manage rather than mine resources. In environmental education materials women should be depicted showing the breadth and depth of their roles. Realistic methods should be developed to meet their concerns.

- *Ensure efforts to formulate policies and programs that support women's environmental roles are guided by better research on women's knowledge of and use and dependence on environmental resources.* Despite recent improvements in the information base on women's environmental roles in the region, there is still comparatively little gender-disaggregated information available on environment and sustainable development. Future research must be guided by an increased awareness of the role that gender plays in the relationships between people and their environment. Researchers across disciplines will need to know how gender-based differences in economic and social roles structure women's use of and dependence on the environment. Gender awareness is important so that, in developing policies and programs to use the environment in a sustainable fashion, environmentalists can take account of the resources women use; health scientists can identify the environmental hazards that threaten women's and their families' health and the roles women can play in reducing those health threats; and development economists and social scientists can determine the losses in women's home production and income that are caused by environmental degradation to develop programs that increase women's income-earning potential in an environmentally sustainable manner.

There has been almost no interdisciplinary collaboration in past efforts to collect information on women's contributions to sustainable development. As a result, studies have presented only partial and fragmented views of women's environmental roles and their potential to contribute to sustainable use of the environment. Multi-disciplinary research drawing on the perspectives of researchers from the social, economic, health, and ecological sciences is necessary to provide a more complete and accurate understanding of the full range of women's environmental roles and their contribution to sustainable development.

Chapter 6

Gender Equity and Changing Institutions

In 1975, the world began to think about men and women in new ways. That year, the First UN World Conference on Women in Mexico City planted the seed of awareness that what happens to women has a profound effect on the well-being of nations. The first three conferences tended to be dominated by political issues such as the Cold War, Palestine, and apartheid in South Africa. But the 1995 Fourth World Conference in Beijing, China, presented a new opportunity to focus on gender issues.

There can be no doubt that international development agencies are much more aware of gender issues today than they were 20 years ago, but progress in carrying out gender-sensitive programs has been slow. Although development agencies and many governments now have WID policies and statements in place, actions on gender issues lag behind.

The concept of "gender" currently used in international development circles contains an implicit challenge for more equitable gender relations. Brouwers' discussion of the term echoes its common, though not universal, use:

> The concept of gender refers to women's and men's socially defined characteristics, which are shaped by historical, economic, religious, cultural and ethnic factors. As a result of gender characteristics, women and men have different experiences in life, different knowledge, perspectives and priorities. With the introduction of the concept of gender in development planning, recognition is given to the causes for and structures of women's subordination in society, to the inequality with men and the power relations involved. Gender analysis emphasizes the context in which women face their problems and stresses the necessity of social change and the need to empower women in this process (Brouwers, 1993).

To be fully realized, gender equity must be a mainstream goal of development (Jahan, 1995). Twenty years after the First UN World Conference marked the birth of what is a discipline, a discrete area for development assistance, and an international movement, we need to look further into the institutional dimensions of mainstreaming. What happens to the goal of gender equity in a new context created by major social, economic, and political changes like as those that have taken place in Latin America and the Caribbean over the last two decades? What happens when a major development institution changes its mandate and organizational structure, as has the Inter-American Development Bank (IDB)?

In international development circles, there is a fondness for "lessons learned." But in today's complex and rapidly changing world, we cannot wait for the lessons to be fully "learned" before acting. Although development professionals still hold to the belief, or at least the hope, that development will improve the well-being of most people, the process does not move in a straight line. We do not complete one task before beginning another. Many tasks are carried out at the same time, all affecting each other. Furthermore, lessons may not be applicable by the time they are actually understood. Lessons still being learned must be examined, even at the risk of using these not yet fully formed "lessons" incorrectly.

Latin America and the Caribbean—and the IDB—are undergoing major institutional changes. At the IDB, this process is still in its early stages. The bank cannot speak yet of a new "model" or institutional structure. But trends are emerging that do provide some insights into present and future struggles and how to win them.

This moment in the history of development cooperation presents many opportunities—and challenges—for promoting gender equity. Renewed and more urgent emphasis is being given to social concerns, including poverty reduction, which means that gender issues cannot be easily ignored. Participatory models of development, especially in the design of development projects, are receiving greater attention. In addition, many institutions are adopting new policies of openness, which will make information on their programs more readily accessible to advocates of gender equity.

But two donor country trends threaten the progress made in addressing gender issues in development cooperation programs—increasing social conservatism and decreasing funding for development cooperation. In many countries, gender equity and some actions that have been used to further this goal (affirmative action, special training programs, public assistance to poor women with small children, reproductive health programs) are under attack from a new wave of social conservatism. And funding for development cooperation is decreasing as donor countries tighten their fiscal belts and with the end of the Cold War as a compelling justification for foreign assistance. Yet, the political changes in Eastern Europe have increased the numbers of potential recipient countries. These factors make it extremely important to use remaining resources strategically to continue the still incipient trend toward promoting gender equity in development assistance.

Most development organizations now have an official policy or mandate for Women in Development (WID) designed to ensure that gender issues take into account both women's and men's needs in the programs they support. They also have an office or an official charged with leading, advising and reviewing policy implementation. The IDB is no exception. The Bank approved its Operating Policy on Women in Development in 1987 and appointed its first women in development advisor in 1989.

This chapter uses the case of the Inter-American Development Bank to examine what promotes or inhibits progress toward gender equity and toward addressing the particular needs and concerns of women within an international development institution. The context in which the IDB operates—particularly conditions in its borrowing member countries (recipients of the IDB's financing and holders of one-half of the voting shares on the IDB's board)—and past progress in implementing a women in development policy are carefully examined. The author also considers how two major institutional changes, the replenishment of the IDB's capital[1] and the Bank's reorganization, will affect implementation of the WID policy.

The Changing Face of Latin America and the Caribbean

In the past 10 years, three important factors have profoundly affected the direction of the IDB's lending and technical cooperation programs:

- the economic crisis of the 1980s, which resulted in dramatic de-

[1] Under each replenishment, the financial resources available for that funding cycle and voting shares among member countries are negotiated, a new volume of lending is authorized, and new policy commitments are made that guide the IDB's programming strategy. The replenishment of capital is the major means through which IDB shareholders (the member country governments: donors and borrowers) can shape the overall policies and programs of the Bank. Each replenishment agreement thus has a major impact on the volume and direction of IDB lending.

clines in incomes and increases in unemployment, and its legacy of persistent poverty and inequality;

• increasing regional economic integration and renewed economic growth in the 1990s (although, as the drop of the Mexican peso has shown, this growth can be very fragile); and,

• democratization, an ongoing process of change from a predominance of authoritarian military and dictatorial governments to a predominance of governments that are chosen through open elections. Decentralization of government functions and increasing importance of civil society in national decision making have accompanied this change.

The economic crisis of the 1980s imposed considerable social costs on the region, particularly on the poor and the middle classes. In addition, numerous studies have indicated that a disproportionate share of the burden of adjustment was placed on women. Women played a vital role in the survival efforts of poor families, compensating for reductions in family income through increased paid and unpaid labor. Yet, their access to economic and social resources remained low or declined.

Today, the overall economic climate in Latin America is improving, but massive poverty remains stubbornly entrenched. The critical question now is how to ensure that women's needs are met, their participation encouraged, and their social and economic contributions supported within the greater focus on social problems and decentralization, issues that are explored in greater detail in the other chapters of this book.

The governments of Latin America and the Caribbean are increasingly focusing their attention on reversing past patterns of social and economic exclusion in response to greater concern with poverty and social issues. As the moribund economies of the 1980s are reactivated, the social ills that worsened during the previous decade now stand out in stark relief. Governments have begun to realize that if their countries' economies are to continue to grow and remain competitive, all of the region's people must be given the opportunity to participate equitably. In particular, although women now make up one-third of the work force in the region—double the proportion of only a generation ago—governments and policy makers are only beginning to understand women's changing economic and social roles.

Addressing Gender and Development Issues in the IDB

The IDB is the largest of the regional development banks. As one of the principal development assistance agencies operating in Latin America and the Caribbean—with over $6 billion in new projects financed each year in this one region—the IDB has a major impact on the direction of development assistance in the region.

The WID Policy

The IDB came late to the WID arena, approving its Operating Policy on Women in Development in 1987, after considerable discussion (IDB, 1987). Unlike bilateral women in development or gender and development policies, the IDB's policy represents a consensus hammered out from differing views expressed by governments of the Latin American and Caribbean borrowing countries and those of the predominantly European and North American donor countries. The IDB policy also reflects the state of development of the policies of all the member countries at the time it was approved.

The objective of the IDB WID policy is to assist member countries in their efforts to integrate women more fully into all stages of the development process and to improve their socioeconomic situation (IDB, 1987). The policy states that the Bank will recognize and enhance women's actual and potential roles in productive and social activities and their contributions to the national development process. This focus recognizes that gender roles are not static and that existing differences and inequities can be changed.

The WID policy is unique among IDB policies in two ways. First, it provides operational directives and administrative guidelines, something rarely seen in policy documents. Second, it also calls for an action plan to be prepared to guide the Bank in implementing the policy and for a progress report on the plan to be given to the IDB Board of Executive Directors every two years. This reporting system allows for periodic readjustment in implementing policy.

Recognizing the increasing economic responsibilities of women in the region, the WID policy outlines objectives for raising their productivity and improving their access to training, income-generating activities, and credit. The policy also emphasizes strengthening institutions that foster women's participation in the social and economic life of their countries.

Most WID programs in development agencies began by focusing on small, separate actions directed exclusively at women, while the larger programs generally continued to exclude women, or at least not consider their participation. Before the approval of the WID policy and in the early days of its implementation, the IDB focussed its efforts to promote women in development on financing small credit and training programs for women microentrepreneurs. Although these programs have been beneficial for many individual women and have yielded valuable lessons, these projects represent less than 1 percent of the IDB's lending each year. The IDB thus devoted only a tiny fraction of its resources to WID and neglected gender equity as an overarching development issue.

Under its 1989-93 Seventh Replenishment funding cycle, the IDB formally reconfirmed its commitment to strengthening women's contribution to the development process and to improving benefits to women and their families from IDB projects (IDB, 1989). However, at the time the IDB's second senior advisor on women in development was hired in 1990, most staff members still remained unaware of the IDB's WID policy. Those that did know of its existence often understood it as a requirement to include a paragraph on how their projects would benefit women in project proposals. A standard paragraph was often repeated from one document to the next, even when the projects were in different sectors.

Such a limited approach to women in development has been typical of international development agencies. In the late 1980s, only 3.5 percent of UN development agency projects were directly targeted to women, which represented a mere 0.2 percent of agency budget allocations. Less than 1 percent of the UN Development Program's $700 million budget was dedicated to funding the $5 million budget of UNIFEM, and less than 1 percent of FAO projects specify strategies to reach women farmers (Staudt, 1990). A report by the OECD Development Assistance Committee showed a similar situation in the bilateral aid programs of DAC member countries, with approximately 5 percent of official development assistance directed to a combination of "WID specific" and "WID integrated" projects in 1991 (Brouwers, 1993).

What Institutional Factors Affect Policy Implementation?

According to a recent study of the World Bank by Nukat Kardem, an international organization's response to new issues and new ways of thinking depends primarily on four factors—"the degree of independence of the [international organization] within the international regime in which it functions; the nature of external pressure on the organization about the new issue; the consistency of the new issue with existing organizational goals and procedures; and the extent of internal advocacy for the issue within the organization"

(Kardam, 1993). These factors differ greatly by type of international organization, such as the United Nations system, bilateral donors, multilateral development banks, and so on. In the case of the IDB, external pressure and internal advocacy have proved the most important. But with the new replenishment and reorganization, the question of how the gender issue fits into the Bank's other goals and procedures has gained increasing importance.

Kardam identifies the efforts of women staff and other advocates for change, whom she labels "policy entrepreneurs," as a crucial element in institutions with a relatively high degree of independence and in which the new policy issue is at least moderately consistent with the institution's existing goals and procedures. External pressure from interest groups may also play an important role, but Kardam argues that "the extent of change will depend on the efforts of the policy advocates in demonstrating the fit between the new issue and organizational goals and procedures" (Kardam, 1993).

The nature of outside pressure on the IDB and other organizations has changed in recent years. With increasing urgency over the last decade, outside pressure from women's organizations on international institutions has called for "mainstreaming the gender perspective." This approach seeks to ensure that large, regular, or "mainstream" programs address the concerns of women as well as men, support the participation of both, and help promote women's empowerment. Reflecting this shift in strategy, in 1989 the IDB formally made women in development objectives one of its main focuses (IDB, 1989).[2] As the Bank moved toward greater emphasis on poverty reduction, the goal of gender equity was an easier fit with its other goals and procedures.

In 1991, the IDB developed an action plan for carrying out its WID policy designed to change fundamentally the way the IDB works in country programming, project development and analysis (IDB, 1991). The focus was on treating women's participation as an integral part of all IDB operations rather than as an isolated component. The action plan stressed the importance of addressing women in development issues at the beginning of the project cycle or, better yet, in the programming process before projects take shape.

[2] Although the IDB's policy is titled Women in Development and does not contain specific references to gender and development, analysis of the policy reveals that it does not target women in isolation from men, it specifically addresses issues of inequality between women and men and advocates for improving the position of women vis-ã-vis men as well as improving women's situation for their own sake and it is generally consistent with a gender and development framework.

Waiting until the final details of project preparation to try to strengthen women's participation, as had too often been the practice in the past, was acknowledged as ineffectual.

Obstacles to Policy Implementation at the IDB

To date, the IDB has made progress in its efforts to integrate women as participants and beneficiaries of its projects. There have been several well-designed projects that successfully incorporate gender concerns, but these are relatively few in number, and many projects still resort to the use of a standard "WID paragraph" in the project document. There is still a lack of true integration of gender concerns in social and economic programs, as well as of knowledge of how women can specifically contribute and benefit.

A variety of factors explain this situation, ranging from those at the personal level to the institutional to the macroeconomic. There are still many staff members who do not understand gender and development issues. Some, although they are well-intentioned, assume that any project in the social sector will benefit women and men equally. Others remain skeptical of the issues but pay lip-service to the WID objectives because it is expected of them. Very few demonstrate hostility or feel threatened by the issue. IDB staff tend to support the WID policy but may not apply it in practice when this means straying from the standard approach to project design in any given sector.

For the staff of development organizations such as the IDB, there are few incentives to take actions recommended in WID policy. In fact, IDB staff face formidable disincentives because of their already heavy workloads, pressure to approve operations quickly, and the administrative complexity of dealing with a cross-sectoral issue. In addition, there is a lack of specialized staff to deal with the issue. Little recognition is given for doing a good job in dealing with the issue, but there are no sanctions for not addressing it. Finally, there is a general lack of methods for analyzing social issues in project analysis.

Another main obstacle is inherent in the bureaucratic environment. The IDB, like many international development agencies, tends to work by replicating models. However, gender and development objectives require staff to change their way of approaching a project fundamentally since they require a much more in-depth knowledge of the beneficiaries. Greater involvement of beneficiaries in decision making at every stage of the project's life cycle is also necessary. Furthermore, research on gender issues that provides the groundwork for innovative project design has not received much support from the IDB.

Macroeconomic policies often have the greatest effects on the lives of men and women, but these policies are rarely evaluated for the different gender impact that they will have. It is both methodologically difficult and politically sensitive to carry out such evaluations. As the IDB increasingly grapples with sectoral reform, including legal and judicial and regional integration issues, greater attention needs to be paid to the impact of gender on these overarching policies.

IDB Progress in Policy Implementation

Despite these problems, progress has been made since the IDB WID policy was approved. In 1993, staff were interviewed for a report to the IDB's Programming Committee (IDB, 1993b). Those who were aware of the IDB's women in development action plan felt the institution had made progress in 1991 and 1992 toward carrying out its women in development policy. They cited greater staff awareness of the WID policy, approval of several technical cooperation projects focusing directly on women in development, increased funding to nongovernmental organizations working with women, close work with national women's bureaus in a number of countries, and increased attention to WID concerns in studies and programming exercises. Several large-scale investment projects also included specific measures to improve the quality of women's contributions to and benefits from projects (IDB, 1993c).

Interviewees felt that the borrowing countries were beginning to recognize the IDB as a resource for assistance in addressing women in development concerns. Many saw the IDB as positioned to be an active leader in women in development in Latin America and the Caribbean (IDB, 1993b).

The WID policy has received considerable high-level backing. IDB President Enrique V. Iglesias, who took office in 1989, immediately made clear his strong support for gender equity both inside the IDB and in its programs. This support was reinforced when Executive Vice-President Nancy Birdsall joined the Bank in 1993.

Funding for the WID program increased from one staff position and $60,000 for consulting services in 1991 to three staff positions and $400,000 for consulting in 1992. Resource levels dropped slightly in 1993 but have held steady since then. As a result, the prevalence of WID issues in programming increased, more people began approaching the WID staff for help, and WID staff were more involved in programming missions. More in-depth advising was possible for project teams, which led to an increase in the WID components and attention to gender issues in projects.

To track progress, the IDB's WID Unit evaluates how well the Bank's project teams analyze and address gender issues in project design. Since 1991, the first year for which statistics are available, the IDB's performance at this level has improved significantly. In 1991, only 6 percent of IDB loans both addressed gender issues in project analysis and included specific actions to improve women's participation as contributors or beneficiaries. By 1994, fully one-third of the loan projects did so. This progress is encouraging, but there is still a long way to go.

New Directions

Recognizing the importance of dialogue on gender equity with different organizations in the member countries, in 1994 the IDB, ECLAC, and UNIFEM co-sponsored a regional forum on Women in the Americas: Participation and Development in Guadalajara, Mexico. The forum focused on four priorities for women in the region: women's political participation, women's economic contribution, the role of women in sustainable development, and the gender dimensions of social reform. Forum participants presented a series of recommendations to the IDB and its member countries, including:

- Gender equity should be part of social reform. Social reform and poverty reduction programs should specifically address the role of women and include concrete measures to strengthen that role.
- IDB programs should help strengthen women's effective exercise of their citizenship, especially their participation in public decision making locally and nationally.
- The IDB should improve its technical and operational capacity to promote and implement its Operating Policy on Women in Development and Agenda for Action, as well as to strengthen the participation of the region's women and men in formulating and executing the IDB's policies and programs.

The full set of recommendations from the forum, the *Agenda for Action,* are included in the annex of this book.

Institutional Changes at the IDB: Replenishment and Reorganization

As Latin America and the Caribbean's development bank, the IDB faces a challenge mirroring that of the region itself—to create a new development strategy based on economic, social, and political modernization. A new replenishment of the IDB's capital (the eighth) was agreed upon at the 1994 Board of Governors Meeting. The IDB's resources increased from $40 billion to $100 billion, boosting support for economic, social, and political reform in Latin America and the Caribbean.

IDB lending will now emphasize such nontraditional areas as social sector reform, modernization of the state (including judicial and regulatory reform), and development of environmental institutions. Lending will also reflect the Bank's growing commitment to improving social conditions and reducing inequities. Fifty percent of IDB operations and 40 percent of its resources are to be directed to social programs, including strengthening women's contribution to development and enhancing their benefits from IDB-financed programs and projects. The IDB is to "monitor this area closely to ensure that the particular needs of women are taken into account in program and project design" (IDB, 1994).

By emphasizing women's roles in the social sectors and poverty reduction efforts, IDB projects should help poor women improve their productivity and incomes. Better education, health, nutrition, and child care services designed to respond specifically to women's needs can decrease the burden of domestic work that usually falls on women's shoulders within the household. But to be successful and equitable, these development programs will have to target and strengthen women's decision-making role.

The IDB has also reorganized its operational structure to respond more efficiently to this new social mandate. Its lending and technical cooperation activities are now grouped along subregional lines. Each department is responsible for programming, project analysis, execution and evaluation—functions centralized units formerly carried out. New central departments have been created to deal with quality enhancement, policy and strategic planning, private sector development, and regional integration and local capacity building in social development. As part of the reorganization, a new Women in Development Unit was created in the Department of Social Programs and Sustainable Development, a central department.

Creating the WID unit has given gender equity greater visibility within the organization. However, the unit has been placed within a central rather than an operational department, and the operational units it will be advising tend to resist "outsider influences." Also worrisome is the possibility that, with the creation of a separate WID unit, IDB staff will feel less commitment to addressing WID concerns themselves. When the post of women in development advisor was created at the World Bank, many saw it as "window dressing that functioned as a good public relations ploy to show that the bank was doing something" (Kardam, 1990).

The challenge is to ensure that the WID Unit is able to play an active and acknowledged role in planning, in programming, and in project design and execution. If its work remains only at the level of policy formulation, goal setting and applied research, past experience of similar units within the IDB shows that it will soon become irrelevant to actual operations and will have little real impact. The unit's effectiveness will depend, in part, on how visible the support it receives from management is.

In addition to increasing the IDB's resources, the 1994 Replenishment Agreement produced a realignment of the IDB's shareholders. Borrowing and donor countries now hold equal shares in the IDB, although the Latin American and Caribbean countries as a regional block still hold 50 percent of the voting shares. The shares held by the non-regional member countries of Europe and Japan have increased. Traditionally, the Europeans and the Canadians have been the strongest supporters of gender equity in IDB programs.

One crucial recommendation from the Forum on Women in the Americas, which coincided with the Bank's Board of Governors meeting in 1994, was that the IDB form an external advisory council to support and review the implementation of the IDB's WID policy. This council would formalize the WID Unit's outreach activities and help to make IDB WID activities more responsive to the needs, priorities and objectives of the member countries.

In 1995, the IDB established the Advisory Council for Women in Development to provide substantive, technical guidance to the Bank on issues affecting women's participation in the programs it finances; to advise the IDB on processes and strategies for strengthening the WID program; and to help improve the network among and communications with interested groups in the Bank's member countries. Council members were selected to represent a mix of NGOs, academic institutions and private individuals with extensive experience in women in development, gender and development, or related fields who understood the institutional workings of agencies such as the IDB. The council includes 11 members from the Bank's borrowing countries and three from the non-borrowing (donor) member countries. Three men and 11 women are on the council. Governor General of Barbados Dame Nita Barrow chairs the council, which also includes a congresswoman from another country. The Bank invited these initial members to join the Advisory Council, but the council itself will decide on its functions and the terms and conditions of membership, including selection of future members.

How could these changes at the IDB help integrate women's issues into mainstream Bank policies and programs? As the IDB places a higher premium on "innovative" programs in new sectors, it is easier to incorporate non-traditional elements in project design. And the IDB's recent, significant reorganization placed many staff members in new, unfamiliar positions in which they must coordinate more, create new allies and learn new skills. But as they are "innovating," they must do so with fewer resources and under the same time constraints they faced before.

Gender and Staff Advocacy within the IDB

Staff advocates are an essential ingredient in bringing about change in development programs (Kardam, 1993). Limited research on this topic at different types of development organizations has found that the presence of a large number of women among the staff has a positive effect on gender policies. But even the presence of more women among the staff may not be enough because "too many other variables, such as organizational structure and culture, intervene to inhibit women's capacity to express oppositional interests.... Incentives to defend the interests of a particular social group pale in comparison to incentives to conform to organizational systems of motivation and reward.... As a minority in most organizations, women have the least interest in challenging dominant agency practices because of the precariousness of individual career positions" (Goetz, 1992).

A dearth of women in positions of authority prevails at almost all development institutions, posing a serious barrier to the work of development (Jahan, 1991). If development institutions are serious about addressing inequitable gender relations through their projects, their first step must be to apply the same standards within their own organization. As Parker and Friedman (1993) point out, "...understanding the structure of gender relations within institutions and throughout the development hierarchy is central to developing the institutional capacity to benefit from the broader changes in society....a desire and an effort to change unequal gender relations within the institution are essential to developing institutions that are sustainable and adaptable to change."

In the past 10 years, the international development agencies—including the UN, World Bank, IMF, and the IDB—have begun to address the issue of women's representation among professional staff seriously. They have taken decisive measures to increase women's representation in senior decision-making positions, but it is too soon to tell how this will affect their policies and operations.

Although women are half of all employees at the IDB, they are only about 30 percent of professional staff and are less than 10 percent of those in management positions. Despite their low levels, these figures compare favorably with the World Bank and other international financial institutions. In the IDB's field offices, however, only 7 percent of professionals are women, and most of them are local employees—a less prestigious position.

In late 1994, the IDB formed a Task Force on Women in response to requests by the Bank's Professional Women's Network. IDB Executive Vice-President Birdsall chairs the task force, which is analyzing gender differences in hiring, pay, assignments, advancement, work quality, and other areas. When it completes its work, the task force will recommend measures to improve the situation of women employees and increase their representation at the IDB.

So far, female staff at the IDB have been extremely supportive of gender equity, and many of them serve as energetic policy advocates within their areas of work. Thus, the IDB's experience has not borne out Goetz's fears that women will not be willing to promote gender equity. In its new executive vice-president, the IDB has also gained a powerful supporter for the agenda of gender equity, both inside the Bank and in its programs.

Although a larger share of women at the IDB are active policy advocates, support for gender equity is not confined to one gender. A significant number of men at the IDB have helped to move the Bank forward on this issue, starting with President Iglesias. Given the greater numbers of men among professional staff and decision makers in the Bank, they are crucial allies. In addition, the different perspectives they bring to the issue are extremely valuable. In most cases, these alliances with men were voluntary. They usually arose from a common interest in improving the quality of Bank projects, especially from the point of view of the beneficiaries, and reducing poverty and inequality. A very strong basic ethic of fairness among IDB staff has helped to bring more allies to the cause of gender equity. Men must play an active role if fervent advocacy of this issue is to be fully legitimized or even rewarded within the institution.

New Strategies for Promoting Gender Equity

Developing New Methods for Working with Development Lenders

The increasingly pronounced shift in development resources from bilateral donors and UN grant-based assistance to lending through the multilateral development banks (MDBs) calls for a different strategy on gender issues. The incentives for change, approaches, and pivotal moments for lobbying the MDBs differ from those with which the supporters of gender equity are familiar. Intergovernmental agencies such as the UN agencies and the MDBs must deal with a greater number of actors than do bilateral donors. In some ways, this makes these agencies an easier target for outside pressure, since there are many points of entry. But these actors the agencies deal with hold different views and represent different interests. Outside pressure must address this diversity and be extremely strong and well organized.

A "moderately independent" institution like the IDB, for example, needs not only staff advocacy demonstrating gender equity's consistency with the institution's goals and procedures but also external pressure to push the institution forward (Kardam, 1993). Constituencies in the borrowing countries need development and support to influence their national governments, which in large measure determine the lending program financed by the MDBs. Receptive donor countries must also look for ways to use scarcer grant resources as leverage over the huge development programs of the MDBs.

Borrowing countries often have quite a lot of leverage in negotiating with the banks because banks are lending institutions. Critical moments for negotiating through bank boards are during replenishment of capital, setting of annual programs and targets, and policy review.

The IDB is learning the importance of such leverage. Concessional funding and donor coordination can be used to create incentives for change in the project and program design process (e.g., to make it more participatory, increase the involvement of women), project components, rules of operation, type of executing agencies (e.g., more NGOs), and applied research (including gender-disaggregated evaluation of program outcomes) in the MDBs.

Uniting Agendas for Equity, Efficiency and Empowerment

Policy statements on gender and development, or women in development, differ in terms of focus and rationale. But they share three areas of emphasis: equity, efficiency, and empowerment.

One lesson of the past two decades is that with more equal rights and benefits for women come different responsibilities. There is a need for a convergence of the two poles of "efficiency" (stressing women's contributions to development) and "equity" (stressing women's benefits from development). If women have nothing to offer to development, their fight for equality will be futile. But even for those who would dress women as mere "instruments" of development to be brought into activities to improve the efficiency of those efforts, an equity perspective must be incorporated. If women do not reap the benefits of their efforts, they will have little incentive to participate.

The goal of empowerment becomes increasingly important in the context of the renewed emphasis on participatory models of development programming and on improving accountability in project execution. The chapter on women and politics addresses these points more fully.

The IDB's WID policy has been based largely on an efficiency argument, although it also contains strong language in support of equity. With the Eighth Replenishment goals of social equity and the IDB's expanded focus on project execution and governance, the Bank has begun to realize the importance of women's empowerment as a goal of its WID activities. The challenge now is to meld these three approaches into successful programs and policies.

A "Modified Mainstreaming" Approach

Although large, mainstream programs continue to represent the principal vehicle for promoting gender equity in development cooperation, there is still a need for separate programs for women in strategic areas. This by no means implies a need to repeat the small, marginal income-generating women's projects of the past. The IDB is learning that women-targeted approaches, or gender-targeted approaches (separate programs or components of projects designed to address specific women's issues or to directly attack unequal gender relations where participants would be both male and female), can have big payoffs, especially when undertaken as part of an overall mainstreaming strategy.

The IDB should evaluate overall programs that will benefit both women and men and address their needs, instead of just integrating women by making small adjustments to existing types of projects. A programmatic approach would try to push the overall mix of projects in directions that promote gender equity, ensuring that there are strategic women-targeted interventions and that, taken as a whole, the program addresses women's needs. Then project-level changes should focus on those projects with greatest potential impact for women. Excessive project focus and failure to prioritize give rise to the "WID paragraph"—a bureaucratic defense mechanism.

Giving Women Leadership and Voices in Decision Making

The IDB's reorganization was intended to decentralize decision making and strengthen the Bank's dialogue with all levels of government and society in its member countries. The IDB's country offices will now have more responsibility for monitoring the impact of projects and will be more involved in strategic studies and loan preparation. This change should help facilitate the influence of external pressure groups by giving the constituency for women's concerns more channels through which to be heard. The IDB WID Unit has learned that the constituency must be strong and well organized if it is to obtain shifts in overall programming and policies.

Conclusions

It is important to recognize that the last 20 years have seen progress on gender equity in development assistance at all levels: a move to the gender and development approach, policy and political mandate, legal and regulatory context, institutional changes at the development agencies, and greater use of these new tools in program implementation. However, the impact of these changes on the lives of women, especially poor women, have been at best very limited, and at worst uneven or even negative, especially as they are tempered by the negative effects of economic crisis and adjustment.

This is an opportune moment for bringing gender equity objectives into the mainstream because of renewed emphasis on the participatory design of programs; openness and accountability of the international agencies; new concern on part of some of these agencies with their image in the aid-recipient countries; and, in most countries in Latin America, the end of long-standing dictatorships, which has created political openings for women.

Although there are new opportunities, the challenges to addressing gender issues continue to be great and there are many obstacles to be overcome. To be effective, an action agenda for change in international development assistance must be created that includes unity and strength among the forces for change, greater sophistication of analysis and action, and strengthening of advocacy skills and capacity in the developing countries.

To improve results, gender issues must be strengthened in policy design and evaluation of overall program impact. At the IDB, much more focus has been placed on the processes in between these two levels of action, particularly on project design and project evaluation. This has contributed to the emergence of a standard "WID menu" of project and policy recommendations, which has had a limited impact. Measures taken must lead to real change in the lives of people. It is no longer acceptable to settle for "window dressing."

Over the past two decades, gender equity has been defined and established as critical to mainstream development. It is vital to the social and economic well-being of women and men and nations. In the aftermath of the Beijing conference, the new challenge is for the diverse and active advocates of gender equity to join forces and present a more united front of action for change.

Bibliography

Abramovitz, Janet M., and Roberta Nichols. 1992. Women and Biodiversity: Ancient Reality, Modern Imperative. *Development* 2: 85-90.

Acosta Vargas, Gladys. 1993. *El Movimiento de Mujeres Latinoamericano y la Construcción de la Democracia.* Instituto Latinoamericano de Servicios Legales Alternativos (ILSA). En edición. Bogota, Colombia.

Allen, David, and Diane Wall. 1987. Behavior of Women State Supreme Court Justices: Are They Tokens or Outsiders? *The Justice System Journal* 21(2).

Alvarez, Sonia. 1990. *Engendering Democracy in Brazil. Women's Movements in Transition Politics.* Princeton, New Jersey: Princeton University Press.

______. 1994. The (Trans)formation of Feminism(s) and Gender Politics in Democratizing Brazil. In *The Women's Movement in Latin America: Participation and Democracy.* See Jaquette, 1994.

Amalric, Franck. 1994. Finiteness, Infinity and Responsibility: The Population-Environmental Debate. In *Feminist Perspectives on Sustainable Development.* See Harcourt, 1994.

Anderson, Joan, and Denise Dimon. 1994. Economic Integration and the Mexican Male/Female Wage Differential. Presented at the XVIII International Congress, LASA, Atlanta.

Antrobus, Peggy, with Barbara Rogers. 1988. *Hanover Street: An Experiment to Train Women in Welding and Carpentry.* New York: SEEDS.

Anderson, A.B., and E.S. Anderson. 1983. *People and the Palm Forest: Biology and Utilization of Babassu Palms in Maranhao, Brazil.* Gainesville, Florida: Department of Botany, University of Florida.

Anderson-Manley, Beverly. 1994. Women and democracy: strengthening women's roles in the democratic process in the anglophone Caribbean region. Prepared for "Women in The Americas: Participation and Development" Regional Forum, April 5-7 1994, Guadalajara, Mexico, IDB-ECLAC-UNIFEM.

Anderson, Jeanine. 1989. Women's Community Service and Child Welfare in Urban Peru. In *Women, Work and Child Welfare in the Third World.* See Leslie and Paolisso, 1989.

______. 1990. Mujeres y Municipios. In *Estrategias de Desarrollo: Intentando Cambiar la Vida,* ed. Patricia Portocarrero. Lima: Ed. Flora Tristán.

______. 1991. *Intereses o Justicia: ¿A Dónde Va la Discusión Sobre la Mujer y el Desarrollo?* Lima: Red Entre Mujeres.

Aranda, J., and C. Botey. 1992. Las reformas al Artículo 27 y las mujeres en el campo. *El Cotidiano* 8(49).

Aranda, Ximena. 1982. *La Mujer Campesina.* Santiago: Grupo de Investigaciones Agrarias.

Arizpe, Lourdes. 1988. La participación de la mujer en el empleo y el desarrollo rural en América Latina y el Caribe: trabajo de síntesis. In *Las Mujeres en El Campo,* ed. J.

Aranda. Mexico City: Universidad Autónoma Benito Juárez de Oaxaca.

———.1990. El Feminismo y la Democratización Mundial. In *Debate Feminista. Amor y Democracia.* 1(1).

——— and Josefina Aranda. 1986. Women Workers in the Strawberry Agribusiness in Mexico. In *Women Work: Development and the Division of Labor by Gender,* eds. Eleanor Leacock and Helen I. Safa. South Hadley, Mass.: Bergin and Garvey Publishers.

——— Michael Paolisso, Margaret A. Lycette, Margarita Velázquez, and Fernanda Paz. 1994. Sustainable Development and Women: Management and Protection of the Environment. Prepared for "Women in the Americas: Participation and Development" Regional Forum, April 5-7, 1994, Guadalajara, Mexico, IDB-ECLAC-UNIFEM.

———. Fernanda Paz, and Margarita Velázquez. 1993. Estudio Sobre la Participación de la Mujer en el Subsector Forestal en México. A report done for the World Bank and the government of Mexico.

Arregui, Marivi, and Clara Baez. 1991. Free Trade Zones and Women Workers. In *Changing Perceptions: Writings on Gender and Development,* ed. Tina Wallace with Candida March. Oxford: Oxfam Publications.

Aspelin, P.L. 1975. External Articulation and Domestic Production: The Artifact Trade of the Maminde of Northwestern Mato Grosso, Brazil. Ph.D. Dissertation, Cornell University.

Astelarra, Judith. ed. 1990. *Participación Política de las Mujeres.* Madrid: Centro de Investigaciones Sociológicas y Siglo XXI.

Ayala-Marin, Alexandra. ed. 1991. *Mujer y Medio Ambiente en América Latina y el Caribe.* See Fundación NATURA and CEPLAES, 1991.

Báez, Clara. 1993. Democracia y Movimientos de Mujeres: Hacia Una Redefinición de los Espacios Políticos. *Género y Sociedad.* 1(1, May-August).

Bakker, Isabel, ed. 1994. *The Strategic Silence: Gender and Economic Policy.* London: ZED Books and the North-South Institute.

Barbieri-Oliveira. 1991. Presencia Política de las Mujeres. *Cuaderno de Ciencias Sociales.* FLACSO.

Barrig, Maruja. 1992. Quejas y Contentamientos: Historia de una Política Social. Los Municipios y la Organización Femenina en la Ciudad de Lima. In *Políticas Sociales, Mujeres y Gobierno Local.* See Raczynski and Serrano, 1992b.

———. 1994a. The Difficult Equilibrium Between Bread and Roses: Women's Organizations and Democracy in Peru. In *The Women's Movement in Latin America: Participation and Democracy.* See Jaquette, 1994.

———. 1994b. Women, Collective Kitchens and the Crisis of the State in Peru. In *Emergences: Women's Struggles for Livelihood in Latin America.* See Friedman, 1994.

———, and Andy Wehkamp. eds. 1994. *Sin Morir en el Intento. Experiencias de Planificación de género en el desarrollo.* Lima: NOVIB.

Barrón, Ma. Antonieta. 1990. Integración de las mujeres en el mercado de trabajo de las hortalizas: causas y condiciones materiales. *Economía Informal* 180(Febuary): 13-23.

______.1994. Mexican Rural Women Wage Earners and Macro-economic Policies. In *The Strategic Silence: Gender and Economic Policy*. See Bakker, 1994.

Barros, Ricardo, Rosane Mendonça, and Louise Fox. 1990. Female Headed Households, Poverty, and the Welfare of Children in Brazil. Paper prepared for joint ICRW/Population Council project, "Family Structure, Female Headship and Maintenance of Families and Poverty."

Bell, Judith Kjellberg. 1992. Women, Environment and Urbanization in a Third World Context: A Guide to the Literature. *Women & Environment* 13(2).

Bellew, R., L. Raney, and K. Subbarao. 1992. Educating Girls. *Finance and Development* (March): 54-56.

Benería, Lourdes. 1991. Accounting for Women's Work: Assessing the Progress of Two Decades. Paper prepared for UNSRID, Meeting on Social Development Indicators, 8-11 April, Rabbat, Morocco.

______. 1992a. Accounting for Women's Work: The Progress of Two Decades. *World Development.* 20(11): 1447-1560.

______. 1992b. The Mexican Debt Crisis: Restructuring the Economy and the Household. In *Unequal Burden: Economic Crises, Persistent Poverty and Women's Work.* See Benería and Feldman, 1992.

______ and Shelley Feldman, eds. 1992. *Unequal Burden: Economic Crises, Persistent Poverty and Women's Work.* Ithaca, New York, and Boulder, Colo.: Cornell University and Westview Press.

______ and Breny Mendoza. 1994. Structural Adjustment and Social Emergency Funds: The Cases of Honduras, Nicaragua and Mexico. Paper prepared for UNRISD's project on Economic Restructuring and New Social Policies, Geneva.

______ and Marta Roldán. 1987. *The Crossroads of Class and Gender: Industrial Homework, Subcontracting, and Household Dynamics in Mexico City.* Chicago: University of Chicago Press.

Bennett, Lisa. 1979. The legal status of rural women: A review of those aspects of legal status which limit the economic participation of women in rural development. Rome: Food and Agriculture Organization (FAO), Institutions and Agrarian Reform Division.

Bennett, Lynn, and Mike Goldberg. 1993. *Providing Enterprise Development and Financial Services to Women: A Decade of Bank Experience in Asia.* World Bank Technical Paper No. 236, Asia Technical Department Series. The World Bank.

Berenbach, Shari, and Diego Guzmán. 1992. *The Solidarity Group Experience Worldwide.* Monograph Series No. 7. Acción International.

Berger, Marguerite, and Mayra Buvinić. eds. 1989. *Women's Ventures: Assistance to the Informal Sector in Latin America.* West Hartford, Conn. Kumarian Press, Inc.

______ Virginia DeLancey, and Amy Mellencamp. 1984. *Bridging the Gender Gap in Agricultural Extension.* Washington, D.C.: International Center For Research on Women (ICRW).

Berryman, Phillip. 1994. The Coming of Age of Evangelical Protestantism. *NACLA Report on the Americas* 27(6, May-June): 6-10.

BID (Banco Interamericano de Desarrollo). 1987. Política Operativa sobre la Mujer en el Desarrollo. Washington D.C.

______. 1990. La Mujer Trabajadora en América Latina. Washington D.C.

______. 1993. Mujer y Desarrollo. Aplicación del Plan de Acción 1991-1992. Washington D.C.

______. 1994. Hacia una Estrategia del Banco Interamericano de Desarrollo (BID) para el Fortalecimiento de la Sociedad Civil. Prepared for IDB conference, September 12-14, 1994, Washington D.C.

______ and PNUD (Programa de las Naciones Unidas Para el Desarrollo). 1993. *Reforma Social y Pobreza: Hacia una Agenda Integrada de Desarrollo.* (Versión Preliminar). Enero.

Blumberg, Rae. 1985. A Walk on the WID Side: Summary of Field Research on Women and Development in the Dominican Republic and Guatemala. U.S. Agency for International Development, Washington D.C. Mimeo.

Bonder, Gloria. 1983. El Estudio de la Política Desde la Perspectiva de las Mujeres. *Revista Internacional de Ciencias Sociales.* 35(4).

Bourque, Susan C. 1989. Gender and the State: Perspectives from Latin America. In *Women, The State and Development,* eds. Sue Ellen Charlton, Jana Everett, and Kathleen Staudt. Albany, N.Y.: State University of New York Press.

Bonilla, Elssy. 1990. La Mujer Trabajadora en América Latina. In *Progreso Económico y Social en América Latina 1990.* Washington, D.C.: Inter-American Development Bank.

______. 1991. La Mujer Latinoamericana en los 90: Recurso Determinante del Crecimiento con Equidad. UNIFEM, Bogota. Mimeo.

______. 1993. Género, Familia y Sociedad: la Aproximación Sociológica. Ponencia Central para el Congreso Latinoamericano de Sociología. Mesa Mujer y Sociedad. Junio, Caracas.

______, Hernán Jaramillo, Cecilia Lopez, et al. 1991. La Mujer en las Políticas del Estado. Propuesta de un marco de referencia. Grupo ad-hoc de apoyo a la Consejería Presidencial para la Mujer, la Familia y la Juventud, Bogota. Mimeo.

Braidotti, Rosi, Ewa Charkiewicz, Sabine Häusler, et al. 1994. *Women, the Environment and Sustainable Development: Towards a Theoretical Synthesis.* London: ZED Books Ltd. and INSTRAW.

Brenes, Ada Julia, Ivania Lovo, Olga Luz Restrepo et al. 1991. *La Mujer Nicaragüense en los Años 80.* Managua, Nicaragua: Ediciones Nicarao.

Brouwers, Ria. 1993. Review of the Integration of Gender Concerns in the Work of the DAC. Theme 1 of the Assessment of WID Policies and Programs of DAC Members. Prepared for the Operations Review Unit of the Directorate General for International Co-operation of the Netherlands, Institute of Social Studies International Services, The Hague, Netherlands. Mimeo.

Bruce, Judith. 1989. *Fundamental Elements of the Quality of Care: A Simple Framework.* Program Division Working Papers No. 1. D.C.: The Population Council, Washington.

______ and Cynthia B. Lloyd. Forthcoming. Beyond Female Headship: Family Research and Policy Issues for the 1990s. In *Intrahousehold Resource Allocation: Policy Issues and Research Methods*, eds. L. Haddad, J. Hoddinott, H. Alderman, et al. Baltimore: The Johns Hopkins University Press.

Brydon, Lynne, and Sylvia Chant. 1989. *Women in The Third World. Gender Issues in Rural and Urban Areas.* New Brunswick, N.J.: Rutgers University Press.

Bulatao, R.A., and R.D. Lee. 1983. *Determinants of Fertility in Developing Countries.* Vol. 1. New York: Academic Press.

Bustillo, Ines. 1993. Latin America and the Caribbean. In *Women's Education in Developing Countries: Barriers, Benefits, and Policies*, eds. E. King and M. Hill. Baltimore: The Johns Hopkins University Press.

Buvinić, Mayra. 1986. Projects for Women in the Third World: Explaining Their Misbehavior. *World Development* 24(5): 653-664.

______. 1990. Women and Poverty in Latin America and the Caribbean: A Primer for Policy Makers. Draft report prepared for the Inter-American Development Bank. Washington D.C.

______. 1994. Women's Situation in Latin America and the Caribbean: Recent Trends and Implications for Public Policy. Paper prepared for Latin American Program Working Papers, The Woodrow Wilson Center, Washington, D.C.

______. Forthcoming. Promoting Employment Among the Urban Poor in Latin America and the Caribbean: A Gender Analysis. ILO Working Paper prepared for the Employment and Development Department, International Labour Office, Geneva, Switzerland.

______. and Marguerite Berger. 1990. Sex Differences in Access to a Small Enterprise Development Fund in Peru. *World Development* 18 (5)695-705.

______, Marguerite Berger, and Cecilia Jaramillo. 1989. Impact of a Credit Project for Women and Men Microentrepreneurs in Quito, Ecuador. In *Women's Ventures: Assistance to the Informal Sector in Latin America.* See Berger and Buvinić, 1989.

______ and G.R. Gupta. 1994. Targeting Poor Woman-Headed Households and Woman-Maintained Families in Developing Countries: Views on a Policy Dilemma. Prepared for the Population Council/ICRW Joint Program on Female Headship and Poverty in Developing Countries.

______ and Margaret A. Lycette. 1988. Women, Poverty, and Development in the Third World. In *Strengthening the Poor: What Have We Learned?*, ed. John P. Lewis. Washington, D.C.: Overseas Development Council.

______ and Margaret A. Lycette. 1994 Women's Contributions to Economic Growth in Latin America and the Caribbean: Facts, Experience, and Options. Prepared for "Women in the Americas: Participation and Development" Regional Forum, April 5-7, 1994, Guadalajara, Mexico, IDB-ECLAC-UNIFEM.

______, Margaret A. Lycette, and William McGreevey, eds. 1983. *Women and Poverty in the Third World.* Baltimore: The Johns Hopkins University Press.

and Rekha Mehra. 1990. *Women in Agriculture: What Development Can Do.* Washington, D.C.: ICRW.

______, Juan Pablo Valenzuela, Temistocles Molina, et al. 1992. The Fortunes of Adolescent Mothers and Their Children: The Transmission of Poverty in Santiago, Chile. *Population and Development Review* 18(2).

Buxell, Ingrid. 1991. Informe de la Misión de Evaluación (Versión Preliminar). La Paz, Bolivia.

Bystydzienski, Jill M. 1992. *Women Transforming Politics: Worldwide Strategies for Empowerment.* Bloomington: Indiana University Press.

Caldeira, Teresa. 1987. Mujeres, Cotidianeidad y Política. In *Participación, Ciudadanía e Identidad. Las Mujeres en los Movimientos Sociales Latinoamericanos,* ed. Elizabeth Jelin. Geneva: Instituto de Investigaciones de las Naciones Unidas para el Desarrollo Social (UNRISD).

CAM (Centro Acción de la Mujer). 1989. *Guía Legal de los Derechos de la Mujer.* Quito: CAM.

Campaña, P. 1982. La Mujer, Trabajo y Subordinación en la Sierra Central del Perú. In *Debate Sobre La Mujer en América Latina y el Caribe II,* ed. M. León. Bogota: Siglo XXI Editores.

Campbell, Tim. 1989. Urban Development in the Third World: Environmental Dilemmas and the Urban Poor. In *Environment and the Poor: Strategies for a Common Agenda,* ed. H. Jeffrey Leonard. Washington, D.C.: Overseas Development Council.

Cañadell, Rosa M. 1993. Chilean Women's Organizations: Their Potential for Change. *Latin American Perspectives* 79 20(4): 43-60.

Cardero, Maria Elena. 1993. The Impact of NAFTA on Female Employment in Mexico. Paper written at the Graduate and University Centre, CUNY on 'Mexican and American Women in Perspective.'

Carillo, Roxanna. 1992. *Battered Dreams: Violence Against Women as An Obstacle to Development.* New York: UNIFEM.

Caro, Dr. Deborah, and Amē Stormer, eds. 1994. *Gender Research Guide for the Agriculture, Environment and Natural Resource Sectors: A Tool for Selecting Methods.* Washington, D.C.: GENESYS and USAID.

Cartaya, Vanessa. 1994. The Gender Issue in Social Policy: The Latin American and Caribbean Case. Prepared for "Women in the Americas: Participation and Development Regional Forum, April 5-7, 1994, Guadalajara, Mexico, IDB-ECLAC-UNIFEM.

Carte, Insko, and Tobias Loeb, eds. 1989. *A Dream Compels Us: Voices of Salvadorean Women.* New Americas Press.

Casanovas, Roberto, et al. 1985. Los Trabajadores por Cuenta Propia el Mercado de Trabajo: El Caso de la Cuidad de La Paz. In *El Sector Informal Urbano en los Paises Andinos.* Quito and Guayaquil: Instituto Latinoamericano de Investigaciones Sociales (ILDIS) and Centro de Formación y Empleo para el Sector Informal Urbano (CEPESIU).

Castaños, María Ines de, et al., 1988. Evaluación de las Acciones y Proyectos del Fondo Social de Emergencia. La Paz, Bolivia.

CEAAL, Red de Educación Popular entre Mujeres. 1991. *Las Mujeres Creando Nuevos Saberes.* Quito: CEAAL.

CEDAW (Comitē para la Eliminación de la Discriminación Contra la Mujer). 1993. *Examen de los Informes Presentados por los Estados Partes de Conformidad con el Artículo 18 de la Convención.* Colombia: United Nations.

CELADE. 1992. Demographic Bulletin, Latin America, Economically Active Population 1970-2000. Santiago, Chile.

CENDOC (Centro de Documentación sobre la Mujer). 1991. *Violencia Doméstica.* Paquete Informativo. Lima, Perú.

Centro de Desarrollo Social y Asuntos Humanitarios, Centro Internacional de Viena, Naciones Unidas. 1989. La Mujer y la Política. División Para el Adelanto de la Mujer. *La Mujer 2000* (2).

CENTRO (Instituto de Estudios Socioeconómicos y Fomento del Desarrollo). 1993. Mujeres Peruanas: La Mitad de la Población del Perú a Comienzos de los 90. Prepared for the Canadian International Development Agency.

CEPAL (Comisión Económica para América Latina y el Caribe). 1989. *Proyectos Productivos de Mujeres en América Latina: Una Compilación.* Santiago: CEPAL.

______. 1990. *Transformación Productiva con Equidad: La Tarea Prioritaria del Desarrollo de América Latina y el Caribe en los Años Noventa,* LC/G.1601-P. Santiago: United Nations.

______. 1993. *Cambios en el Perfil de las Familias: La Experiencia Regional.* Santiago: United Nations.

______. 1994a. *Las Mujeres en América Latina y el Caribe en los Años Noventa: Elementos de Diagnóstico y Propuestas.* Santiago: CEPAL.

______. 1994b. Las Mujeres en América Latina y el Caribe en los Años 90. *Notas Sobre la Economía y el Desarrollo.* (562-563, septiembre).

______. 1994c. *Mujeres en el Proceso de Toma de Decisiones en América Latina y el Caribe.* Santiago: CEPAL.

______ and CELADE. 1993. Población, equidad y trasformación productiva. Presented at Conferencia Regional Latinoamericana y del Caribe Sobre Población y Desarrollo, United Nations, April 4-May 4, 1993, Mexico City.

CEPLAES (Centro de Planificación y Estudios Sociales) and ACDI (Agencia Canadiense para el Desarrollo Internacional), eds. 1992. *Entre los Límites y las Rupturas: Las Mujeres Ecuatorianas en la Década del 80.* Quito: CEPLAES.

Cernea, Michael. ed. 1985. *Putting People First: Sociological Variables in Rural Development.* Washington D.C.: World Bank and Oxford University Press.

Chambers, Robert. 1983. *Rural Development: Putting the First Last.* London: Longman.

Chaney, Elsa. 1977. *Supermadre: Women in Politics in Latin America.* Austin: University of Texas Press, Institute of Latin American Studies.

Chant, Sylvia. 1985. Single-Parent Families: Choice or Constraint? The Formation of Female Headed Households in Mexican Shanty Towns. *Development and Change.* 16(4): 635-656.

Chase, Vasantha. 1988. Farming Systems Research in the Eastern Caribbean: an Attempt at Analyzing Intra-Household Dynamics. In *Gender Issues in Farming Systems Research and Extension,* eds. Susan V. Poats, Marianne Schmink, and Anita Spring. Boulder, Colo.: Westview Press.

Chauhan, Sumi Krishna, et al. 1983. *Who Puts the Water in Taps? Community Participation in Third World Drinking Water, Sanitation and Health.* London: Earthscan.

Chinchilla, Norma Stoltz. 1994. Feminism, Revolution, and Democratic Transitions in Nicaragua. In *The Women's Movement in Latin America: Participation and Democracy.* See Jaquette, 1994.

Chuchryk, Patricia M. 1989. Feminist Anti-Authoritarian Politics: The Role of Women's Organizations in the Chilean Transition to Democracy. *The Women's Movement in Latin America: Feminism and the Transition to Democracy.* See Jaquette, 1989.

______. 1994. From Dictatorship to Democracy: The Women's Movement in Chile. In *The Women's Movement in Latin America: Participation and Democracy*. See Jaquette, 1994.

CIDA (Canadian International Development Agency). 1993. *Women and Fisheries Development.* Ottawa: CIDA

CIM (Comisión Interamericana de Mujeres). 1989a. *Plan de Acción de CIM: Participación Plena e Igualitaria de la Mujer en la Política.* Washington, D.C.: Organization of American States.

______. 1989b. Comité Directivo 1988/90, Doc, 16/89, 02/10/89.

CINTERFOR (Inter-American Center for Research and Documentation for Vocational Training) and ILO (International Labour Organization). 1991. *Vocational Training on the Threshold of the 1990s.* PHREE Background Paper Series, PHREE/91/35. The World Bank, Washington, D.C.

CLACSO. Biblioteca de Ciencias Sociales (autores varios). 1989. *Centralización/ Descentralización del Estado y Actores Territoriales.* Buenos Aires: CLASCO.

CLADEM (Latinamerican Committee for the Defense of Women's Rights). 1994. *Women: Watched and Punished. Regional Seminar "Criminal Law and Women in Latin America and the Caribbean."* Lima: CLADEM.

Clavel G., Carlos, et al. 1987. *Estudio Sobre Programas Especiales de Empleo: Tomo I.* Santiago: Departamento de Economía, Universidad de Chile.

Coady International Institute. 1991. *A Handbook for Social/Gender Analysis.* Hull, Canada: Canadian International Development Agency.

Collinson, Helen. ed. 1990. *Women and Revolution in Nicaragua.* London: Zed Books Ltd.

Commonwealth Secretariat. 1983. *Ladies in Limbo.* London: Commonwealth Secretariat.

______. 1985. *Ladies in Limbo Revisited: The Fate of Women's Bureaux, Case Studies from the Caribbean.* London: Commonwealth Secretariat.

______. 1990. *Engendering Adjustment for the 1990s.* London: Commonwealth Secretariat.

Conde, Eulalia D. de. 1986. Evaluation and High-Level Employment: The Case of Latin American Women. *Bulletin of the OAS* 8(1-2).

Consejería para la Juventud, la Mujer y la Familia (Colombia). 1993. *Política Integral Para las Mujeres.* Bogota.

Corcoran-Nantes, Yvonne. 1993. Female Consciousness or Feminist Consciousness?: Women's Consciousness Raising in Community-Based Struggles in Brazil. In *Viva: Women and Popular Protest in Latin America.* See Radcliffe and Westwood, 1993.

Cornia, G.A. 1984. A Survey of Cross-sectional and Time Series Literature on Factors Affecting Child Welfare. In *The Impact of World Recession on Children,* eds. Richard Jolly and G.A. Cornia. Oxford: Pergamon Press.

______, Richard Jolly, and Frances Stewart eds. 1987. *Adjustment with a Human Face.* Oxford: Clarendon Press.

Corvalán, Graziella, Mirtha Rivarola, and Olga Zaiza. 1987. Discriminación de la Mujer en la Actualidad en el Paraguay. Encuentro Nacional de Mujeres "Por nuestra igualdad ante la ley" Paraguay.

Cruz, Maria Concepcion, Carrie A. Meyer, Robert Repetto, et al. 1992. *Population Growth, Poverty, and Environmental Stress: Frontier Migration in the Philippines and Costa Rica.* Washington, D.C.: World Resources Institute.

Cuvi, María. 1992. Políticas Agrarias y Papel de la Mujer en el Desarrollo del Ecuador. In *Entre los Límites y los Rupturas: Las Mujeres Ecuatorianas en la Década del 80.* See CEPLAES and ACDI, 1992.

Dasso, Mónica, and Daniel Barraza. 1993. Proyecto Descentralización, Desarrollo Social y Pobreza: Presentación Resultados Focus Group (La Pintana). *Centro de Estudios Públicos* (2).

DeGraff, Deborah, and Richard E. Bilsborrow. 1993. Female-Headed Households: Family Welfare in Rural Ecuador. *Journal of Population Economics.* 6(4, November), 317-336.

De Vanzo, Julie, and John Haaga. 1991. *Women in Development: Issues for Latin America and the Caribbean Region.* Latin America and the Caribbean Technical Department. Regional Studies Program, Report No 2. The World Bank, Washington D.C.

De la O-Martinez, María Eugenia. 1984. *Innovación Tecnológica y Clase Obrera.* Mexico City: Universidad Autónoma Metropolitana-Iztapalapa.

De Barbieri, Teresita. 1992. *Las Mujeres y la Crisis en América Latina.* Lima: Red Entre Mujeres.

Deere, Carmen Diana. 1987. The Latin American Reform Experience. In *Rural Women and State Policy: Feminist Perspectives on Latin American Agricultural Development,* eds. Carmen Diana Deere and Magdalena León. Boulder, Colo.: Westview Press.

______ and Magdalena León de Leal. 1982. *Women in Andean Agriculture: Peasant Production and Rural Wage Employment in Colombia and Peru.* Geneva: International Labour Office.

Dennis, Frances, and Dulce Castleton. 1989. *Case Studies in Population and Natural Resources.* Costa Rica: International Union for the Conservation of Nature.

DeWalt, Billie R., and Kathleen M. DeWalt. 1982. *Cropping Systems in Pespire, Southern Honduras.* Report No. 1. Farming Systems Research in Southern Honduras. University of Kentucky.

DeWalt, Billie R., Susan C. Stonich, and Sarah L. Hamilton. 1993. Honduras: Population, inequality, and resource destruction. In *Population and Land Use in Developing Countries, Report of a Workshop,* eds. Carole L. Jolly and Barbara Boyle Torrey. Washington, D.C.: National Academy Press.

Dimenstein, Gilberto. 1994. Little Girls of the Night. *NACLA: Report on the Americas* 27(6, May-June): 29-34.

Dixon-Mueller, Ruth. 1985. *Women's Work in Third World Agriculture: Concepts and Indicators.* Women, Work, and Development No. 9. International Labour Office and United Fund for Population Activities, Geneva.

______. 1993. *Population Policy & Women's Rights.* Westport, Conn: Praeger.

______ and Richard Anker. 1988. *Assessing Women's Economic Contribution to Development.* Training in Population, Human Resources and Development Planning, World Development Programme, Paper No. 6. International Labor Organization, Geneva.

Donaldson, Jamie K. 1992. Finding Common Ground: Redefining Women's Work in Colombia. *Grassroots Development* (16)1: 2-11.

Dufour, K.L. 1984. The Time and Energy Expenditure of Indigenous Women Horticulturalists in the Northwest Amazon. *American Journal of Physical Anthropology* 65: 37-46.

Dwyer, Daisy, and Judith Bruce. 1988. *A Home Divided: Women and Income in the Third World.* Stanford: Stanford University Press.

ECLAC (Economic Commission for Latin America and the Caribbean). 1976. The Participation of Women in the Development of Latin America. (ESA/CSDHA/AC, 10/4), rev. 1. Santiago, Chile.

______. 1990. *Growth with Equity.* Santiago: ECLAC.

______. 1991. *Sustainable Development: Changing Production Patterns, Social Equity and the Environment.* Santiago: ECLAC.

______. 1994. Achieving Social Justice, Equity and Development: A Review of the Status of Women of the Caribbean Subregion in Preparation for the Fourth World Conference on Women, 1995. DDR/9, 20 September 1994.

ECOGEN: Thomas-Slayter, Barbara, and Diane Rocheleau. 1993. *Essential Connections: Linking Gender to Effective Natural Resource Management and Sustainable Development.* Worcester, Mass.: Clark University.

ECOGEN: Thomas-Slayter, Barbara, A.L. Esser and M. D. Shields. 1993. *Tools of Gender Analysis: A Guide to Field Methods for Bringing Gender Into Sustainable Resource Management.* Worcester, Mass.: Clark University.

Ellis, Pat, ed. 1986. *Women of the Caribbean.* London: Zed Books.

Elson, Diane, ed. 1991. *Male Bias in the Development Process.* Manchester: Manchester University Press.

______. 1994. Micro, Meso, Macro: Gender and Economic Analysis in the Context of Policy Reform. In *The Strategic Silence: Gender and Economic Policy.* See Bakker, 1994.

Encuentro Nacional de Mujeres (autoras varias). 1987. *Por Nuestra Igualdad Ante la Ley.* Paraguay.

Engle, Carole. 1982. Aquacultural Technology: a Tool for Women in Development. *Women in Natural Resources: An International Perspective.* Moscow, Idaho: Forest, Wildlife and Range Experiment Station, University of Idaho.

Engle, Patrice. 1993. Influences of Mothers' and Fathers' Income on Children's Nutritional Status in Guatemala. *Social Science and Medicine* 37(11): 1303-1312.

Erickson, B., ed. 1990. *Call to Action: Handbook for Ecology, Peace and Justice.* San Francisco: Sierra Club Books.

Escandón, Carmen Ramos. 1994. Women's Movements, Feminism, and Mexican Politics. In *The Women's Movement in Latin America: Participation and Democracy.* See Jaquette, 1994.

Escobar de Pabon, Silvia. 1993. Mujer y Trabajo en Unidades Económicas de Pequeña Dimensión. Reflexiones Sobre la Situación Actual y Perspectivas. Presented at Seminario de Apoyo Técnico sobre Aspectos de Género y Desarrollo, ACDI-Contrapartes, Cochabamba, Bolivia.

Espinal, Rosario, and Sherri Grasmuck. 1993. Gender, Households and Informal Entrepreneurship in the Dominican Republic. Paper presented at the Sixth International Forum, Association for Women in Development, October 21-24, 1993, Washington, D.C.

Estremadoyro, Julieta. 1992. *Violencia en la Pareja.* Comisarías de Mujeres en el Peru. Cuadernos de Trabajo. Lima: Ediciones Flora Tristán.

Facio, Alda. 1992. *Cuando el Género Sueña Cambios Trae.* Metodología para el análisis de género del fenómeno legal. ILANUD. Proyecto Mujer y Justicia Penal. San José de Costa Rica.

______. 1993. Origen de la Legislación Protectora del Trabajo Femenino. In *Sobre Patriarcas, Jerarcas, Patrones y Otros Varones* (una mirada género sensitiva del Derecho). Programa Mujer, Justicia y Género. ILANUD. San José de Costa Rica.

______, Beverly Anderson-Manley, Ligia Delgadillo, and Gladys Acosta. 1994. Women and Democracy: Consolidating the Role of Women in the Democratic Process in Latin America and the Caribbean. Prepared for "Women in the Americas: Participation and Development Regional Forum, April 5-7, 1994, Guadalajara, Mexico, IDB-ECLAC-UNIFEM.

FAO (Food and Agriculture Organization). 1987. *Mujeres Campesinas en América Latina: Desarrollo Rural, Acceso a la Tierra, Migraciones, y Legislación.* Santiago: FAO.

______. 1988. *Women in Fishing Communities.* Rome: FAO.

FEDESARROLLO and Instituto SER de Investigación. 1992. Indicadores Sociales. Mujer. *Coyuntura Social,* (6).

Feijoó, María del Carmen. 1992. Mujer y Políticas Sociales a Nivel Local: El Caso Argentino. In *Políticas Sociales, Mujeres y Gobierno Local.* See Raczynski and Serrano, 1992b.

and Elizabeth Jelin. 1987. Women from Low-Income Sectors: Economic Recession and Democratization of Politics in Argentina. In *The Invisible Adjustment. Poor Women and Economic Crisis,* ed. UNICEF. Santiago: Alfabeta Editores.

and Marcela María Alejandra Nari. 1994. Women and Democracy in Argentina. In *The Women's Movement in Latin America: Participation and Democracy.* See Jaquette, 1994.

Feldman, Shelley. 1992. Crises, Poverty and Gender Inequality: Current Themes and Issues. In *Unequal Burden: Economic Crises, Persistent Poverty and Women's Work.* See Benería and Feldman, 1992.

Fempress. 1993. *mujer/fempress.* (144).

Ferguson, Anne, and Marina Flores. 1987. *Resource Guide, Women in Agriculture: Guatemala.* East Lansing: Michigan State University, Center for International Programs.

Fernandez, Maria. 1988. Technological Domains of Women in Mixed Farming Systems of Andean Peasant Communities. In *Gender Issues in Farming Systems Research and Extension.* See Chase, 1988.

Finnida (Finnish International Development Agency). 1993. *Looking at Gender And Forestry: Operational Issues for Project Planners, Implementors and Administrators.* Helsinki: Finnida.

Fisher, Jo. 1993. Women and Democracy: For Home and Country. *NACLA Report on the Americas* 27 (1): 30-36).

Fisseh, Yacoob. 1985. *The Contribution of Small-Scale Forest-Based Processing Enterprises to Rural Non-Farm Employment and Income in Selected Developing Countries.* Rome: FAO.

FLACSO (Facultad Latinoamericana de Ciencias Sociales). 1992-1993. *Mujeres Latinoamericanas en Cifras: Argentina, Brasil, Chile, Colombia, Costa Rica, Ecuador, El Salvador, Guatemala, Perú, Uruguay*, eds. Teresa Valdés and Enrique Gomáriz. Instituto de la Mujer, Ministerio de Asuntos Sociales de España and FLACSO.

Flora, Cornelia Butler, and Blas Santos. 1986. Women in Farming Systems in Latin America. In *Women and Change in Latin America.* See Nash and Safa, 1986.

Flórez, Carmen Elisa. 1992. Generación de Ingresos y Estructura Familiar. Las Mujeres Urbanas Jefes de Hogar. Banco Interamericano de Desarrollo and gobierno de Colombia. Misión de Cooperación Técnica de Corta Duración ATN/SF-3837-CO. Bogota. Mimeo.

Floro, Maria. 1994. Work Intensity and Women's Time Use. In *Color, Class and Country: Experiences of Gender*, eds. G. Young and B. Dickenson. London: Zed Press.

Folbre, Nancy. 1991a. Women on Their Own: Global Patterns of Female Headship. Paper prepared for the Population Council-ICRW Seminar on the Determinants and Consequences of Female Headed Households. International Center for Research on Women, Washington, D.C.

______. 1991b. Mothers on Their Own: Policy Issues for Developing Countries. Paper prepared for the Population Council-ICRW Seminar on the Determinants and Consequences of Female Headed Households. International Center for Research on Women, Washington D.C.

______. 1994. *Who Pays for the Kids? Gender and the Structures of Constraint.* London and New York: Routledge.

Ford-Smith, Honor. 1989. *Ring Ding in a Tight Corner. A Case Study of Funding and Organizational Democracy in Sistren, 1977-88.* Toronto: ICAE.

Francke, Marfil. 1988. Nature and Evolution of Economic Crisis in Peru: 1975-1987. Prepared for the Conference on Weathering Economic Crises: Women's Responses to the Recession in Latin America and the Caribbean, Racine, Wis., June 15-17.

______. 1992. Women and the Labor Market in Lima, Peru: Weathering Economic Crises. Paper prepared for the ICRW Seminar on Weathering Economic Crises: Women's Responses to Recession in Latin America, August 11, Washington, D.C.

French, Joan. 1994. Hitting Where it Hurts Most: Jamaican Women's Livelihoods in Crisis. In *Mortaging Women's Lives: Feminist Critiques of Structural Adjustment*, ed. Pamela Sparr. London: Zed Books Ltd.

Friedman, John. 1994. *Emergences: Women's Struggles for Livelihood in Latin America.* Los Angeles: UCLA, Latin American Studies Program.

Frohmann, Alicia, and Teresa Valdés. 1993. *Democracy in the Country and in the Home.* Serie Estudios Sociales No.33. The Women's Movement in Chile. FLACSO, Santiago, Chile.

Fundación NATURA and CEPLAES. 1991. *Mujer y Medio Ambiente en America Latina y el Caribe.* Quito: Fundación NATURA and CEPLAES.

García, Ana Isabel, and Enrique Gomáriz. 1989. Tendencias Estructurales. Información Estadística por Sexo. In *Mujeres Centroamericanas ante la Crisis, la Guerra y el Proceso de Paz.* Tomo I. San José: FLACSO, CSUCA, and Universidad para la Paz.

García Guadilla, María-Pilar. 1993. *Ecología*: Women, Environment and Politics in Venezuela. In *Viva: Women and Popular Protest in Latin America.* See Radcliffe and Westwood, 1993.

Gaskin-Reyes, Camille. 1992. The Changing Social and Economic Context of Caribbean Society. Implications for Women and Areas of Bank Support. In *Women and Development: Caribbean Perspectives.* Washington D.C.: Inter-American Development Bank.

GENESYS. 1992a. *Gender and Agriculture and Natural Resource Management in Latin America and the Caribbean: An Overview of the Literature.* Washington, D.C.: The Futures Group.

______. 1992b. *Women and the Transition to Democracy in Latin America and the Caribbean: A Critical Review.* Washington, D.C.: USAID.

______. 1994. *Gender and Sustainable Development: A Training Manual.* Washington, D.C.: USAID.

Gliessman, Stephen R. 1990. Understanding the Basis of Sustainability for Agriculture in the Tropics: Experiences in Latin America. In *Sustainable Agricultural Systems,* Clive A. Edwards and others. Ankeny, Iowa: Soil and Water Conservation Society

Goetz, Anne Marie. 1992. Gender and Administration. *IDS Bulletin.* 23 (4): 6-17.

Goldschmidt-Clermont, Luisella. 1989. Valuing Domestic Activities. Paper submitted to the Second ECE/INSTRAW Joint Meeting on Statistics of Women, Geneva, November 13-16.

Gomez, Adriana, Lezak Shallat, Carmen Torres and Victor Toledo Liancaqueo. 1992. Amerindian and Black Women: 500 Years of Neglect. *Isis International/Women in Action* (2).

Gonzalez de la Rocha, Mercedes. 1986. Lo Público y lo Privado: El Grupo Doméstico Frente al Mercado de Trabajo Urbano. In *Cambio Regional: Mercado de Trabajo y Vida Obrera,* eds. Guillermo De la Peña and Agustín Escobar. Jalisco: Colegio de Jalisco.

Green, Cathy. 1994. *Poverty, Population and Environment: Does 'Synergism' Work for Women?* University of Sussex Discussion Paper 343 (May). Institute of Development Studies, Brighton.

Grosh, M. 1993. *Social Spending in Latin America. The Story of the 1980s.* World Bank Discussion Papers. Number 106. Washington, D.C.

Guzman, Maria Margarita, and Maria Clemencia Castro. 1992. From a Women's Guarantee Fund to a Bank for Microenterprise Process and Results. In *Women's Ventures: Assistance to the Informal Sector in Latin America.* See Berger and Buvinić, 1992.

Guzmán, Virginia. 1991. Desde los proyectos de desarrollo a la sociedad. In *Una Nueva Lectura: Género en el Desarrollo.* See Guzmán, Portocarrero, and Vargas, 1991.

______, Patricia Portocarrero and Virginia Vargas. eds. 1991. *Una Nueva Lectura: Género en el Desarrollo.* Lima: Entre Mujeres and Flora Tristán Ediciones.

Handa, Sudhanshu. 1994. Gender, Headship and Intrahousehold Resource Allocation. *World Development.* 22(10): 1535-1547.

Harcourt, Wendy, ed. 1994. *Feminist Perspectives on Sustainable Development.* London: Zed Books Ltd. and the Society for International Development.

Häusler, Sabine. 1994. Women and the Politics of Sustainable Development. In *Feminist Perspectives on Sustainable Development.* See Harcourt, 1994.

Heindl, Erin, Ema Budinich, and Ignacio Irrazaval. 1989. *Gasto Social Efectivo.* Santiago: ODEPLAN.

Hernández, Teresita, and Clara Murguialday. 1992. *Mujeres Indígenas Ayer y Hoy. Aportes Para la Discusión desde una Perspectiva de Género.* Madrid: Talasa Ediciones.

Hirschmann, David. 1993. *Democracy and Gender: A Practical Guide to USAID Programs.* Special Study No. 9. GENESYS and USAID, Washington, D.C.

Howden, Sarah. 1993. The Impact of the 1980s Economic Crisis on Latin American and Caribbean Women: Assessment from a Gender Perspective. Mimeo.

Huffman, Sandra L., et al. 1990. *Prevention of Maternal Malnutrition through a Community Kitchen in Peru.* Maternal Nutrition and Health Care Program. Research Report Series No 7. International Center for Research on Women, Washington, D.C.

IBGE (Instituto Brasilero de Geografía y Estadística). 1990. *Pesquisa Nacional por Amostragem a Domicilio.* Brasilia: IBGE.

ICAE (International Council for Adult Education, Women's Program). 1989. *The Moon Also Has Her Own Light: The Struggle to Build a Women's Consiousness Among Nicaraguan Farmworkers.* Toronto:ICAE.

ICRW (International Center for Research on Women). 1992. Weathering Economic Crises: Women's Responses to the Recession in Latin America and the Caribbean. Selected Country Studies. Washington, D.C.

IDB (Inter-American Development Bank). 1987. "Operating Policy on Women in Development." Document No. GP-114-3. Washington, D.C.

______. 1989. "Report on the Seventh General Increase in the Resources of the Inter-American Development Bank." Document No. AB-1378. Washington, D.C.

______. 1990. *Economic and Social Progress in Latin America 1990.* Washington, D.C.: The Johns Hopkins University Press.

______. 1991. "Strategy and Plan of Action for Implementing Bank Policy." Document No. GP-114-5. Washington, D.C.

______. 1992. Women's Participation in Latin America: Background paper presented at Women in Development: Caribbean Perspectives, June 30, IDB, Washington, D.C.

______. 1993a. *Economic and Social Progress in Latin America 1993.* Washington, D.C.: The Johns Hopkins University Press.

______. 1993b. The Current Status of IDB Activities in Women in Development and Recommendations for the Future: A Report to the Programming Committee. Washington, D.C. Mimeo.

______. 1993c. Women in Development: Implementation of the Action Plan, 1991-1992. Washington, D.C. Mimeo.

______. 1994. "Report on the Eighth General Increase in the Resources of the Inter-American Development Bank." Document No. AB-1704. Washington, D.C.

______. 1995a. *Gender/Women in Development Guide for Technical Training and Vocational Education.* Draft.

______. 1995b. Minutes of the Third Meeting of the Task Force on Women, April 18, 1995. Washington, D.C. Mimeo.

______ and the Government of Chile. 1993. Programa de Capacitación Laboral. Borrador del Informe de Evaluación Preliminar. Washington D.C.

______ and UNDP (United Nations Development Program). 1990. *Our Own Agenda.* New York and Washington, D.C.: Latin American and Caribbean Commission on Development and Environment.

______. 1993. *Reforma Social y Pobreza. Hacia una Agenda Integrada de Desarrollo.* Washington D.C.: IDB and UNDP.

IFAD (International Fund for Agricultural Development). 1992. *Informe Sobre las Mujeres Rurales que Viven en Condiciones de Pobreza.* Rome: IFAD.

IICA (Instituto Interamericano de Cooperación para la Agricultura). 1994. *Productoras de Alimentos: Políticas Agrícolas Frente a las Mujeres Productoras de Alimentos en América Latina y el Caribe.* San José: IICA.

INSTRAW. 1993. Women and Environment. *INSTRAW NEWS* 19.

IPPF (International Planned Parenthood Federation). 1993. Data translated into Spanish by *Profamilia.* 10 (22).

IPU (Inter-Parliamentary Union). 1992. *Women and Political Power.* Series Reports and Documents No. 19. Geneva.

Isis Internacional. 1990. *Violencia en Contra de la Mujer en América Latina y el Caribe. Información y Políticas.* Santiago: Isis Internacional.

______, Centro de Información y Documentación. 1993. Violencia en Contra de la Mujer. Boletín Bibliográfico. Documentos 2/93.

______, IULA, and CELCADEL. 1993. *El Espacio Posible: Mujeres en el Poder Local.* Ediciones de las Mujeres No. 19. Santiago de Chile.

IWHC (The International Women's Health Coalition). 1993. Women's declaration on population policies. New York.

Jackson, Cecile. 1993. Doing What Comes Naturally? Women and Environment in Development. *World Development* 21(12): 1947-1963.

Jacobson, Jodi L. 1992. *Gender Bias: Roadblock to Sustainable Development.* Worldwatch Paper 110. Washington, D.C.: Worldwatch Institute.

Jahan, Rounaq. 1991. Promoting Gender Awareness and Analysis in Development Bureaucracies. Paper presented at AWID forum in Washington, D.C., 1991. Cited in A. Rani Parker and Michelle Friedman, "Gender and Institutional Change in International Development." In *Women at the Center: Development Issues and Practices for the 1990s,* eds. Gay Young, Vidyamali Samarasinghe, and Ken Kusterer. West Hartford, Conn.: Kumarian Press, 1993.

______. 1995. *The Elusive Agenda: Mainstreaming Women in Development.* London: Zed Books.

Jaquette, Jane S., ed. 1989. *The Women's Movement in Latin America: Feminism and the Transition to Democracy.* Boston: Unwin Hymen.

______, ed. 1994. *The Women's Movement in Latin America: Participation and Democracy, Second Edition.* Boulder, Colo.: Westview Press.

Jarvis, L.S. 1986. *Livestock Development in Latin America.* Washington, D.C.: World Bank.

Jazairy, Idriss, Mohiuddin Alamgir, and Theresa Panuccio. 1992. *The State of World Rural Poverty: An Inquiry into Its Causes and Consequences.* New York: New York University Press and IFAD.

Jelin, Elizabeth, ed. 1990. *Women and Social Change in Latin America.* London: Zed Books.

______. 1992. *Ante, de, en, y: Mujeres, Derechos Humanos.* Lima: Red Entre Mujeres, Diãlogo Norte-Sur.

Joekes, Susan. 1987a. *Employment in Industrial Free Zones in the Dominican Republic: A Report with Recommendations for Improved Worker Services.* Washington, D.C.: International Center for Research on Women.

______. 1987b. Women's Work and Social Support for Childcare in the Third World. International Center for Research on Women, Washington D.C. Mimeo.

and Roxana Moayedi. 1987. *Women and Export Manufacturing: A Review of the Issues and AID Policy.* Washington, D.C.: International Center for Research on Women.

______, Noeleen Heyzer, Ruth Oniango'o, et al. 1993. *Gender, Environment and Population.* Geneva: U.N. Research Institute for Social Development.

Johnson, F. Catherine, and Beatrice Lorge Rogers. 1993. Children's Nutritional Status in Female-Headed Households in the Dominican Republic. *Social Science and Medicine* 37(11): 1293-1301.

Johnson, Kirsten, and Silvana Castillo. 1990. *Evaluation of the WID Initiative in CARE Guatemala's Agroforestry and Integrated Aquaculture Projects: 1988-1990.* Guatemala: CARE.

Jones, E. 1992. *Development Administration: Jamaican Adaptations.* Jamaica: Caricom Publishers.

Jusidman, C. 1988. Women and Labor in the Mexico City Metropolitan Area: Effects of the Economic Crisis. Prepared for the Conference on Weathering Economic Crises: Women's Responses to the Recession in Latin America and the Caribbean, Racine, Wis., June 15-17.

Kabeer, Naila. 1992. *From Fertility Reduction to Reproductive Choice: Gender Perspective on Family Planning.* Discussion Paper No. 299. Institute of Development Studies, Brighton, England.

______. 1994. *Reversed Realities: Gender Hierarchies in Development Thought.* London: Verso.

and Susan Joekes. 1991. Researching the Household: Methodological and Empirical Issues. *IDS Bulletin* 22(1): 1-4.

Kardam, Nüket. 1990. The Adaptability of International Development Agencies. The Response of the World Bank to Women in Development. In *Women, International Development, and Politics: The Bureaucratic Mire.* See Staudt, 1990.

______. 1993. Development Approaches and the Role of Policy Advocacy: The Case of the World Bank. *World Development.* 21 (11): 1773-1786.

Kelly, Petra. 1993. Feminicemos el Poder. *Mujeres en Acción.* (3).

Kennedy, Eileen. 1992. Effects of Gender of Head of Household on Women's and Children's Nutritional Status. Paper presented at the International Food Policy Research Institute Workshop on The Effects of Policies and Programs on Women, January 16, 1992.

King, Elizabeth. 1990. *Does Education Pay in the Labor Market? The Labor Force Participation, Occupation and Earnings of Peruvian Women.* Living Standards Measurement Study. Working Paper No. 67. The World Bank, Washington D.C.

Kirkwood, Julieta. 1986. *Ser Política en Chile: Las Feministas y los Partidos.* Santiago: FLACSO.

Koblinsky, Marge, Oona Campbell, and Siobán Harlow. 1993. More than Mothers. *Populi: The UNFPA Magazine* 20(3).

Koblinsky, Marge, Judith Timyan, and Jill Gay. 1993. *The Health of Women: A Global Perspective.* Boulder, Colo.: Westview Press.

Krawczyk, Miriam. 1993. Women in the region: Major changes. *CEPAL Review* (April): 7-13.

Kreye, Otto, Jurgen Heinrichs and Folker Frobel. 1987. *Export Processing Zones in Developing Countries: Results of a New Survey.* Multinational Enterprises Programme Working Paper No. 43. International Labour Office, Geneva.

Kusterer, Ken. 1993. Women-Oriented NGOs in Latin America. In *Women at the Center: Development Issues and Practices for the 1990s.* See Jahan, 1991.

______, Maria Regina Estrada de Batres, and Josefina Xuya Cuxil. 1981. *The Social Impact of Agribusiness: A Case Study of ALCOSA in Guatemala.* A.I.D. Evaluation Special Study No. 4. USAID, Washington, D.C.

Lafosse, Violeta. 1989. Los Comedores y la Promoción de la Mujer. In *La Mujer y los Comedores Populares*, eds. N. Galer and P. Núñez. Lima: SEPADE.

Lago, María Soledad. 1986. La Mujer Rural en el Modelo Neoliberal Chileno. In *La Mujer y la Política Agraria en América Latina*, eds. M. León de Leal and C.D. Deere. Bogota: Siglo XXI and Editores de Colombia.

Lago Cruz, M. 1990. ¿Qué Nos Dicen las Encuestas sobre Cómo Participa la Mujer en Política Hoy? In *¿Existe la vocación política de la mujer?.* Santiago: PARTICIPA.

Lara, Flores, and Sara María. 1988. El papel de la mujer en el campo: nuevas estrategias. In *Las Sociedades Rurales Hoy*, ed. Zepada. Zamora, Mexico: El Colegio de Michoacán and CONACYT.

Larguia, Isabel, and John Dumoulin. 1986. Women's Equality and the Cuban Revolution. In *Women and Change in Latin America.* See Nash and Safa, 1986.

Lazarte Rojas, J. 1991. *Mujeres y Problemas de Participación Política en Bolivia.* La Paz: Centro de Información y Desarrollo de la Mujer (CIDEM).

Leach, Melissa. 1991. Gender, Environment and Resources: Issues, Approaches and a West African Case Study. Paper presented at conference, SIDA Seminar on Gender and Environment, 15 October, Stockholm, Sweden.

Lechner, Norbert. 1990. De la Revolución a la Democracia. In *Debate Feminista: Amor Democracia.* 1 (1).

León, Magdalena. 1989. The Invisible Worker: Health Conditions of the Domestic Worker in Colombia. In *Mid-life and Older Women in Latin America and the Caribbean.* Washington, D.C.: AARDP and the Pan American Health Organization.

______. 1993. El Gênero en la Polîtica Pûblica de América Latina: Neutralidad y Distención. *Análisis Político* (20).

Leonard, H. Jeffrey. 1987. *Natural Resources and Economic Development in Central America.* London: International Institute for the Environment and Development.

Leslie, Joanne. 1989. Women's Work and Child Nutrition in the Third World. In *Women, Work and Child Welfare in the Third World.* See Leslie and Paolisso, 1989.

______ and Michael Paolisso. eds. 1989. *Women, Work and Child Welfare in the Third World.* Boulder, Colo.: Westview Press.

Little, Peter, and Michael Horowits, eds. 1987. *Lands at Risk in the Third World: Local Level Perspectives.* Boulder, Colo.: Westview Press.

Lloyd, Cynthia B. 1991. The Contribution of the World Fertility Surveys to an Understanding of the Relationship Between Women's Work and Fertility. *Studies in Family Planning* 22(3): 144-161.

______. 1993. What is the Family (and Who Does the Planning)? *Populi: The UNFPA Magazine* 20(4).

Lohmann, L. 1990. Whose common future? *The Ecologist* 20(3): 82-84.

Lopez, Cecilia, and Molly Pollack. 1992. La Incorporación de la Mujer en las Políticas de Desarrollo. In *Género, Mujer y Mercado de Trabajo en América Latina. Proceso y Dilemas.* See Lopez, Pollack, and Villarreal, 1992.

______, Molly Pollack, and Marcela Villarreal. eds. 1992. *Género, Mujer y Mercado de Trabajo en América Latina. Proceso y Dilemas.* Santiago: PREALC and OIT.

______ and Margarita Ronderos Torres. 1994. Reforma Social con Perspectiva de Género: Aportes para la Discusión. Prepared for "Women in the Americas: Participation and Development" Regional Forum, April 5-7, 1994, Guadalajara, Mexico, IDB-ECLAC-UNIFEM.

Louát, Frederich, Margareth Grosh, and Jacques van der Gaag. 1993. *Welfare Implications of Female Headship in Jamaican Households.* Living Standard Measurement Study. Working Paper No 96. The World Bank, Washington D.C.

Machado, Leda María Vieira. 1993. "We Learned to Think Politically": The Influence of the Catholic Church and the Feminist Movement on the Emergence of the Health Movement of the Jardim Nordeste Area in São Paulo, Brazil. In *Viva: Women and Popular Protest in Latin America.* See Radcliffe and Westwood, 1993.

Mann, Charles C. 1993. How many is too many? *The Atlantic Monthly* 271(2): 4767.

Mason, Karen O. 1984. *The Status of Women: A Review of Its Relationship to Fertility and Mortality.* New York: The Rockefeller Foundation.

Massiah, Joycelin. 1983. *Women as Heads of Households in the Caribbean: Family Structure and Feminine Status.* UNESCO.

______. 1989. Women's Lives and Livelihood: A View from the Commonwealth Caribbean. *World Development* (17)7. 965-977.

Mathurin Mair, Lucille. 1975. *The Rebel Woman in the West Indies.* Kingston: The Institute of Jamaica.

McKay, Lesley. 1993. Women's Contribution to Tourism in Negril. In *Women and Change in the Caribbean: A Pan-Caribbean Perspective,* ed. Janet Momsen. London: James Currey, Ltd.

Mehra, Rekha. 1993. Gender in Community Development and Resource Management. In *Women at the Center: Development Issues and Practices for the 1990s*. See Jahan, 1991.

Melo, Cándida. 1991. Contaminación Ambiental: Su Impacto en la cotidianidad de la Mujer. In *Mujer y Medio Ambiente en America Latina y El Caribe*. See Fundación NATURA and CEPLAES, 1991.

Meynen, Wicky, and Virginia Vargas. 1991. La Autonomía Como Estrategia para el Desarrollo Desde los Múltiples Intereses de las Mujeres (Apuntes para una Discusión). Mimeo.

Milicic, Neva, and Luz Eugenia Cereceda. 1992. *Resultados de una Encuesta de Opinión*. Serie Documentos de Estudios No. 2. *Mujer y Política*. Corporación PARTICIPA, Santiago, Chile.

Molyneux, Maxine. 1985. Mobilisation Without Emancipation? Women's Interests, the State, and Revolution in Nicaragua. *Feminist Studies* 11(2); 227-54.

Morley, Samuel A. 1994. Poverty and Distribution in Latin America: Evidence from the Past, Prospects for the Future. Social Agenda Policy Group, Inter-American Development Bank, Washington, D.C.

Moser, Caroline. 1987. *The Impact of Recession and Adjustment Policies at the Microlevel: Low Income Women and Their Households in Guayaquil, Ecuador*. UNICEF.

______. 1989. The Impact of Recession and Adjustment at the Microlevel: Low Income Women and their Households in Guayaquil, Ecuador. In *The Invisible Adjustment: Poor Women and the Economic Crisis*. New York: UNICEF.

______. 1993a. Adjustment from Below: Low-income Women, Time and the Triple Role in Guayaquil, Ecuador. In *Viva: Women and Popular Protest in Latin America*. See Radcliffe and Westwood, 1993.

______. 1993b. *Gender Planning and Development: Theory, Practice and Training*. London and New York: Routledge.

______. 1993c. Women, Gender and Urban Development. Challenges for the 1990s. Paper prepared for Final Workshop of Ford Foundation Research Project "Urban Research in the Developing World: Towards an Agenda for the 1990s." Cairo. Mimeo.

______, Alicia Herbert, and Roza Makonnen. 1993. *Urban Poverty in the Context of Structural Adjustment: Recent Evidence and Policy Response*. TWU Discussion Paper No 4. The World Bank, Washington D.C.

Murguialday, Clara. 1989. *Movimiento de Mujeres: Nuevo Sujeto Emergente en América Latina y el Caribe*. Cuadernos de Trabajo de HEGOA, No. 1. Spain.

Myers, Robert G. 1994. Toward a Program of Investment in Early Childhood Care and Development: A Review of Experience. Draft prepared for the Inter-American Development Bank, Washington, D.C.

Nash, June. 1983. *Implications of Technological Change for Household Level and Rural Development*. Working Paper #37. East Lansing Office of Women and Development, Michigan State University, East Lansing, Mich.

______ and Helen Safa. eds. 1986. *Women and Change in Latin America*. South Hadley, Mass.: Bergin and Garvey.

Navarro, Milagro. 1992. *La Mujer en los Hechos y en el Derecho*. Argentina: Editorial Advocatus.

O'Connell, Helen. 1994. *Women and the Family*. London: Zed Books Ltd.

Olivera, Mercedes, and Ana María Fernández. 1991. *Subordinación de Género en las Organizaciones Populares Nicaragüenses*. Cuadernos de Trabajo #2. Cenzontle, Managua.

Olivera, Mercedes, Malena De Montis, and Mark Meassick. 1990. *Mujeres: Panorámica de su Participación en Nicaragua*. Managua: Cenzontle, Colección Realidades.

Ortuzar, Carmen. 1992. Sowing Hope in Family Plots. In *The Power to Change*. India: Women's Feature Service.

Osmond, Marie Withers. 1993. Women's Status in Contemporary Cuba. In *The Women and International Development Annual. Volume 3*, eds. Rita Gallin, Anne Ferguson, Janice Harper. Boulder, Colo.: Westview Press.

Otero, María. 1989. *A Question of Impact: Solidarity Group Programs and Their Approach to Evaluation*. New York: Private Agencies Collaborating Together (PACT).

Østergaard, Lise. ed. 1992a *Gender and Development: A Practical Guide*. London: Routledge.

______. 1992b. Health. In *Gender and Development: A Practical Guide*. See Østergaard, 1992a.

Padoch, Christine, and Miguel Pinedo-Vasquez. 1991. Floodtime on the Ucayali. *Natural History* (May): 48-57.

Panayotou, Theodore. 1993. *Green Markets: The Economics of Sustainable Development*. San Francisco: International Center for Economic Growth.

Palacio, Germán. 1993. Sueños de Género Durante la Época de Esplendor y Decadencia del Derecho Laboral. In *Pluralismo Jurídico*. Bogota: Facultad de Derecho, Ciencias Políticas y Sociales, Universidad Nacional de Colombia.

PAHO (Pan American Health Organization). 1990. *Perfil Epidemiológico de la Salud de la Mujer en la Región de las Américas*. Washington D.C.: PAHO.

Paolisso, Michael, and Sally W. Yudelman. 1991. *Women, Poverty and the Environment in Latin America*. Washington, D.C.: ICRW.

Parker, A. Rani, and Michelle Friedman. 1993. Gender and Institutional Change in International Development. In *Women at the Center: Development Issues and Practices for the 1990s*. See Jahan, 1991.

Pateman, Carole. 1990. Feminismo y Democracia. In *Debate Feminista: Amor y Democracia* 1(1).

Peake, Linda. 1993. The Development and Role of Women's Political Organizations in Guyana. In *Women and Change in the Caribbean: A Pan-Caribbean Perspective*. See McKay, 1993.

Pearson, Ruth. 1993. Gender and New Technology in the Caribbean: New Work for Women? In *Women and Change in the Caribbean: A Pan-Caribbean Perspective*. See McKay, 1993.

Perelli, Carina. 1994. The Uses of Conservatism: Women's Democratic Politics in Uruguay. In *The Women's Movement in Latin America: Participation and Democracy*. See Jaquette, 1994.

Pérez-Alemán, Paola. 1990. *Organización, Identidad y Cambio: Las Campesinas en Nicaragua*. Managua: Centro de Investigación para la Promoción de los Derechos de la Mujer.

______. 1992. Economic Crisis and Women in Nicaragua. In *Unequal Burden: Economic Crises, Persistent Poverty, and Women's Work*. See Benería and Feldman, 1992.

Phillips, Lynne. 1987. Women, Development and the State in Rural Ecuador. In *Rural Women and State Policy: Feminist Perspectives in Latin American Agricultural Development*. See Deere and León de Leal, 1987.

Pitanguy, Jacqueline, and Solene Herculano. 1993. To Rio and Beyond: The Case of Brazil. INSTRAW NEWS 19:11-21.

Pollack, M.E. 1990. Mujer y Producción de Alimentos en América Latina y el Caribe. Work prepared at the request of the IDB for the 1990 IPES Report.

______. 1992. Los Grupos Vulnerables del Mercado de Trabajo: los Casos de Chile y Paraguay. In *Genero, Mujer y Mercado de Trabajo en América Latina. Procesos y Dilemas*. See Lopez, Pollack, and Villarreal, 1992.

______. 1993. Feminization of the Informal Sector in Latin America and the Caribbean? *Serie Mujer y Desarrollo*, No. 11, LC/L.731. ECLAC, Santiago, Chile.

Portugal, Ana María. 1986. ¿Qué es ser Feminista en América Latina? *Movimiento Feminista, Balance y Perspectivas*. Ediciones de las Mujeres No. 5. Isis Internacional, Santiago, Chile.

PREALC (Programa Regional del Empleo para América Latina y el Caribe). 1988. *Sector Informal: Funcionamiento y Políticas*. Santiago: PREALC, Oficina Internacional del Trabajo.

Presidencia del Consejo de Ministros, Consejo Nacional de Población. 1990. *Programa Nacional de Promoción de la Mujer (1990-1995)*. Lima, Peru.

PROFAMILIA and DHS. 1991. *Colombia: Encuesta de Prevalencia, Demografía y Salud. 1990*. Bogota: PROFAMILIA and DHS.

Psacharopoulos, George, and Zafiris Tzannatos. eds. 1992a. *Case Studies on Women's Employment and Pay in Latin America*. Washington, D.C.: The World Bank.

______. 1992b. *Women's Employment and Pay in Latin America: Overview and Methodology*. World Bank Regional and Sectoral Studies. The World Bank, Washington, D.C.

Psacharopoulos, George. et al. 1993. *Poverty and Income Distribution in Latin America: The Story of the 1980s*. LAC Technical Department Regional Studies Program, Report No. 27. The World Bank, Washington, D.C.

Quisumbing, Agnes R. 1993. Improving women's agricultural productivity as farmers and workers. The World Bank, Washington, D.C. Draft.

Raczynski, Dagmar, and Claudia Serrano. 1992a. Abriendo el debate: Descentralización del estado, mujeres y políticas sociales. In *Políticas Sociales, Mujeres y Gobierno Local*. See Raczynski and Serrano, 1992b.

Raczynski, Dagmar, and Claudia Serrano. eds. 1992b. *Políticas Sociales, Mujeres y Gobierno Local*. Santiago: CIEPLAN.

Radcliffe, Sarah. 1993. 'People Have to Rise Up - Like the Great Women Fighters': The State and Peasant Women in Peru. In *Viva: Women and Popular Protest in Latin America*. See Radcliffe and Westwood, 1993.

Radcliffe, Sarah A., and Sallie Westwood. eds. 1993. *Viva: Women and Popular Protest in Latin America*. London: Routledge.

Rakowski, Cathy. 1989. Gender, Family and Economy in a Planned, Industrial City: The Working and Lower Class Households of Ciudad Guayana. Michigan State University. Mimeo.

Ramírez, Socorro. 1988. Las Mujeres Resisten la Crisis Económica y Reclaman Participación. *Mujeres, Crisis y Movimiento. América Latina y el Caribe.* Ediciones de Mujeres No. 9. Isis Internacional, Santiago, Chile.

Ravallion, Martin. 1991. Reaching the Rural Poor Through Public Employment. *World Bank Research Observer* 6(2): 153-175.

Reichmann, Rebeca L. 1984. *Women's Participation in Progreso: A Microenterprise Credit Program Reaching the Smallest Businesses of the Poor in Lima, Peru.* Cambridge, Mass.: Acción Internacional and AITEC.

Repetto, Robert, and Thomas Holmes. 1983. The role of population in resource depletion. *Population and Development Review* 9(4): 609-632.

Restrepo, Darío. 1989. Nueva Fase de Acumulación del Capital, Reestructuración del Estado y Relocalización de los Procesos Productivos y de los Conflictos Sociales. In *La Reforma del Estado en América Latina.* Colombia: Fescol.

______. 1992. Neoliberalismo y Reestructuración Capitalista. In *Rompiendo la Corriente: Un Debate al Neoliberalismo.* Bogota: Centro de Estudios de Investigaciones Sociales.

Rigat-Pflaum, María (comp.). 1993. *Equiparación de la Mujer en Alemania.* Argentina: Fundación Friedrich Ebert.

Rivera Bustamante, Tirza, ed. 1991. *Las Juezas en Centroamérica y Panamá.* San José: Centro para la Administración de Justicia.

Rivera-Cira, Tirza. 1993. *Las Mujeres en los Parlamentos Latinoamericanos.* Valparaíso, Chile: Centro de Estudios y Asistencia Legislativa, Universidad Católica de Valparaíso.

Rodda, Annabel. prepared by. 1991. *Women and the Environment.* London: Zed Books Ltd.

Rodríguez, Marcela V. 1993. *Sobre la Constitucionalidad de la Cuota Mínima de Participación de Mujeres en los Partidos Políticos.* A.A.D.C. Boletin Informativo.

Rodríguez, Lilia. 1994. Barrio Women. Between the Urban and the Feminist Movement. *Latin American Perspectives* Issue 82, 21(3): 32-48.

Rojas, Mary Hill. 1994. Women and the Environment: Themes from a Literature Review. Presentation for the Gender and Environment Network Series, Development Strategies for Fragile Lands (DESFIL). USAID, Washington, D.C.

Roldán, Marta. 1988. Renegotiating the Marital Contract: Intrahousehold Patterns of Money Allocation and Women's Subordination among Domestic Outworkers in Mexico City. In *A Home Divided: Women and Income in the Third World*, eds. Daisy Dwyer and Judith Bruce. Stanford: Stanford University Press.

______. 1991 JIT Technological Innovation, Industrial Restructuring and Gender Relations. Paper presented at the Conference on Women Organizing in the Process of Industrialization, Institute of Social Studies, The Hague, April 15-26.

Rosales Villavicencio, Osvaldo. 1979. *La Mujer Chilena en la Fuerza de Trabajo: Participación, Empleo y Desempleo (1957-1977).* Santiago: Universidad de Chile.

Rosenhouse, Sandra. 1988. Identifying the Poor: Is Headship a Useful Concept? Prepared for Joint ICRW/Population Council Seminar I. Concepts and Classifications of Female-Headed Households: Implications and Applications for National Statistics. New York, December 12-14, 1988.

______. 1989. *Identifying the Poor: Is "Headship" a Useful Concept?* LSMS Working Paper Number 58. The World Bank, Washington, D.C.

Safa, Helen Icken. 1990. Women's Social Movements in Latin America. *Gender and Society* 4(3): 354-369.

______. 1993. The new woman worker: Does money equal power? *NACLA Report of the Americas* 17(1). 24-29.

______. 1994. *The Myth of the Male Breadwinner.* Boulder, Colo.: Westview Press.

______ and Peggy Antrobus. 1992. Women and the Economic Crisis in the Caribbean. In *Unequal Burden: Economic Crisis, Persistent Poverty and Women's Work.* See Benería and Feldman, 1992.

Saint Victor, Rosalind. 1986. Family Relations and Support Systems. In *Women of the Caribean.* See Ellis, 1992.

Santa Cruz, Adriana. 1986. Feminismo Latinoamericano: Los Retos Frente al Poder. *Movimiento Feminista, Balance y Perspectivas.* Ediciones de las Mujeres No.5. Isis Internacional, Santiago, Chile.

Schaffner, Gertrude, and Eleanor Kremen. 1990. *The Feminization of Poverty: Only in America?* New York: Praeger.

Schild, Verónica. 1994. Recasting Popular Movements. Gender and Political Learning in Neighborhood Organizations in Chile. *Latin American Perspectives* Issue 81, 21(2): 59-80.

Schirmer, Jennifer. 1993. The Seeking of Truth and the Gendering of Consciousness: the Comadres of El Salvador and the Conavigua Widows of Guatemala. In *Viva: Women and Popular Protest in Latin America.* See Radcliffe and Westwood, 1993.

Schkolnik, Mariana. 1992. Chile: Impacto del Gasto Social en los Hogares con Jefatura Femenina. In *Género, Mujer y Mercado de Trabajo en América Latina. Proceso y Dilemas.* See Lopez, Pollack and Villarreal, 1992.

Schmink, Marianne. 1984. *Administración Communitaria del Reciclamiento de Desechos: EL SIRDO.* New York: SEEDS.

______. 1990. Gender Factors in the Mayarema Project, Guatemala. Consulting report submitted to Tropical Resources for Development, Inc., USAID, and USAID/Guatemala. TRD, Inc., Gainesville, Florida.

Schuler, Margaret, ed. 1992. *Freedom from Violence. Women's Strategies from Around the World.* New York: UNIFEM.

Secretaría de Salud. 1992. Encuesta Nacional de Fecundidad. Secretaría de Salud de México, Mexico City.

Sefchovich, Sara. 1980. *América Latina: La Mujer en Lucha.* Mexico City: FEM.

Sen, Amaryta K. 1990. Gender and Cooperative Conflicts. In *Persistent Inequalities: Women and World Development,* ed. Irene Tinker. New York: Oxford University Press.

Sen, Gita. 1992. Women, Poverty and Population: Issues for the Concerned Environmentalist. Paper prepared for collaborative project of the International Social Sciences Association, the Social Science Research Council, and Development Alternatives with Women for a New Era (DAWN) on Rethinking Population and the Environment.

———. 1994. Women, Poverty and Population: Issues for the Concerned Environmentalist. In *Feminist Perspectives on Sustainable Development.* See Harcourt, 1994.

Serrano, Claudia. 1992. Estado, Mujer y Políticas Sociales en Chile. In *Políticas Sociales, Mujeres y Gobierno Local.* See Raczynski and Serrano, 1992.

Shiva, Vandana. 1988. *Staying Alive: Women, Ecology and Development.* London: Zed Books.

SIDA (Swedish International Development Authority). 1994. *Workshop on Gender and Water Resources Management: Lessons Learned and Strategies for the Future. Volumes 1 and 2.* Stockholm: SIDA.

Silva, María Angélica. 1992. Estudio Comparado de las Legislaciones Vigentes en Materia Civil, Penal y Laboral en Paises Seleccionados de América Latina. Documento CEPAL.

Singh, Susheela, and Deirdre Wulf. 1990. *Today's Adolescents, Tomorrow's Parents: A Portrait of the Americas.* New York: The Alan Guttmacher Institute.

Smyke, Patricia. 1991. *Women and Health.* London: Zed Books Ltd.

Society for International Development. 1993. *Development Connections.* 13(6). Solís, Vivienne and Marta Trejos. 1990. *Women and Sustainable Development in Central America.* San José: International Union for the Conservation of Nature and Regional Central American Office-Centro Feminista de Información y Acción.

Sollis, Peter and Charles MacDonald. 1994. *Guyana's Social Impact Amelioration Programme.* Women's Participation in Social Investment Funds, Inter-American Development Bank.

Sontheimer, Sally, ed. 1991. *Women and the Environment: A Reader. Crisis and Development in the Third World.* London: Earthscan Publications.

Standing, Guy. 1989. Global Feminization Through Flexible Labor. *World Development* 17(7): 1077-1095.

Staudt, Kathleen. ed. 1990. *Women, International Development and Politics: The Bureaucratic Mire.* Philadelphia: Temple University Press.

Steady, Filomina Chioma, ed. 1993. *Women and Children First: Environment, Poverty, and Sustainable Development.* Rochester, Vermont: Schenkman Books, Inc.

Stephen, Lynn. 1992. Women in Mexico's Popular Movements: Survival Strategies Against Ecological and Economic Impoverishment. *Latin America Perspectives* 72, 19(1): 73-96.

Summers, Lawrence. 1992. Investing in All the People. Educating Women in Developing Countries. Mimeo.

Tamayo, Giulia. 1989. *Las Garantías Constitucionales en una Estrategia para la Defensa de los Derechos de la Mujer.* Informativo No.1. CLADEM, Lima, Peru.

Tendler, Judith. 1982. *Turning Private Voluntary Organizations into Development Agencies: Questions for Evaluation.* A.I.D. Program Evaluation Paper No. 12. USAID, Washington, D.C.

Thomas, Duncan. 1990. Intra-Household Resource Allocation: An Inferential Approach. *The Journal of Human Resources* 25(1): 635-664.

Tiano, Susan. 1986. Maquiladoras in Mexico: Integration or Exploitation. Mimeo.

Tiefenhaler, J. 1992. Female Labor Force Participation and Wage Determination in Brazil, 1989. In *Case Studies on Women's Employment and Pay in Latin America.* See Psacharopoulos and Tzannatos, 1992a.

Tochman, V. 1989. Policies for the Heterogeneous Informal Sector in Latin America. *World Development* 17(7): 1067-1076.

Tornaria, Carmen. 1986. Las Mujeres y el Proyecto Democrático Uruguayo. *Movimiento Feminista, Balance y Perspectivas.* Ediciones de las Mujeres No.5. Isis Internacional, Santiago, Chile.

Torres-Rivas, Edilberto. 1989. *The Struggle for Democracy in Central America.* Latin American Perspective Series, No.6. Westview Press.

Tovar, Teresa. 1992. Estado, Pobladores y Pobladoras en Perú. *Políticas Sociales, Mujeres y Gobierno Local.* See Raczynski and Serrano, 1992.

UN (United Nations). 1991a. *The World's Women 1970-1990: Trends and Statistics.* Social Statistics and Indicators, Series K(8). United Nations, New York.

______. 1991b. *Women. Challenges to the Year 2000.* New York.

______. Forthcoming. The World's Women: Trends and Statistics. New York.

UNFPA (United Nations Population Fund). 1989. *State of the World Population Report.* New York.

UNICEF. 1987. *The Invisible Adjustment. Poor Women and Economic Crisis.* Santiago: Alfabeta Editores.

UNDP (United Nations Development Program). 1993. *Human Development Report.* New York: Oxford University Press.

USAID (United States Agency for International Development). 1982. "Women in Development." Policy Paper. USAID, Washington, D.C.

______. 1988. *Social cultural setting of small farm agriculture in the Eastern Caribbean. Annex F: Social Analysis.* CARDI FSR/D Project Paper (538-0099). Regional Development Office/Caribbean (RDO/C), Barbados.

Valdez, Carmen Teresa. 1994. Amor a Golpes: Un Problema de Salud Pública. *Revista Pandora. Diario El Nacional.* February 26, Caracas.

van Herpen, Dorien, and Jacqueline Ashby. 1991. *Gender Analysis in Agricultural Research.* Proceedings of an Internal Workshop, CIAT, Palmira, Colombia, 13-14 June 1991. Cali, Colombia: Centro Internacional de Agricultura Tropical (CIAT).

von Braun, Joachim, David Hotchkiss, and Maaren Immink. 1989. Nontraditional Export Crops in Guatemala: Effects on Production, Income, and Nutrition. IFPRI Research Report 73. International Food Policy Research Institute (IFPRI), Washington, D.C.

van den Oever, Pietronella. 1993. Women's Roles, Population Issues, Poverty, and Environmental Degradation. In *Women and Children First: Environment, Poverty, and Sustainable Development.* See Steady, 1993.

Vargas, Virginia. 1992. The Feminist Movement in Latin America: Between Hope and Disenchantment. *Development and Change* 23(3): 195-214.

Velázquez, Margarita. 1993. *Mujer y Medio Ambiente en América Latina y el Caribe: Propuestas para la Investigación*. Mexico City: LEAD.

Vial, Isabel, and Eugenia Muchnik. 1989. *Impacto del P.N.A.C. en Preescolares de Santiago*. Santiago: Departamento de Economía Agraria, Universidad Católica de Chile.

Vigier, María Elena. 1986. *El Impacto del PAIT en al Empleo y los Ingresos: Lima Metropolitana 1986*. Lima: Proyecto Planificación del Mercado Laboral, Organización Internacional del Trabajo.

———. 1988. Perú: El Impacto Social del PAIT. In *Empleos de Emergencia*. Santiago: PREALC and OIT.

Villarreal, Marcela. 1992. La Dimensión de Género en los Proyectos de Desarrollo Social. In *Género, Mujer y Mercado de Trabajo en América Latina. Proceso y Dilemas*. See Lopez, Pollack, and Villarreal. 1992.

Wainerman, Catalina H. 1992. *Improving the Accounting of Women Workers in Population Censuses: Lessons from Latin America Population and Labor Policies Programme Research*. Geneva: International Labor Organization.

——— and Zulma Recchini de Lates. 1981. *El Trabajo Femenino en el Banquillo de los Acusados*. Mexico City: Population Council and Terra Nova.

Ward, Kathryn. 1990. *Women Workers and Industrial Restructuring*. Ithaca: Cornell University. ILR Press.

Waring, Marilyn. 1989. *If Women Counted*. London: HarperCollins.

Warren, Sarah T. ed. 1992. *Gender and Environment: Lessons from Social Forestry and Natural Resource Management. A Source Book*. Toronto: Aga Khan Foundation Canada.

Watson, Judith, and Kathleen Drayton. 1990. *Report on Social Soundness and Gender Analysis of the Environmental and Coastal Resources (ENCORE) Project*. Washington, D.C.: The Futures Group.

Waylen, Georgina. 1992. Rethinking Women's Political Participation and Protest: Chile 1970-1990. *Political Studies* 40(2): 299-314.

White, Karen, Maria Otero, Margaret Lycette, et al. 1986. *Integrating Women into Development Programs: A Guide for Implementation for Latin America and the Caribbean*. Washington, D.C.: ICRW.

WHO (World Health Organization). 1994. *AIDS: Images of an Epidemic*. Geneva: WHO.

Wieringa, Saskia. 1994. Women's Interests and Empowerment: Gender Planning Reconsidered. *Development and Change* 25: 829-848.

Wiltshire, Rosina. 1993. Problems of Environmental Degradation and Poverty with Particular Emphasis on Women and Children of Island Nations. In *Women and Children First: Environment, Poverty, and Sustainable Development*. See Steady, 1993.

Wood, Charles H. 1989. Woman-Headed Households and Child Mortality in Brazil, 1960-1980. Draft presented at the joint ICRW/Population Council Seminar II: Consequences of Female Headship and Female Maintenance. Washington, D.C., February 27-28.

The World Bank. 1984. *World Development Report 1984*. New York: Oxford University Press.

______. 1992. Costa Rica: Women's Country Assessment. Human Resources Operations Division. Latin America and the Caribbean Regional Office. Washington D.C.

______. 1993a. Honduras: Women's Country Assessment. Country Department II. Human Resources Operations Division. Latin America and the Caribbean Regional Office. Washington D.C.

______. 1993b. *Human Resources in Latin America and the Caribbean. Priorities and Actions.* Washington D.C.: The World Bank.

______. 1993c. *World Development Report 1993.* New York: Oxford University Press.

______. 1993d. Venezuela: WID Report. Draft Version. Human Resources Operations Division. Latin America and the Caribbean Regional Office. Washington D.C.: The World Bank.

______. 1994. *Enhancing Women's Participation in Economic Development. A World Bank Policy Paper.* Washington D.C.: The World Bank.

______ and the Inter-American Development Bank. 1993. Meeting the Needs of Poor Urban Women in Social Investment Funds and Fund-like Programs in Latin America and the Caribbean. Paper prepared for the November 1993 Workshop on Social Investment Funds in Latin America: Meeting the Needs of Poor Urban Women. Organized by the World Bank's Urban Development Division and the Inter-American Development Bank's Women in Development Unit, Washington, D.C. Mimeo.

WRI (World Resources Institute). 1990. *World Resources 1990-1991.* New York: Oxford University Press.

______. 1992. *World Resources 1992-1993.* New York: Oxford University Press.

Wurgaft, José. 1988. Lecciones de los Programas de Empleo. Una Visión de Conjunto. In *Empleos de Emergencia.* See Vigier, 1988.

______. 1992. Los Fondos de Inversión Social y la Reestructuración Económica en América Latina. *Revista Internacional del Trabajo* 11(3): 291-301.

Young, Gay. 1990. Hierarchy and Class in Women's Organizations: A Case from Northern Mexico. In *Women, International Development and Politics: The Bureaucratic Mire.* See Staudt, 1990.

Yamada, Gustavo. 1992. Peru's Popular Kitchens (Comedores Populares). In *From Platitudes to Practice: Targeting Social Programs in Latin America,* ed. M. Grosh. Washington D.C.: The World Bank.

Yousesef, Nadia H., Mayra Buvinić and Ayse Kudat. 1979. *Women in Migration: A Third World Focus.* Washington, D.C.: ICRW.

Yudelman, Sally W. 1987. *Hopeful Openings. A Study of Five Women's Development Organizations in Latin America and the Caribbean.* West Hartford, Conn: Kumarian Press.

Yudelman, Montague. 1989. Sustainable and Equitable Development in Irrigated Environments. In *Environment and the Poor: Development Strategies for a Common Agenda.* See Campbell, 1989.

Zabin, Carol. 1992. Binational Labor Markets and the Segmentation by Gender. Paper presented at the XVII Congress, LASA, Los Angeles.

Zuckerman, Elaine. 1990. *Social Funds in Latin America: Where Do We Stand?* Washington, D.C.: Inter-American Development Bank.

Table 1: Life Expectancy

	1970-1975		1990-1995	
	Women	Men	Women	Men
Argentina	71	64	75	68
Bahamas	70	63	76	69
Barbados	72	67	78	73
Bolivia	49	45	64	59
Brazil	62	58	69	64
Chile	67	60	76	69
Colombia	63	60	72	66
Costa Rica	70	66	79	74
Cuba	73	69	78	74
Dominican Republic	62	58	70	65
Ecuador	60	57	69	65
El Salvador	61	57	69	64
Guadeloupe	71	65	78	71
Guatemala	55	53	67	62
Guyana	62	58	68	62
Haiti	50	47	58	55
Honduras	56	52	68	64
Jamaica	71	67	76	71
Martinique	72	66	79	73
Mexico	65	61	74	67
Nicaragua	57	54	69	65
Panama	68	65	75	71
Paraguay	68	64	70	65
Peru	57	54	67	63
Puerto Rico	76	69	78	72
Suriname	67	62	73	68
Trinidad and Tobago	68	63	74	69
Uruguay	72	66	76	69
Venezuela	69	64	74	67

Source: The World's Women 1995: Trends and Statistics. UN publication forthcoming.

Table 2: Reproductive Health Indicators

	Contraceptive use (%) among married women of reproductive age, 1990		% births attended by trained attendant, 1986-90	Maternal mortality ratio (per 100,000 live births), 1990	Fertility rate of women aged 15-19 (per 1,000), 1990
	Any Method	Modern Method			
Antigua and Barbuda	53[d]	50[d]	86	20[b]	-
Argentina	74	-	92	140	66
Bahamas	62	60	100	21	61
Barbados	55[d]	53[d]	98	27	53
Belize	47[d]	42[d,e]	87	36	-
Bolivia	30	12	29	600	83
Brazil	66	57	73	200	41
Chile	-	-	98	67	66
Colombia	66	55	51	200	71
Costa Rica	70	58	97	25	93
Cuba	70	67	100	32	82
Dominica	50[d]	48[c, d]	96	58[b]	-
Dominican Republic	56	52	44[f]	90	70
Ecuador	53	42	26	170	77
El Salvador	47	44	66	127	131
Grenada	54[d]	49[d, g]	81	142[b]	-
Guadeloupe	44[a, d]	31[a, d]	-	103[a]	36
Guatemala	23	19	23	200	123
Guyana	31[a, d]	28[a, d]	93	200[b]	61
Haiti	10[d]	9[d]	40	340	54
Honduras	41	33	63	117	100
Jamaica	67[d]	64[d]	88	115	87
Martinique	51[a, d]	38[a, d]	-	95	32
Mexico	53	45	45	60	88
Nicaragua	49	45	42	103	153
Panama	58[b, h]	54[b]	85	60	83
Paraguay	48	35	30	300	76
Peru	59	33	78	240	68
Puerto Rico	70[b]	62[b, c]	-	19	64
St. Kitts and Nevis	41[b, d]	37[b, d]	-	183[b]	-
St. Lucia	47[d]	46[d]	-	26[b]	-
St. Vincent and the Grenadines	58[d]	55[d, e]	-	13[b]	-
Suriname	-	-	91	65	62
Trinidad and Tobago	53[d]	44[d]	95	80	72
Uruguay	-	-	100	26	60
Venezuela	49[a]	38[a]	82	55	71

Source: The World's Women 1995: Trends and Statistics. UN publication forthcoming.

[a] Data refer to a year between 1975 and 1979.
[b] Data refer to a year between 1980 and 1984.
[c] Excluding vaginal barrier methods.
[d] Including women in visiting unions.
[e] Excluding vaginal barrier methods and male sterilization.
[f] In institutions.
[g] Excluding vaginal barrier methods and sterilization.
[h] Excluding abstinence, douche and folk methods.

Table 3: Literacy and Education, 1990

(by percentage and age)

	Illiterate, 15-24		Illiterate, 25+		Ratio of female to male enrolment (x100)	
	Women	Men	Women	Men	Second Level	Third Level
Argentina	2.7[d]	3.6[d]	7.5[d]	6.4[d]	107	88[b]
Bahamas				-	105	216
Barbados	-	-	-		88	110
Bolivia	8.3	3.7	36.6	15.8	85	-
Brazil	9.8	14.6	24.7	22.2	116[d]	110
Chile	1.3	1.8	7.6	6.7	106	80
Colombia	6.0	8.0	19.0	16.0	116	107
Costa Rica	2.4[d]	3.3[d]	10.1[d]	9.6[d]	101	-
Cuba	1.2[a]	1.9[a]	7.2[a, g]	5.8[a, g]	108	136
Dominica	-	-	-	-	117	83
Dominican Rep.	15.8[d]	18.9[d]	31.0[d]	29.1[d]	122[i]	-
Ecuador	4.0	3.0	19.0	12.0	101	64[b]
El Salvador	29.5[a, h]	27.1[a, h]	56.1[a, f]	44.5[a, f]	102	49
French Guiana	10.8[d]	6.9[d]	20.5[d]	20.4[d]	-	-
Guadeloupe	1.1[d]	1.9[d]	13.3d	14.8[d]	113	-
Guatemala	-	-	-	-	90	-
Guyana	-	-	-	-	104	75
Haiti	49.0[d]	48.7[d]	76.0[d]	69.4[d]	96	35
Honduras	20.0	23.0	43.0	40.0	122	75[e]
Jamaica	6.2	17.1	17.3	26.4	107	149[e]
Martinique	0.8[d]	1.4[d]	9.0[d]	11.6[d]	110	-
Mexico	5.1	4.0	20.4	12.7	99	75[b]
Netherlands Antilles	1.7[d]	2.8[d]	8.5[d]	7.2[d]	111[d]	-
Nicaragua	-	-	-	-	137	122
Panama	5.0	5.0	15.0	13.0	105	139
Paraguay	6.4[d]	5.3[d]	19.9[d]	12.1[d]	101	86[b]
Peru	10.2	3.5[d]	34.6[d]	13.2[d]	88	54[d]
Puerto Rico	5.4[d]	6.6[d]	13.8[d]	11.8[d]	-	144[d]
St. Kitts and Nevis	0.9[d]	1.1[d]	3.2[d]	3.8[d]	102	67
St. Lucia	-	-	-	-	156	120
St. Vincent and the Grenadines	-	-	-	-	121	209
Suriname	-	-	-	-	118	111
Trinidad and Tobago	0.7	0.7	5.8	2.4	101	94[e]
Uruguay	1.2	1.9	5.3	6.6	112[d]	140[e]
U.S. Virgin Islands	-	-	-	-	143	281[c]
Venezuela	3.6	5.3	14.1	10.9	133	89

Source: The World's Women 1995: Trends and Statistics. UN publication forthcoming.

[a] Data refer to a year between 1975 and 1979.

[b] Data refer to universities and equivalent degree-granting institutions only.

[c] Data refer to full-time students only.

[d] Data refer to a year between 1980 and 1984.

[e] Data refer to the university/universities only.

[f] Age 30+.

[g] Age 25-49.

[h] Age 10-29.

[i] Data refer to general secondary education only.

Table 4: Economic Activity Rate over Age 15 and Women's Share of Labor Force
(percentage)

	Estimated adult economic activity rate				Estimated women's share of the adult labor force	
	1980		1994			
	Women	Men	Women	Men	1980	1994
Antigua and Barbuda	-	-	56*	74*	-	46*
Argentina	27	76	28	74	27	29
Bahamas	38	78	39	82	34	34
Barbados	59	76	61	78	47	46
Belize	28	82	29	81	25	26
Bolivia	23	85	26	82	22	25
Brazil	30	82	31	80	27	28
Chile	26	73	29	75	27	29
Colombia	22	77	22	79	23	23
Costa Rica	23	84	24	83	21	22
Cuba	32	73	38	76	31	33
Dominica	-	-	43*	75*	-	42*
Dominican Republic	12	86	16	85	12	15
Ecuador	19	83	20	81	19	19
El Salvador	29	87	29	83	26	28
French Guiana	-	-	51*	75*	-	38*
Grenada	-	-	57*	71*	42	44*
Guatemala	14	85	18	83	14	18
Guyana	26	84	29	85	25	26
Haiti	61	84	54	83	44	41
Honduras	17	87	23	86	17	21
Jamaica	65	83	68	83	46	46
Martinique	47	71	53	73	42	44
Mexico	30	83	30	82	27	28
Netherlands Antilles	41	73	43	75	38	39
Nicaragua	23	84	30	81	22	30
Panama	29	79	31	79	26	28
Paraguay	23	89	23	88	20	20
Peru	25	80	25	79	24	24
Puerto Rico	26	68	26	68	29	29
St. Vincent and the Grenadines	-	-	44*	81*	-	36*
Suriname	27	71	31	75	28	30
Trinidad and Tobago	31	79	34	81	29	30
Uruguay	31	76	32	74	30	32
U.S. Virgin Islands	-	-	60*	72*	-	48*
Venezuela	29	81	32	81	26	28

Source: The World's Women 1995: Trends and Statistics. UN publication forthcoming.

* Data are the results of the 1990 round of censuses or the latest available national labour force or households survey, as reported in the International Labour Office Year Book of Labour Statistics (Geneva, various years up to 1994) or in national census and survey reports and national statistical yearbooks.

Table 5: Latin American Urban Economically Active Rates

(by age and percentage)

	Total		15-24		25-34		35-44		45-54		55+	
Country	1980	1990	1980	1990	1980	1990	1980	1990	1980	1990	1980	1990
Argentina												
Women	32.4	38.2	44.9	41.1	45.4	52.5	42.7	52.9	34.1	49.1	10.0	12.8
Men	75.6	75.7	66.1	61.7	98.1	97.4	98.1	97.1	[illegible]	[illegible]	[illegible]	[illegible]
Bolivia												
Women	-	46.6	-	33.8	-	56.7	-	62.0	-	55.4	-	30.8
Men	-	73.2	-	45.2	-	90.4	-	97.2	-	92.2	-	58.4
Brazil												
Women	37.2	45.1	42.9	48.1	43.9	55.7	42.3	55.3	31.9	43.0	12.5	15.7
Men	81.5	82.5	74.5	77.6	96.5	96.3	95.3	95.9	86.7	87.6	50.2	49.1
Colombia												
Women	41.8	45.7	42.3	41.2	52.1	61.2	49.2	56.8	35.2	39.2	16.7	15.3
Men	79.3	79.2	61.3	59.0	95.8	94.4	97.1	92.9	92.9	92.0	64.5	54.6
Costa Rica												
Women	33.6	39.1	33.2	39.2	45.6	52.6	44.4	51.8	26.5	33.0	11.3	9.4
Men	77.6	77.6	64.0	61.8	93.3	95.8	95.4	96.8	92.6	90.3	44.7	50.8
Chile												
Women	-	34.0	-	26.4	-	46.1	-	46.8	-	40.0	-	15.2
Men	-	73.2	-	47.8	-	95.3	-	97.4	-	92.1	-	46.2
Guatemala												
Women	-	42.9	-	42.1	-	50.1	-	50.0	-	43.1	-	25.2
Men	-	84.4	-	69.4	-	97.0	-	97.4	-	96.7	-	46.2
Honduras												
Women	-	43.4	-	34.5	-	53.8	-	57.2	-	51.6	-	25.2
Men	-	80.2	-	65.7	-	94.8	-	96.5	-	95.0	-	64.9
Mexico												
Women	-	35.9	-	36.4	-	44.6	-	42.3	-	32.4	-	15.4
Men	-	77.3	-	59.6	-	93.4	-	96.5	-	91.8	-	58.3
Panama												
Women	44.5	42.8	40.0	35.5	63.3	58.7	58.3	60.6	41.7	47.5	14.6	11.0
Men	76.2	75.6	55.9	58.8	97.3	98.5	98.5	97.0	94.8	93.7	51.3	44.3
Paraguay												
Women	-	49.7	-	50.6	-	62.8	-	61.4	-	46.3	-	20.9
Men	-	84.2	-	69.0	-	96.9	-	99.6	-	94.4	-	67.6
Uruguay												
Women	37.3	43.8	43.2	46.5	56.6	69.3	54.5	65.7	41.4	55.5	11.9	15.0
Men	74.6	74.7	73.9	67.7	97.7	97.8	97.4	97.4	91.4	95.2	38.1	43.9
Venezuela												
Women	31.2	37.5	25.7	24.8	42.6	50.8	42.0	53.7	30.3	41.5	11.3	15.6
Men	78.4	77.9	57.9	55.0	95.3	92.7	98.1	96.4	94.2	92.9	67.0	63.3
Total												
Women	36.9	41.7	38.9	39.5	49.9	57.3	47.6	56.7	34.4	44.1	12.6	13.5
Men	77.6	77.6	64.8	63.1	96.3	95.7	97.1	96.8	92.1	92.2	52.7	50.3

Source: Statistics and Economics Projections Division, ECLAC

Table 6: Economically Active Rates for Selected Latin American Countries
(by age and percentage)

Country	Total 1980	Total 1990	15-24 1980	15-24 1990	25-34 1980	25-34 1990	35-44 1980	35-44 1990	45-54 1980	45-54 1990	55+ 1980	55+ 1990
Brazil												
Women	35.9	40.1	42.1	43.3	35.5	44.3	37.1	47.5	36.0	41.2	20.1	20.5
Men	91.1	90.8	90.3	91.3	98.2	97.4	97.8	97.5	95.6	95.4	72.6	72.0
Costa Rica												
Women	23.2	26.6	28.4	30.9	24.1	30.9	26.2	32.1	16.3	18.6	7.1	8.3
Men	84.0	86.3	80.0	83.4	96.4	96.5	96.5	98.0	91.8	92.5	56.7	59.1
Chile												
Women	-	15.9	-	16.3	-	18.9	-	20.6	-	16.9	-	8.1
Men	-	85.1	-	78.0	-	97.5	-	96.6	-	95.1	-	67.0
Guatemala												
Women	-	18.8	-	18.1	-	18.7	-	21.8	-	20.9	-	15.3
Men	-	93.1	-	89.3	-	98.6	-	99.3	-	97.4	-	83.9
Honduras												
Women	-	22.3	-	17.7	-	23.8	-	29.1	-	27.9	-	18.3
Men	-	91.7	-	87.9	-	97.4	-	98.4	-	96.6	-	81.9
Panama												
Women	17.9	24.8	19.1	24.4	22.7	35.4	21.8	35.1	14.0	21.6	8.1	9.8
Men	87.0	85.3	75.3	78.6	98.1	98.1	98.9	98.0	97.2	95.4	75.4	67.7
Venezuela												
Women	18.7	20.0	15.1	13.9	23.1	24.4	24.7	30.7	21.8	22.6	10.6	14.3
Men	87.9	87.6	76.1	78.5	97.7	96.1	98.0	97.6	97.0	94.8	83.6	80.5
Total												
Women	23.9	27.9	26.2	26.1	26.4	33.8	27.5	36.4	22.0	26.0	11.5	13.2
Men	87.5	87.5	80.4	83.0	97.6	97.0	97.8	97.8	95.4	94.5	72.1	69.8

Source: Statistics and Economics Projections Division, ECLAC

Table 7: Number of Women in Occupational Groups, 1990

(per 100 men)

	Professional, technical and related workers	Administrative and managerial workers	Clerical and related workers	Sales workers	Service workers	Agricultural and related workers	Production, transport equipment operators and laborers
Argentina	-	-	-	-	-		
Bahamas	100	50	193	167	162	19	17
Barbados	110	48	216	138	132	53	29
Belize	108 [a]	14 [a]	93 [a]	53 [a]	126 [a]	3 [a]	14 [a]
Bolivia	72	20	81	250	263	10	16
Brazil	133 [a]	21 [a]	57 [a]	39 [a]	237 [a]	15 [a]	18 [a]
Chile	108	24	84	89	263	10	13
Colombia	72	37	121	66	229	17	25
Costa Rica	81	30	102	49	146	6	26
Cuba	91 [a]	23 [a]	181 [a]	129 [a]	84 [a]	13 [a]	15 [a]
Dominica	118	56	300	-	200	20	38
Dominican Rep.	98 [a]	27 [a]	83 [a]	37 [a]	267 [a]	11 [a]	16 [a]
Ecuador	79	35	96	59	174	14	18
El Salvador	76	22	104	174	261	18	39
French Guiana	68 [a]	21 [a]	103 [a]	107 [a]	337 [a]	55 [a]	13 [a]
Grenada	113	46	192	165	140	47	39
Guatemala	82	48	89	129	261	8	35
Guyana	90 [a]	15 [a]	90 [a]	72 [a]	64 [a]	10 [a]	10 [a]
Haiti	65	48	146	846	188	33	44
Honduras	100	38	124	155	263	3	42
Jamaica	147 [c]	- [c]	192 [e]	- [c]	255	61	31
Mexico	76	24	115	47	82	4	14
Netherlands Antilles	72	34	273	146 [b]	- [c]	13	41
Nicaragua	-	-	-	-	-	-	-
Panama	103	41	275	74	126	3	14
Paraguay	105	19	80	89	255	12	20
Peru	69	28	99	113	60	18	22
Puerto Rico	115	40	226	56	72	2	24
St. Kitts and Nevis	138 [a]	16 [a]	151 [a]	154 [a]	192 [a]	43 [a]	34 [a]
St. Lucia	135 [a]	23 [a]	166 [a]	209 [a]	247 [a]	30 [a]	22 [a]
St. Vincent and the Grenadines	119 [a]	25 [a]	125 [a]	115 [a]	215 [a]	30 [a]	24 [a]
Suriname	232	27	102	85	150	29	7
Trinidad and Tobago	121	29	222	92	112	21	15
Uruguay	157	26	101	67	210	10	24
U.S. Virgin Islands	135	200	546	666	231	10	15
Venezuela	123	23	158	53	136	5	12

Source: The World's Women 1995: Trends and Statistics. UN publication forthcoming.

[a] Data refer to a year between 1980 and 1984.

[b] Sales workers; service workers.

[c] Data for this category are included elsewhere.

[d] Professional, technical and related workers; administrative and managerial workers.

[e] Clerical and related workers; sales workers.

Table 8: Distribution of Labor Force by Sector, 1994
(percentages)

	Agriculture		Industry		Services	
	Women	Men	Women	Men	Women	Men
Argentina	2	13	12	41	86	45
Bahamas	2	16	4	26	94	58
Barbados	9	6	18	24	73	69
Belize	2	16	4	26	94	58
Bolivia	28	45	11	22	61	34
Brazil	10	21	19	37	71	42
Chile	2	14	9	27	89	60
Colombia	3	37	20	25	77	38
Costa Rica	4	24	22	28	74	48
Cuba	13	23	21	35	66	41
Dominican Republic	5	41	3	19	92	40
Ecuador	11	31	11	21	78	48
El Salvador	5	42	18	27	77	32
Guadeloupe	5	13	5	33	90	54
Guatemala	8	60	17	17	74	23
Guyana	7	27	18	26	76	47
Haiti	54	73	9	10	38	16
Honduras	8	66	34	15	58	19
Jamaica	18	41	8	22	75	38
Martinique	6	11	5	29	89	60
Mexico	12	38	35	34	53	28
Netherlands Antilles	2	16	4	26	94	58
Nicaragua	8	52	14	17	79	31
Panama	7	27	7	23	86	50
Paraguay	11	53	16	22	73	25
Peru	26	36	9	22	65	42
Puerto Rico	1	5	31	36	68	58
Suriname	15	15	9	23	76	62
Trinidad and Tobago	4	7	22	48	74	45
Uruguay	2	18	21	33	76	49
Venezuela	4	13	17	35	79	52

Source: The World's Women 1995: Trends and Statistics. UN publication forthcoming.

Table 9: Women in Political Party Directorates

Country	Year	Number of leaders		Percentage who are women
		Total	Women	
Bolivia	1991	50	6	12.0
Brazil	1985-91	702	33	4.7
Chile	1991	133	17	12.8
Costa Rica	1990	42	4	9.5
Cuba	1988	24	3	12.5
Dominican Rep.	1991	520	76	14.6
Honduras	1991	35	5	14.3
Mexico	1990-91	94	16	17.0
Paraguay	1991	154	22	14.3
Peru	1990	111	9	8.1
Venezuela	1988	182	20	11.0

Source: Latin American Women in Statistics, FLACSO, Santiago, 1993.

Table 10: Women Candidates in Legislative Elections as of 1991

Country[a]	Last election held	Total number of candidates	Number female candidates	% female candidates	% of female elected[b]
Barbados	1991				
Senate		All appointed	-	-	-
House of Assembly		90	13	14.4	7.7
Chile	1989				
Senate		110	7	6.4	42.8
Chamber of Deputies		363	29	8.0	24.1
Dominica	1990				
House of Assembly		60	9	15.0	55.5
Guyana	1985				
National Assembly		315	71	22.5	33.8
Nicaragua	1990				
National Assembly		767	164	21.4	9.1
Panama	1989				
Legislative Assembly		394	34	8.6	14.7
Saint Lucia	1987				
Senate		All appointed	-	-	-
House of Assembly		38	0	0.0	0.0

Source: Women and Political Power, Inter-Parliamentary Union, Geneva, 1992.

[a] Only those countries for which figures were available.

[b] Women elected vis-à-vis the women candidates, not the percentage of women elected vis-à-vis the total membership of the House.

Table 11: Women in Public Life
(percentage)

	Parliamentary seats women occupy			Women in decision-making positions in government ministries			
	Mono-cameral or lower chamber, 1987	Upper chamber, 1994	Mono-cameral or lower chamber, 1994	Ministe-rial level, 1987	Sub-ministerial level, 1987	Ministe-rial level, 1994	Sub-ministerial level, 1994
Antigua and Barbuda	0	18	6	0.0	0.0*	0.0	43.8*
Argentina	5	2	16	0.0	3.1*	0.0	3.0
Bahamas	4	19	8	0.0	30.8	23.1	34.5
Barbados	4	29	4	0.0	19.4	0.0	16.2
Belize	4	22	4	0.0	8.3	6.3	12.5
Bolivia	3	4	7	0.0	5.0*	0.0	7.7
Brazil	5	3	6	3.4	4.1*	4.5	10.8
Chile	-	7	8	0.0	3.8*	13.0	0.0
Colombia	-	7	11	6.7	0.0	11.1	5.6
Costa Rica	11	-	14	0.0	13.6*	9.5	9.1
Cuba	34	-	23	2.9	0.0	0.0	9.1
Dominica	10	-	13	22.2	26.5	9.1	37.8
Dominican Rep.	5	-	-	0.0	-	4.2	14.3
Ecuador	1	-	5	0.0	-	5.6	0.0*
El Salvador	3	-	11	0.0	-	10.0	6.7*
Grenada	13	15	13	0.0	25.0*	10.0	13.6
Guatemala	7	-	5	14.3	4.2	18.8	6.5
Guyana	37	-	20	7.1	12.0	11.5	25.0
Haiti	-	0	4	0.0	8.3*	13.3	9.5*
Honduras	5	-	8	0.0	5.4	10.5	21.7*
Jamaica	12	14	12	0.0	20.0	5.0	17.0
Mexico	11	5	8	0.0	2.0*	5.0	5.0
Nicaragua	15	-	16	5.0	3.2	10.0	8.0
Panama	6	-	8	0.0	8.3*	13.3	15.4
Paraguay	2	11	3	0.0	0.0	0.0	3.3
Peru	6	-	9	0.0	2.8*	5.6	11.1
St. Kitts and Nevis	7	-	6	0.0	-	-	-
St. Lucia	0	36	0	0.0	13.3*	8.3	0.0
St. Vincent and the Grenadines	5	-	13	0.0	0.0*	0.0	0.0*
Suriname	8	-	6	0.0	0.0*	0.0	0.0*
Trinidad and Tobago	17	23	14	9.5	20.8*	18.5	12.5
Uruguay	0	0	6	13.3	0.0*	0.0	5.0
Venezuela	4	8	6	0.0	14.3	10.7	0.0*

Source: The World's Women 1995: Trends and Statistics. UN publication forthcoming.
* may not include all subministerial levels.

Table 12: Women Officials of Local Governments in Selected Countries, 1979-1993

(percentage)

Country	1979	1981	1982	1983	1984	1986	1989	1990	1991	1992	1993
Chile		-	-	-	-	-	-	-	-	-	11.9
Costa Rica[a]	-	-	8.9	-	-	11.2	-	13.7	-	-	-
Cuba[b]	-	7.8	-	-	-	17.1	-	-	-	-	13.5
Dominican Rep.			2.1	-	-	4.0	-	4.9	-		-
Guatemala				-	-	-	-	-	-	1.0	-
Paraguay	-	-	-	-	-	-	-	-	13.9	-	-
Peru[c]	-	-	-	10.0	-	-	9.5	-	-	-	9.5
Venezuela[d]	14.0	-		-	-	21.5	-	12.8 -	-	-	-

Source:

[a] Includes the municipal posts of executive, councilman and representative, both officials and substitutes.

[b] Results of the first round with 433 delegates to elect in the second round.

[c] Information available only for districts of the Lima metropolitan area.

[d] Represents the presence of women on municipal councils.

Agenda for Action

Regional Forum on Women in the Americas: Participation and Development

Guadalajara, April 5-7, 1994
IDB-ECLAC-UNIFEM

Preamble

The Forum on Women in the Americas, sponsored by the Inter-American Development Bank (IDB), the Economic Commission for Latin America and the Caribbean (ECLAC), and the United Nations Development Fund for Women (UNIFEM), held in Guadalajara, Mexico, on April 5-7, 1994, attracted more than 400 women and men from all over Latin America and the Caribbean. They came representing their governments, the private sector—NGOs, community groups, academic bodies and business associations—and other international organizations. The objective was to assist the IDB and the other sponsoring institutions in setting priorities and devising concrete steps to strengthen the participation of women in their programs. The forum discussed four top priority issues for women in the region: women's political participation, women's economic contribution, the role of women in sustainable development, and the gender dimension in proposals for social reform.

The forum presented the IDB and its member countries with a set of major recommendations, not only on how to promote the participation of women in its programs, but also on how to work more effectively towards economic growth, social reform, management of the environment, modernization of the state, and the strengthening of the role of civil society.

Women have a vital contribution to make to the economic and social development of Latin America and the Caribbean and to the reduction of poverty in the region. During the crisis of the 1980s, the survival of poor families depended largely on the efforts made by women. Women now form a large portion of the workforce, are participating in politics in the region, and play a broadly recognized role in the social sectors and in management of the environment.

The Inter-American Development Bank has a policy towards women in development, approved by the Executive Board in 1987, which commits it to taking the steps needed to increase and enhance the participation of women in all of its programs. That mandate has become even more pressing since the 35th Meeting of the Board of Governors of the Bank held in Guadalajara. At that meeting, the members agreed on the Eighth Replenishment of the IDB's capital, which is especially geared to social development and the reduction of poverty.

This Agenda for Action records and summarizes the recommendations that arose out of the discussions held during the forum in the expectation that they will be appropriated and implemented by the IDB and the governments of the region. These recommendations have also been of use in the preparation of the Action Platform for the Fourth World Conference on Women, to be held in Beijing in 1995, through the submission of the Agenda for Action to the preparatory meeting for the Latin American and Caribbean region in Mar del Plata, Argentina.

The Agenda for Action reflects the consensus reached by the representatives of different sectors in IDB member countries in Latin America and the Caribbean who attended the forum. It is a synthesis of debates and recommendations put forward in nine workshops on specific topics and in the plenary sessions of the forum. In Guadalajara, these recommendations were brought to the attention of the Meeting of the Board of Governors of the IDB, who represent IDB member countries.

It is important to note that the Agenda for Action includes the main recommendations made during the forum but does not claim to be an exhaustive list of all the ideas discussed. Its purpose is to serve as a guide for concrete action.

A preliminary draft of the Agenda for Action was submitted for consideration by participants at the forum. Comments from participants were incorporated into this final version, which will be presented to the Board of Governors of the IDB to guide it in planning concrete actions to be undertaken by the Bank over the next few years.

Agenda for Action: Major Recommendations

The Agenda for Action is a response to the main concerns addressed at the forum—the need to strengthen the participation of women in the economic and social development of the region, promotion of sustainable and equitable development, social integration, and an active role for civil society in defining, planning, and building the future of the region. The Agenda establishes priority objectives and concrete measures, both for the IDB and for the governments of Latin America and the Caribbean, in three main areas:

- Promotion of equitable and sustainable economic and social reform.
- Promotion of the participation of women in the public decision-making process.
- Strengthening of the institutional capacity of the IDB to enable it, in conjunction with its counterparts, to implement the Agenda for Action.

Area A: Promotion of Equitable and Sustainable Economic and Social Reform

One basic recommendation to emerge from the forum concerned the need to combine social and economic reform, since the two areas have a complementary impact on the populations of Latin American and Caribbean countries, and especially on women, given the links between poverty and gender. There is general agreement on the need to combine the expansion of economic opportunities, investment in human capital, and activities designed to enhance the productivity and income of women workers, with improvement of social services, social policy reform, and the strengthening of poverty reduction programs. The following recommendations reflect this approach and point to the priority areas that, from that point of view, should be taken into consideration by the IDB and the governments of member countries.

Overall Objective: *Gender equity should be part of social reform. Social reform and poverty reduction programs should specifically address the role of women and include concrete measures to strengthen that role.* The main areas needing attention are:

- enhancement of economic opportunities and urban and rural women's labor productivity;
- equitable and higher quality education for girls and women;
- expansion of health care coverage and improvement of health services, including preventive health care and the prevention of domestic violence; and
- enhancement of the ways women contribute to and benefit from sustainable development.

In all these activities, it is important to bear in mind class, ethnic, cultural, and generational differences among women, and, in particular, the special characteristics of indigenous communities.

Objective 1: Improve Women's Access to the Labor Market and Labor Mobility and Increase Women's Productivity and Income.

1. Improve women's access to job opportunities and productive resources that could help them increase their productivity and income as workers and business owners through loans, training, extension courses, access to technical information, support services, and title deeds.
2. Provide women with information and guidance concerning job opportunities and on-the-job training to improve their job readiness.
3. Create affirmative action measures in favor of women in training programs, while at the same time ensuring that programs match labor market requirements.
4. Educate employers to eliminate prejudices against the hiring of women in certain professions. Disseminate information about successful employment of women in non-traditional occupations.

5. Organize and finance seminars for trade union leaders and senior staff in professional associations geared to eliminating job discrimination between men and women. Provide training to increase women's participation in labor organizations.

6. Procure that the state bears the social cost of reproduction. Provide public funding to cover provisional and health care costs associated with maternity so that for an employer, from a cost point of view, there is no difference between men and women as factors of production. Promote the establishment of day care centers for infants.

7. Ensure that there are no legal barriers in social and labor legislation to the equal participation of women in the labor force.

8. Improve the quality of women's jobs by supervising physical working conditions and setting up mechanisms for denouncing and punishing discrimination against women in terms of job opportunities, sexual harassment, wage discrimination, etc.

Objective 2: Improve the Conditions under Which Rural Women Contribute to Economic and Social Development.

1. Incorporate the gender perspective into the IDB's new rural development strategy in each of its components, especially in activities related to lending, technology, training, land titling and water management.

2. Extend proposals for creating and developing financing systems, including those designed to support microenterprises, to rural areas.

3. Support international research centers in developing research methods and agricultural and livestock extension courses for productive systems using technology and instruments designed with a gender perspective.

4. Promote measures improving the legal status of rural women as a basis for access to every kind of productive resource.

5. Promote the participation of NGOs, producer organizations and women's organizations in agricultural and rural development programs, to strengthen their capacity to articulate their demand for services and ability to administer development programs.

6. Support integral training projects for rural women in different fields (technical, organizational, and entrepreneurial and, with respect to self-esteem, civil rights, and participation in political life) that help to create the conditions for equality of opportunity.

Objective 3: Improve the Quality of Education and Equality of Access to It.

1. Incorporate the principle of equal opportunities for men and women at every level of the educational system. Eliminate gender-based discrimination in educational programs and materials.

2. Promote teacher training at every level of the educational system aimed at making teachers sensitive to gender discrimination and at familiarizing them with equitable and effective practices.

3. Improve systems for informing and counselling women about the educational opportunities open to them.

4. Establish temporary fellowship systems in those professions that, because of discrimination, no or only a very few women have joined.

5. Increase investment in the education of women and men from poor homes.

6. Develop and support programs and policies designed to strengthen the connection between education and employment, especially for women.

Objective 4: Broaden the Approach to Women's Health to Address Issues throughout Their Life Cycle.

1. Adopt an integral approach for health and demographic programs, based on a human development strategy and considering women's health from the point of view of their complete life cycle, not just their reproductive cycle.

2. Promote access to updated health and legal systems guaranteeing men and women the right to decide freely about reproduction issues.

3. Define targets and support concrete steps to reduce maternal and infant mortality. Create mechanisms to support women's ability to breastfeed their infants.

4. Promote policies and programs designed to increase and enhance the participation of men and children in preventive health care in the family and in the community.

5. Take measures to ensure that reforms in the way national health systems and services are organized and financed do not reduce access to health care for women or for low-income families.

6. Increase emphasis on, and investment in, preventive health care in national health policies and programs.

Objective 5: Implement Comprehensive Policies to Prevent Domestic Violence and to Treat and Attend to Its Victims.

1. Support programs for preventing domestic violence and for attending to its victims. Include training for those who deal with the victims of domestic violence in all sectors, paying special attention to the cultural patterns and values underlying it.

2. Support government initiatives with community participation—of women's groups, NGOs, and others—that raise awareness and sensitivity to the problem of domestic violence.

3. Promote and encourage activities seeking to prevent violence through the dissemination of information by the media, thereby helping to make people more aware of and sensitive to the problem.

4. Carry out studies of the social and economic costs of domestic violence.

5. Promote the creation of laws and policies to protect victims of violence and punish aggressors.

6. Update and improve the legal procedures used in the treatment of domestic violence cases.

7. Support the Inter-American Development Convention on the Prevention, Punishment and Eradication of Violence against Women.

Objective 6: Maximize Both the Contributions Women Make to Sustainable Development and the Benefits They Derive as a Result of Their Participation.

1. Facilitate women's access to use and ownership of land, extension services, credit, and information on the environment and technology.

2. Support women's efforts to conserve and administer the urban environment and ensure that they participate at every level of environmental policy.

3. Remove cultural and social barriers preventing true participation by indigenous groups, and indigenous women in particular, in the design and implementation of sustainable development strategy.

4. Support interdisciplinary research related to the impact of sectoral policies on the environment from a gender perspective.

Objective 7: Support All Programs and Projects Capable of Improving the Situation of Indigenous Women.

1. Include participation by indigenous women and their perspective in all the activities recommended in the Agenda for Action.

2. Set priorities on the use of funds for programs and projects in order to give preference to those helping to reduce indigenous women's poverty and discrimination against them.

3. Promote the organization and training of indigenous women and their access to loans and resources needed to increase their productivity and income.

Area B: Promotion of Women's Participation in Public Decision Making

Overall Objective: *The Bank's programs should help strengthen women's effective exercise of their citizenship, especially their participation in public decision-making at the local and national levels.* Priority tasks are:

- promoting constitutional, legal and judicial amendments needed to ensure equal rights for men and women;

- encouraging and strengthening women's participation in the social and political sphere;
- strengthening public institutions for implementing programs and mechanisms helping to increase equality of opportunity for men and women; and
- strengthening organizations in civil society that represent women.

Objective 1: Promote Constitutional, Legal and Judicial Amendments Needed to Ensure Equal Rights For Women and Men.

1. Promote the ratification and implementation, via parliament, of all national and international conventions on equal rights for women and men.
2. Finance studies and seminars for political leaders and members of the judiciary.
3. Promote equal opportunities in the economic sphere, in particular by eliminating gender-based discrimination in lending for housing and business purposes.
4. Improve women's access to proper administration of justice. This entails a number of changes, ranging from office hours that allow women to comply with their multiple roles to greater sensitivity in dealing with women's charges, including, where necessary, the creation of a women's police force to attend to women's charges of domestic violence, sexual assault, rape, etc.

Objective 2: Support and Encourage Participation by Women in Social and Political Life by Improving Their Access to Decision-Making Bodies.

1. Encourage the establishment of affirmative action mechanisms enabling women to participate actively in the leadership of political parties and social organizations.
2. Finance studies and seminars for social and political leaders to make them more sensitive to this issue and turn them into agents for change.
3. Promote the formation of non-partisan political women's groups.
4. Broaden the participation of women's organizations from civil society in the organization and supervision of political processes.
5. Provide training to develop women's leadership skills, particularly in politics.

Objective 3: Create or Strengthen Public Institutions for Implementing, Following up on, and Evaluating Policies and Programs Designed to Increase Equality of Opportunity for Man and Women

1. Support the appointment of an "ombudsman" devoted to eliminating discrimination and guaranteeing equal opportunities for both sexes within the State bureaucracy.
2. Provide incentives and support to countries to produce an Equal Opportunity for Women Plan that would guide policy-making and program development.

3. Provide training and technical assistance to strengthen the institutional and technical capacity of the women's offices or ministries to incorporate the gender dimension in public policies and programs. Provide financing for research and the publication of research findings.

4. Promote the inclusion and active participation of women's offices in the main decision and policy-making bodies in government. Promote coordination and institutional cooperation among these offices and the other ministries.

5. Strengthen relations and communications between women's offices and organizations in civil society that represent women at the national and local levels.

Objective 4: Support Measures to Make the Different Actors in Society More Open to the Gender Perspective.

1. Finance country and regional studies analyzing the contributions that women make to economic and social development and the barriers that they face.

2. Organize seminars, workshops, and projects to make the different strata in society aware of the discrimination to which women are subjected and ways to correct it.

3. Finance media programs to make the population aware of discrimination, how much it costs, and what can be done about it.

4. Promote the elimination of discriminatory images in the mass media. Promote an image of women that reflects their current situation and future possibilities.

Objective 5: Invest in the Development and Improvement of Nongovernmental Organizations Working with Women and on Poverty Issues, Especially Those That Can Collaborate with Governments.

1. Promote and boost communications between the state and organizations in civil society representing women's interests.

2. Provide technical and financial resources to support the institutional strengthening of NGOs working with women and adopting a gender perspective.

Area C: Strengthening of the Institutional Capacity of the IDB to Enable It, in Conjuction with Its Caounterparts, to Implement the Agenda for Action

Overall Objective: *The technical and operational capacity of the IDB should be improved to promote and implement its policy of women in development and the Agenda for Action and to strengthen the participation of women and men from the region in the formulation and execution of the IDB's policies and programs,* through such measures as:

- encouraging the participation by potential women and men beneficiaries in the design, execution, and evaluation of projects financed by the IDB;

- providing funds for programs benefiting women and based on a gender perspective;
- establishing an external advisory council for the IDB to support and review the implementation of its policy on women and the recommendations made at the forum;
- strengthening the IDB's women in development unit; and
- training IDB staff and their counterparts and making them more sensitive to the situation of women and aware of measures that can be taken to increase women's participation.

Objective 1: Promote Greater Participation by Women and Men in Programs and Projects Financed by the IDB.

1. Facilitate the direct participation of women and men beneficiaries in the design, execution and evaluation of development projects and programs.
2. Incorporate the gender perspective at each stage of the project cycle: identification, design, execution, and evaluation. All the information on the target population—initial, follow-up, and evaluation data—should be disaggregated by sex and include the socio-economic characteristics, needs, and potential of each.
3. Allocate funds on concessional terms for projects promoting gender equality.
4. Prioritize policies, programs, and projects designed to enhance equality of opportunity and reduce the gap between men and women.
5. Introduce conditionalities in projects to ensure that they have a positive effect on women, and, if possible, reduce inequality between the sexes.
6. Strengthen the Bank's and its counterparts' capacity to provide a breakdown by gender when evaluating the impact of projects.

Objective 2: Enhance Ties and Improve Communication between the IDB and Latin American and Caribbean Women.

1. Form an External Advisory Council to support the implementation of the policy on women in development and the Agenda for Action in the IDB.
2. Enhance the dissemination and exchange of information with women in IDB member countries.
3. Take advantage of the network of organizations and individual women mobilized by the forum as a future reference group and as focal points in the different countries.
4. Establish mechanisms which facilitate the monitoring, in the Bank and in the member countries, of the steps taken to fulfill the Agenda for Action.

Objective 3: Strengthen the Women in Development Unit of the IDB and the Capability of Bank Staff to Address Gender Issues.

1. Increase the human resources allocated to the women in development unit within the IDB to facilitate coordination, supervision, and execution of IDB policy in this area and to ensure implementation of the recommendations made at the forum.

2. Appoint a person to be in charge of gender issues in each of the IDB's representative offices in member countries to facilitate implementation of the recommendations.

3. Set up mechanisms capable of increasing and facilitating communication between the women in development unit and other divisions in the Bank to achieve with greater efficiency the goal of incorporating a gender perspective in all the Bank's projects.

4. Finance and disseminate diagnostic studies regarding women's participation in different sectors and their situation in different countries. Conduct evaluations of projects from a gender perspective. Exchange information, initiatives and success stories from the region.

5. Conduct training courses and workshops for Bank staff, IDB Executive Directors, and member governments of the IDB to raise their awareness of gender issues and their ability to address them.

Objective 4: Set Up Mechanisms to Ensure Participation by Local Women's Organizations in the Design, Execution and Evaluation of IDB Projects.

1. Devise and support investment policies and mechanisms capable of tapping the wealth of energy and creativity shown by grassroots, political, and business organizations, such as the ones that attended the forum.

2. Promote the integration of NGO activities with governmental efforts and support by government institutions for NGOs.

3. Encourage consultation between national women's offices and the IDB.

ACRONYMS

ANMUCIC	Asociación Nacional de Mujeres Campesinas e Indígenas de Colombia
ASSEMA	Associação em Areas de Assentamento no estado do Maranhão
ATC	Asociación de Trabajadores del Campo - Nicaragua
BID	Banco Interamericano de Desarrollo
CAFRA	Caribbean Association for Feminist Research and Action
CE MUJER	Centro de Solidaridad para el Desarrollo de la Mujer
CEDAW	United Nations Convention on the Elimination of all Forms of Discrimination Against Women
CELADE	Centro Latinoamericano de Demografía
CENDOC	Centro de Documentación sobre la Mujer - Peru
CEPAL	Comisión Económica para América Latina y el Caribe
CLADEM	Comité Latinoamericano para la Defensa de los Derechos de la Mujer
CODIMCA	Consejo para el Desarrollo Integral de la Mujer Campesina
ECLAC	Economic Commission for Latin America and the Caribbean
EPZ(s)	Export Processing Zone(s)
FAO	Food and Agriculture Organization
FLACSO	Facultad Latinoamericana de Ciencias Sociales
FOSIS	Social Solidarity and Investment Fund - Chile
FSE	Social Emergency Fund - Bolivia
GNP	Gross National Product
GTA	Grupo de Tecnologia Alternativa - Mexico
HBI	Programa de Hogares de Bienestar Familiar
IABA	Inter-American Bar Association
IAWJ	International Association of Women Judges
ICDP(s)	Integrated Conservation and Development Project(s)
IDB	Inter-American Development Bank
IICA	Inter-American Institute for Cooperation on Agriculture
IOCU	International Organization of Consumer Unions
IPPF	International Planned Parenthood Federation
ISIS	ISIS International
IWHC	International Women's Health Coalition
NACLA	North American Congress on Latin America
NAFTA	North American Free Trade Agreement
NGOs	Non-governmental Organization(s)
OAS	Organization of American States
PAHO	Pan-American Health Organization
PAIT	Temporary Income Support Program - Peru
PAN	National Food Program - Argentina
PEM	Minimum Employment Program - Chile
POJH	Employment Program for Heads of Households - Chile
SERNAM	Servicio Nacional de la Mujer - Chile

SIRDO	Integrated System for Recycling Organic Wastes - Mexico
UN	United Nations
UNAG	Unión Nacional de Agricultores y Ganaderos - Nicaragua
UNCED	United Nations Conference on Environment and Development
UNDP	United Nations Development Program
UNEP	United Nations Environment Program
UNFPA	United Nations Family Planning Agency
UNICEF	United Nations Children's Fund
WAND	Women and Development Unit, University of the West Indies - Barbados
WHO	World Health Organization
WID	Women in Development
WRC	Women's Rights Committee (of the IABA)
WRI	World Resources Institute